TALAWA THEATRE COMPANY

TALAWA THEATRE COMPANY

A THEATRICAL HISTORY AND THE BREWSTER ERA

David Vivian Johnson

methuen | drama

LONDON • NEW YORK • OXFORD • NEW DELHI • SYDNEY

METHUEN DRAMA
Bloomsbury Publishing Plc
50 Bedford Square, London, WC1B 3DP, UK
1385 Broadway, New York, NY 10018, USA
29 Earlsfort Terrace, Dublin 2, Ireland

BLOOMSBURY, METHUEN DRAMA and the Methuen Drama logo are trademarks of Bloomsbury Publishing Plc

First published in Great Britain 2021
This edition published 2022

Copyright © David Vivian Johnson, 2021

David Vivian Johnson has asserted his right under the Copyright, Designs and Patents Act, 1988, to be identified as author of this work.

For legal purposes the Acknowledgements on p. xii constitute an extension of this copyright page.

Cover design: Charlotte Daniels
Cover image: *Five Conversations* by Lubaina Himid at the *En Plein Air* exhibition at the High Line, New York (photo by Timothy Schenck)
Background © Getty Images

All rights reserved. No part of this publication may be reproduced or transmitted in any form or by any means, electronic or mechanical, including photocopying, recording, or any information storage or retrieval system, without prior permission in writing from the publishers.

Bloomsbury Publishing Plc does not have any control over, or responsibility for, any third-party websites referred to or in this book. All internet addresses given in this book were correct at the time of going to press. The author and publisher regret any inconvenience caused if addresses have changed or sites have ceased to exist, but can accept no responsibility for any such changes.

A catalogue record for this book is available from the British Library.

A catalog record for this book is available from the Library of Congress.

ISBN: HB: 978-1-3501-0797-7
PB: 978-1-3501-8748-1
ePDF: 978-1-3501-0796-0
eBook: 978-1-3501-0798-4

Typeset by Deanta Global Publishing Services, Chennai, India

To find out more about our authors and books visit www.bloomsbury.com and sign up for our newsletters.

To Lloyd and Edna,
Thank you for your wit and inspiration.

CONTENTS

Preface		x
Acknowledgements		xii
1	**Voicing an identity**	1
	Why Brewster and Talawa?	1
	Defining black in Britain	4
	Defining voice	6
	The sociology of language	6
	Language style as audience design and related theories	8
	The burden of representation	9
2	**Post-traumatic slavery disorder**	13
	Ritual: A survival technique	13
	Storytelling	21
	Jamaican theatre 1700s–1980s	23
	Louise Bennett's lineage and legacy	27
	Lest we forget: Black British theatre and the post-war pioneers	33
	By happenstance: Earl Cameron, 1917–2020	34
	A black trap: Cy Grant, 1919–2010	37
	Bottom of the pile: Barry Reckord, 1926–2011	42
	Unequal opportunities: Pearl Connor, 1924–2005	47
3	**A stranger in non-paradise**	57
	Brewster's beginnings	57
	The Barn	60
	The making of contemporary black British theatre: Brewster's role	64
	Dark and Light	69
	Theatre of Black Women	71
	Carib Theatre	72
	Black Theatre Cooperative	74
	Black Theatre Forum	76
	Talawa	79
	When the time is right: Talawa's residency at the Cochrane	82

Contents

4	**The island plays**	**91**
	Contextualizing Talawa's Caribbean genre with *An Echo in the Bone* and *Maskarade*	91
	The Black Jacobins	94
	The motivation to revolt	94
	Oral language of performance: We speak black	95
	Non-spoken performance vocabulary: Colonialism and Voodoo	103
	The Dragon Can't Dance	109
	A chosen ethnicity	109
	Oral language of performance: It ain't reach yet	110
	Non-spoken performance vocabulary: 'All A We Is One' – music, calypso and Carnival	112
	The Lion	122
	Oral language of performance: Speaky spokey	122
	Notions of black identity: Black . . . ish Brit . . . ish	128
	Beef, No Chicken	133
	Brewster: Directing language	134
5	**The black south**	**143**
	Refusing exclusion from the American genre	143
	The Love Space Demands	146
	Piecing it together: The structure of the work	146
	Oral language of performance: Speaking from her heart	148
	Non-spoken performance vocabulary: The psyche and dancing the dialogue	150
	From the Mississippi Delta	154
	Oral language of performance: Delta voices	154
	A cappella actresses: The performances	156
	Critical reception	159
	Flyin' West	162
	We need heritage facts: Research package and the company's response to it	163
	Critical reception	171
	My eyewitness account	174

Contents

6	**Stay in your box**	**177**
	The British classical genre: No voice for blacks	177
	Antony and Cleopatra	184
	King Lear	188
	Tis Pity She's a Whore	191
	The Importance of Being Earnest	195
	A critical reception	199
	Contemporary black Victorians	202
	White words black mouths	203
	O to hell go Othello	206
	Audience response	210
	Production reviews	212
	The language of the text versus the colour of the performers: Even Cassio is black	213
	Playing Othello: The actors' perspective	215
7	**Don't tell massa**	**221**
	The contribution to black British theatre and identity	221
	The end	223
Images		227
Bibliography		242
Index		250

PREFACE

Between 1986 and 2001, Talawa's twenty-nine productions under Dr Yvonne Brewster OBE put black theatre practitioners and black British life centre stage. This exposure presented black British identity from the insiders' perspective. The innovative performance work was the foreground to a number of equally pioneering subsidiary projects initiated by Brewster. These aimed at developing new generations of black British artists, whilst also celebrating those that had gone before. The projects included education and community-based projects with the Hackney Theatre Education Focus and the Paul Hamlyn Foundation, the Black Women Writers' Programme, Talawa Summer School and the oral history projects *Blackgrounds* and *Blackstages*.

Brewster's creative projects were accompanied by a simultaneous and relentless commitment to board membership including the British Council's Drama and Dance Advisory Committee, the Black Theatre Forum, the London Arts Board, the Royal Victoria Hall Foundation, the Theatres' Trust and the Riverside Mental Health Trust. Additionally, Brewster contributed to numerous theatre enquiries including the Gulbenkian enquiry into director training in Britain.

Brewster was doubly honoured for her work in 1993 and 2001. In 1993 she received an OBE 'For Talawa's hard work, not because we were accepted by the establishment'.[1] The wording of the award was critical in her decision to accept it: 'For your contribution to British theatre.'[2] In the same year she won the Arts Council Woman of Achievement Award. In 2001 the US National Black Theatre Festival honoured her with the Living Legend Award, and back home in Britain the Open University made her a Doctor of Philosophy in recognition of her body of work. Additional awards include two Baftas in 1996 for directing Shakespeare for television.

---

[1] Allister Harry, 'The Voice Interview: Yvonne Brewster, Enter, Stage Left!', *The Voice*, 7 November 1995.
[2] Yvonne Brewster, Personal Interview by David Johnson, London, 26 November 2018.

Preface

I first met Brewster in 1995. This was to speak with her about Jamaican writer and performer Louise Bennett. My interest in Bennett stemmed from my love of Jamaican language, which came from my Jamaican parents. This in turn was my basis for becoming a linguist. Whilst I am praised for fluency in four European languages, any serious linguistic knowledge of Jamaican patois is generally considered a joke. I wanted to know more about the performance history of the language of my cultural roots. Brewster obliged. I then worked for Talawa between 1996 and 2002 as a researcher for Brewster's productions of Derek Walcott's *Beef, No Chicken* and Pearl Cleage's *Flyin' West*, as a researcher and interviewer on the *Blackgrounds* project and as a consultant on the Louise Bennett interview for the *Blackstages* project. During this time I also sat on Talawa's board and wrote my PhD thesis on the company's achievements and performance work under Brewster. It is this personal interest and experience of Talawa, along with interviews from 1996 to 2019, that form the backbone of the following chapters.

ACKNOWLEDGEMENTS

I thank the following:

Dr Yvonne Brewster OBE for decades of riveting discussion on theatre and life.

Dr John Gilmore for calm advice throughout the initial creation of this project.

Professor Richard Cave for seeing potential in this work.

Anna Brewer and Meredith Benson at Bloomsbury for enthusiastically guiding me through this publication process.

Ramona Riedzewski for access to Talawa's archives at the Victoria and Albert Museum, and to Talawa for permitting use of production images.

Lubaina Himid for graciously allowing me to use her paintings from her 'Five Conversations' series for the front cover.

Calliope Mefsut for providing invaluable guidance at every stage of this journey.

Ben Thomas for many long and helpful conversations.

Claire Gager-Hughes for reminding me to 'connect or disconnect'.

CHAPTER 1
VOICING AN IDENTITY

'May I always be a credit to my race.'[1]

Why Brewster and Talawa?

This book is the first detailed history of Talawa Theatre Company under its co-founder and first artistic director Dr Yvonne Brewster OBE. Following a detailed contextualization of theatre history in the opening chapters, the period between 1986 and 2001 is discussed. This is Talawa's foundation era, during which Brewster started, developed and gracefully began to bow out of the company. Along with Brewster's contribution to the history of black British theatre, both prior to and through her work with Talawa, the origins of the company, its key early productions and Brewster's ability to develop and question notions of black British identity through her work are examined. This is a celebratory, though tough journey that marks Brewster's pioneering legacy in helping to forge the identity of contemporary black British theatre.

Whilst there have been a number of academic books that discuss black theatre and Brewster specifically, most offer only an excellent glance at both. This is seen in Duggan and Ukaegbu's *Reverberations Across Small-Scale British Theatre*, Godiwala's *Alternatives Within the Mainstream: British Black and Asian Theatres*, and Saunders's *British Theatre Companies 1980–1994*. Each honours Talawa's work by dedicating a full chapter to it.[2] Others

---

[1] *Black Hollywood, They've Got to Have Us: Legends and Pioneers* (2018), [TV programme] BBC1, 13 October.
[2] Kene Igweonu, 'Keeping It Together: Talawa Theatre Company, Britishness, Aesthetics of Scale and Mainstreaming the Black-British Experience', in *Reverberations Across Small-Scale British Theatre; Politics, Aesthetics and Forms*, ed. Patrick Duggan and Victor Ukaegbu (Bristol: Intellect, 2013), 83; Victor Ukaegbu, 'Talawa Theatre Company: The "Likkle" Matter of Black

have focused on plays and playwrights, as seen in Goddard's *Contemporary Black British Playwrights: Margins to Mainstream*.[3] Others still have produced comprehensive histories. Chambers's *Black and Asian Theatre in Britain: A History* provides impressive detail spanning the thirteenth to twenty-first centuries.[4] Such writing highlights the need for individuals and specific companies to be examined in greater detail.

African-Caribbean artists in Britain have produced a body of work that merits its own analysis. It constitutes a substantial contribution to British theatre and need no longer be included in, for example, Asian theatre. Whilst the lumping together of huge bodies of work serves a need, it also generalizes, dilutes and sometimes reduces the work of a formidable artist to part of a list, or a footnote. It is often the wider mainstream and funding bodies that necessarily force culturally different groups into the same non-white category in order to more 'conveniently' deal with them as a single unit. In fact, these groups are usually more different than they are alike and they do not develop a tangible commonality by being bound in this way, except to those who create the categories. In reality, they remain marginalized and 'other'. Brewster explains why Tara Arts, for example, cannot be a black theatre company, but why it is associated with others that are: 'They are Asian and they are Asian-culture-based, this BAME business. I call it BLAME. Just blame everybody else for everything.'[5]

The central aim here is to avoid the BLAME game and provide a detailed theatrical history for, and highlight the work of, Brewster and Talawa. Anthologies and compilations that include both also often highlight the work of other female and black directors, many of whom merit having their individual story told. Writers and other artists will focus their energies on those they wish to illuminate. This was seen when West Africans felt that Caribbean theatre dominated the black British theatre landscape and

---

Creativity and Presentation on the British Stage', in *Alternatives Within the Mainstream: British Black and Asian Theatres*, ed. Dimple Godiwala (Newcastle: Cambridge Scholars Press, 2006), 123; Yvonne Brewster, 'A Short Autobiographical Essay Focusing on My Work in the Theatre', in *Alternatives Within the Mainstream British Black and Asian Theatres*, ed. Dimple Godiwala (Newcastle: Cambridge Scholars Press, 2006), 390; Kene Igweonu, 'Talawa', in *British Theatre Companies 1980–1994*, ed. Graham Saunders (London: Bloomsbury, 2015), 237.
[3]Lynette Goddard, *Contemporary Black British Playwrights: Margins to Mainstream* (Basingstoke: Palgrave Macmillan, 2015).
[4]Colin Chambers, *Black and Asian Theatre in Britain: A History* (Oxon: Routledge, 2011).
[5]Yvonne Brewster, Personal Interview by David Johnson, London, 20 November 2018.

founded Tiata Fahodzi in 1997: 'it became the company's central mission statement to produce work that emanated from West Africans for West Africans in West African bubbles of London.'[6] Their aim was to tell their particular stories in their specific voices, just as Brewster did for her communities through Talawa.

Brewster was born in Jamaica in 1938. This was the year before Hattie McDaniel starred as Mammy in *Gone with The Wind* and sixteen months before McDaniel became the first African American woman to win an Oscar for best supporting actress for her portrayal of Mammy. Being the only guest in her segregated seat at the Oscars, McDaniel was acutely aware that her win was a huge accolade for the entire black diaspora.[7] The seemingly tenuous link between Brewster's birth and McDaniel's win is much less spurious when the irregularity with which black life is generally celebrated is considered. Brewster's birth, unremarkable in itself, becomes significant when looking at her life's work. What chance was there that a black woman born in Jamaica at that time, even if from a privileged background, would have a notable impact on British theatre? Brewster achieved this because she was unable to live up to stereotypes and was skilled at carving out her own path and identity in equal measure. Mahone comments, 'The very act of a black woman telling her story, speaking her truth, can be perceived as an act of resistance to oppression; the real power in her exercise of artistic freedom is casting her own image of her own hand.'[8]

Brewster's work cast a clear image of black identity that could not fail to resonate with those African, Caribbean and black British people whose stories it told, in their own spoken and non-spoken language forms. It was also a catalyst for many performers who would not have been given the same welcome, opportunity, experience and sense of self from the mainstream. Most importantly, Brewster's theatre exposed the identity of Britain's marginalized black communities to the white space, whilst legitimately illustrating the widest possible range of performance styles indigenous to the genre of black British theatre.

---

[6]Ekua Ekumah, 'Second Generation Africans in British Theatre', in *Reverberations Across Small-Scale British Theatre; Politics, Aesthetics and Forms*, ed. Patrick Duggan and Victor Ukaegbu (Bristol: Intellect, 2013), 71.
[7]*Black Hollywood*, BBC1, 13 October 2018.
[8]Sydné Mahone, 'Moon Marked and Touched by Sun', in *Black Theatre: Ritual Performance in the African Diaspora*, ed. Paul Carter Harrison, Victor Leo Walker II and Gus Edwards (Philadelphia: Temple University Press, 2002), 259.

Talawa Theatre Company

Defining black in Britain

Brewster and her work at Talawa are analysed here through the prism of black identity in Britain. Since their first encounters with white people, black people have been redefined by them. The free black people of Africa were renamed slaves, niggers, coons and darkies. Then followed the array of words to label anyone that was mixed, including sambo, mulatto, mestizo, mixed-blood, coloured, half-caste, Creole and quadroon. Contemporary branding now justifies the terms mixed, mixed race, multiracial, biracial, multiethnic and polyethnic. Here, 'black' refers to African-Caribbean people and their British descendants.

The foundations of present-day black Britain and black identity within it began in the 1500s, as there have been black people living and being born in Britain since that time.[9] It was, however, after Britain had been bombed in the Second World War and needed to be rebuilt that the arrival of black British invitees from the colonies darkened the complexion of British society.

When the *Empire Windrush* docked in Tilbury in 1948 with 492 Jamaicans, they were welcomed as 'Five Hundred Pairs of Willing Hands'.[10] This, along with the arrivals that followed in the ensuing decade, gives an impression that most Caribbean people arriving at this time came in this way, as skilled non-professionals seeking work in the 'Motherland'.[11] Many had been enticed by the promise of secure well-paid work and educational opportunities. These opportunities saw them taking up posts on London transport and in nursing.[12] They were British, they 'took their British citizenship seriously, and many regarded themselves not as strangers, but as kinds of Englishmen'.[13] This status was, however, disputed by the likes of Enoch Powell: 'The West Indian does not by being born in England become

---

[9]Peter Fryer, *Staying Power: The History of Black People in Britain* (London: Pluto Press, 1984), xi.
[10]*Daily Worker*, no. 5226 (23 June 1948), 3 as quoted by ibid., 372.
[11]Fryer, *Staying Power*, 372. Fryer points to the fact that the larger numbers of arrivals came from 1954 onwards and not immediately after the arrival of the *Windrush*. By 1958 Britain had received 125,000 West Indians.
[12]Elyse Dodgson, *Motherland: West Indian Women in Britain in the 1950s* (London: Heinemann, 1984), 7, 31 and 33.
[13]Nicholas Deakin and others, *Colour, Citizenship and British Society* (London: Panther Books, 1970), 283.

an Englishman. In law he becomes a United Kingdom Citizen by birth; in fact he is a West Indian or an Asian still.'[14]

Powell's notion was voiced at a time when those who were later defined by British society as the first generation of black Britons were babies. Whilst the West Indian parents of these children often saw their offspring as British, their children were not always treated as equal to their white counterparts. In keeping with Powell's above notion of suggested difference these children were made to feel as foreign as their parents had, particularly in the key areas of education and later in employment and housing.[15]

Such discrimination encourages questions around the complex cultural identity of later generations of black Britons. For them, seldom accepted as British and always having to explain their cultural heritage, the question 'No, I mean where do you *really* come from?' encourages a sense that the 'black' in 'black Briton' is synonymous with unequal. This has a two-pronged effect: some black Britons reject their Britishness whilst others are firm in their knowledge that Britain is their home and they are here to stay. To affirm the latter and encourage other black Britons to recognize their British roots, the documentation and publicizing of black contribution in all areas of British life must be acknowledged.

Brewster's work at Talawa ensured that black people saw themselves, along with all aspects of black life, on stage. The questions of race, racism, belonging, forging and articulating an identity in a new place were raised both directly and indirectly through character, plot and production. Along with the topical issues performed was the language they were presented in. Black language forms were used as a device to forge the identity of complex characters, and illustrate how black identity is intrinsically linked to language.

---

[14]Mary Karen Dahl, 'Postcolonial British Theatre: Black Voices at the Center', in *Imperialism and Theatre: Essays on World Theatre, Drama and Performance*, ed. J. Ellen Gainor (London and New York: Routledge, 1995), 38–55 (52–3). Quoting Enoch Powell's speech in Eastbourne on 16 November 1968.
[15]David J. Smith, *Racial Disadvantage in Britain: The PEP Report* (Harmondsworth: Penguin Books, 1977), 13.

Defining voice

'Voice is me, it is my way of being me in my going out from myself.'[16]

The sociolinguistic theories used to discuss language use, as it relates to black identity in Talawa's productions, fall under the sociology of language and language style as audience design and related theories.

The sociology of language

Joshua A. Fishman's theory of the sociology of language is used as an umbrella term referring to all aspects of language linked with language behaviour and the responses to it. It examines the characteristics of language varieties, their functions and those that speak them.[17] Within the general theory of the sociology of language is the theory of the dynamic sociology of language. This is used to explain selective language change within a single community for different events, and examines both the factors that led to this change and the responses to it. The dynamic sociology of language further encompasses three sociolinguistic concepts used throughout this book when discussing Talawa's performances. These are overt language, verbal repertoire and antilanguage speech.

Overt language shows how speech forms at risk of dying out are given a higher status to help revive them. In the case of Caribbean and other related speech forms, overt language behaviour is demonstrated in the publication of Caribbean language texts and by performance artists using Caribbean language in their work. Talawa's African and Caribbean productions illustrate this linguistic reclamation and show that Brewster made a concerted effort to connect language with black British identity, thus exemplifying what Maggie Inchley describes as 'cultural audibility'.[18]

Verbal repertoire is the language of a community that uses many forms of speech.[19] The speaker decides which speech form is most appropriate

---

[16]Steven Connor, *Dumbstruck: A Cultural History of Ventriloquism* (Oxford: Oxford University Press, 2000), 4; Mladen Dolar, *A Voice and Nothing More* (Cambridge, MA: MIT Press, 2006), 112.

[17]Joshua A. Fishman, 'The Sociology of Language', in *Sociolinguistics: A Reader and Coursebook*, ed. Nikolas Coupland and Adam Jaworski (London: Macmillan, 1997), 25–30.

[18]Maggie Inchley, *Voice and New Writing, 1997–2007: Articulating the Demos* (Basingstoke: Macmillan, 2015), 1.

[19]Fishman, 'The Sociology of Language', 28.

for a particular occasion. This dexterity is in continual development amongst black Britons whose language choices combine African, British and Caribbean influences. This has equipped these speakers with a range of speech styles that differ from and include 'standard English' speech.[20]

The ability to authentically change voice depending on interlocutor and environment develops with need. This is about fitting in and, in its crudest form, survival. It is unsurprising that Talawa's black British performers display considerable verbal repertoire in performance. In some cases, this is their life experience performed. Where identity is gauged on the basis of language alone, black Britons who use a sophisticated verbal repertoire are able to belong to an environment that represents only a percentage of their entirety. When staged, this means black British performers can often comfortably move between regional accents, received pronunciation and African-Caribbean voices due to their large reservoir of linguistic resources.

Antilanguage speech is the language created from a more dominant speech form, to show a rejection of the original form and what it represents. Antilanguage is the preferred form of speech for the antigroup: the speakers who use it. The aim of antilanguage is to 'exclude outsiders and express the ideology of the antigroup'.[21] The message at the core of an antilanguage is often one of hostility from those in the marginalized group to those in the mainstream. Antilanguage speech can be used as the result of a range of factors including the desire to express difference, create internal solidarity and shut others out. All of this may be expressed through a particular use of accent, grammar, unique phrases and themes that help to give the antilanguage group its identity whilst excluding others.[22]

Although most ways of speaking are produced with a sense of how speakers wish to be perceived, it is those who adopt an antilanguage-style speech that rely most heavily on the expected reception of their voice. This expectation drives voice production. When this voice was used in Talawa's productions, often in Caribbean plays, critics commented on not being able to understand the speech. The unintentional by-product of this language use then was that white critics briefly sampled the daily black experience

---

[20]The term 'standard English' is written in inverted commas, as is 'standard American English', in Chapter 5, 'The Black South'. This is to illustrate the notion that, based on sound and grammar, no single form of English speech has a higher status than another.
[21]Robert Hodge and Gunther Kress, 'Social Semiotics, Style and Ideology', in *Sociolinguistics: A Reader and Coursebook* (London: Macmillan, 1997), 53.
[22]Ibid., 54.

of being 'other' in British society. More importantly, Brewster knew her antilanguage speech choices would send a strong message of inclusion to those it was meant for. They would need no explanation of the fact that 'to deny the legitimacy of Africanized English is to deny the legitimacy of black culture and the black experience'.[23]

Language style as audience design and related theories

The theory of language style as audience design is linked to Allan Bell's 1984 Audience Design Framework. Bell suggests that speech adaptation often stems from the speaker's view of his or her audience, which may be made up of a single individual or a group, along with what the speaker intends to achieve from the interaction.[24] Here the audience is generally the literal theatre audience. The language of Talawa's performance work is often premeditated and aims to attract a target audience that naturally uses similar speech to that being performed. This is a subversion of Bell's theory, which ordinarily examines the speaker's change of speech once the interlocutor has spoken. For the length of the performance there is no dialogue between the actors and the audience. The performers then have a form of linguistic control over the silent spectators, although their speech has been guided by the genre of the work performed and what the target audience expects to hear.

Two further concepts related to this theory are referred to in the discussion of Talawa's work. These are linguistic accommodation and linguistic behaviour. Giles and Powesland use their accommodation theory to argue that speakers adapt their language to sound more like their listeners and thus gain a favourable impression from them.[25] In addition to creating a favourable impression other factors for speech change may include the subject under discussion, where the discussion takes place, the speaker's attempt to be better understood, and the speaker's ability to make the change. Effort and external pressures may also lead to the attributions for accommodation.[26]

---

[23]Geneva Smitherman, *Talkin and Testifyin* (Boston: Houghton Mifflin, 1977), 174.
[24]Allan Bell, 'Language Style as Audience Design', in *Sociolinguistics: A Reader and Coursebook* (London: Macmillan, 1997), 243.
[25]Howard Giles and Peter Powesland, 'Accommodation Theory', in *Sociolinguistics: A Reader and Coursebook* (London: Macmillan, 1997), 232.
[26]Ibid., 235.

Voicing an Identity

R. B. Le Page's concept of linguistic behaviour describes how speakers change their language in an attempt to identify with another speaker or group. This concept differs to the accommodation theory as it is essentially concerned with the temporary nature of the language change and the reasons for it.[27] In performance, brief changes in speech most obviously occur when delivering songs, poems and jokes, or when intentionally imitating another known voice in the production.

Finally, the phrase, 'accuracy of language use' is employed to describe the performers' skill in producing a credible spoken voice for the character being played. Authenticity comes from the performers' ability to produce a sound that enables the audience to know precisely where the character comes from. This kind of oral realism is not always essential in theatre. American actors play Shakespeare in theatre and film using American accents. Similarly, British actors perform American playwrights on the British stage with varying degrees of success in their accuracy of language use. These are widely accepted conventions and audiences can reasonably be asked to suspend their disbelief and accept the oral 'inaccuracies' of a performer.

The burden of representation

For Talawa's performances generally, and for its Caribbean productions in particular, the case for accuracy of language use in performance is strengthened because the work often highlights voices that customarily go unheard. The performance of such voices brings with it a burden of representation as the work becomes politicized by virtue of its 'minority' status. As Inchley explains, 'The care and craft exerted by practitioners in the acts of listening to, scripting and speaking voices for theatre are . . . not only artistic but also political . . . especially where claims of articulating non-standard or rarely heard voices with authenticity and accuracy are made.'[28] This accidental politicization of voices, with the multilayered ethical and other issues surrounding it, meant that the result of Brewster's efforts to give audibility to rarely heard black voices

---

[27]Peter Trudgill, 'Acts of Conflicting Identity: The Sociolinguistics of British Pop-Song Pronunciation', in *Sociolinguistics: A Reader and Coursebook* (London: Macmillan, 1997), 253.
[28]Inchley, *Voice and New Writing*, 2.

had to be as authentic as possible to maintain credibility in a hostile environment where the overt staging of black lives was both silently and sometimes loudly challenged.

McDaniel's desire to be a credit to her race illustrates the burden of representation that Brewster and others have carried throughout their careers. Brewster used this responsibility to ensure not only that space was made for her work on the British stage, but that it provided a training ground and a nurturing environment for the individual growth for her actors. In this regard, Brewster mirrors her American predecessor Barbara Ann Teer, who founded the National Black Theatre of Harlem (NBT) in 1968.[29] When Teer was asked by the director of the off-Broadway show she was rehearsing to roll her eyes like Butterfly McQueen in *Gone With The Wind*, she found this insulting. Equally insensitive was the request from another director for her to remove her hat. This was her hair. Faced with the choice of getting rid of her hair or getting that job, Teer kept her hair.[30] She also made a choice not to play roles she knew would demean her and her people and perpetuate negative stereotypes, even when this meant working less or having no job at all. These types of experiences led her to create her own theatre.

Whilst Teer developed courses to create a theatre where black performers could embrace their black identity, Brewster offered this less overtly. Talawa's objectives under Brewster nonetheless aimed to ensure exposure and accurate representation. This would be achieved by using black culture and experience to further enrich British theatre, providing high-quality productions that reflect the significant creative role that black theatre plays within the national and international arena, and by enlarging theatre audiences from the black community.[31] By accomplishing this, Talawa's Brewster era marks a didactic period in the company's history that was dedicated to giving accurate linguistic and cultural representations of black British people. This was at a time when second and third generations of black Britons were coming of age. A time when black Britons wanted

---

[29]Further detail of Teer is given in Chapter 2, 'Post-Traumatic Slavery Disorder', as Brewster's intentions and results are likened to Teer's at various points throughout.
[30]Lundeana M. Thomas, 'Barbara Ann Teer: From Holistic Training to Liberating Rituals', in *Black Theatre: Ritual Performance in the African Diaspora*, ed. Paul Carter Harrison, Victor Leo Walker II and Gus Edwards (Philadelphia: Temple University Press, 2002), 368.
[31]http://www.talawa.com/index.htm – Who Is Talawa?: Talawa's Profile and Mission Statement, 6 March 2001.

more than to be reduced to the most simplistic of negative stereotypes both on and off stage.

To discuss Brewster and her work with Talawa as outlined above, *Talawa Theatre Company: A Theatrical History and the Brewster Era* is structured into six further chapters. Whilst Chapters 2 and 3 provide a substantial theatre history context for the company Brewster created, the plays discussed in Chapters 4 to 6 inevitably draw on black British experience and culture, highlight productions seldom discussed in detail, and illustrate how breathing black life into performance work makes it relevant to contemporary British society. As almost all of Talawa's work during the period under discussion was initially analysed by the mainstream from a white perspective, the present exploration offers a necessary black British view of the same work. This is necessary because the work was created with black Britons in mind, but their reaction to it was seldom considered or documented.

In Chapter 2, 'Post-traumatic slavery disorder', Talawa's theatrical lineage is set out. This is shown to start in West Africa through ritual and storytelling, develop in Jamaica over two centuries of theatre from 1700 to the 1980s, and continue in Britain after the Second World War through the pioneering post-war work of black British artists from the Caribbean.

In Chapter 3, 'A stranger in non-paradise', a biography of Brewster's life and work, both in Jamaica and Britain, is presented. The latter work specifically illustrates the breadth and depth of Brewster's contribution to the genre of black British theatre prior to her time at Talawa. Her involvement in the pioneering work that she and others did with Dark and Light, the Theatre of Black Women, Carib Theatre, Black Theatre Cooperative, and the Black Theatre Forum highlights the growing voice of black Britons and their determination to articulate an identity that was rarely represented on the British stage. This also provides a backdrop to the discussion of how and why Brewster started Talawa and how she was able to get Talawa a three-year residency in London's West End.

Chapter 4, 'The island plays', demonstrates how Brewster established Talawa through the Caribbean plays she produced and how she dared to put black Caribbean and black British lives at the forefront of her work. It shows how, by giving a literal voice to black language through producing Caribbean work, Brewster also gave a black British voice to the Caribbean genre. The chosen oral language forms of the productions and their impact on Talawa's audience and on black British theatre generally is explored. Additionally, the chapter reveals varying non-spoken Caribbean performance forms in Talawa's work. These include ritual, storytelling, colonialism, Voodoo, calypso and Carnival. Brewster shines a light on how these African-Caribbean forms permeate contemporary black British existence, whilst also demonstrating the cultural and linguistic differences between Caribbean and black Britons. The shows discussed are *An Echo in the Bone*, *Maskarade*, *The Black Jacobins*, *The Dragon Can't Dance*, *The Lion* and *Beef, No Chicken*.

Chapter 5, 'The black south', explains the genre of American work within the context of the modern British stage. This highlights the uniqueness and bravery of Talawa's work. Three of Talawa's productions that take place in the American black south are examined. Each show presented Talawa's audience with the struggles of black American life, often those of women, along with female discourses on sex and love, and little advertised black existences. The latter is illustrated in the presentation of the tough pioneer lives of black cowboys who ventured out west on the promise of land. The stories are told in the performances of *Love Space Demands*, *From the Mississippi Delta* and *Flyin' West*.

Chapter 6, 'Stay in your box', focuses on Brewster's productions of British classics. The discussion illustrates how Brewster shows this work belongs to black as well as other Britons. The initial debate explores the genre of British classics and looks specifically at the mainstream theatrical conflict between the language of the classics and their performance by black actors. Through Brewster's productions of *Antony and Cleopatra*, *King Lear*, *'Tis Pity She's a Whore*, *The Importance of Being Earnest* and *Othello*, the theatrical mainstream was given multiple opportunities to show its readiness to accept black performers working within this most quintessential of genres. Would 'white' words coming from black mouths be abhorred, applauded, celebrated or ignored? The chapter looks at critical receptions, notions of black actors playing Shakespeare and the roles created for white Victorians, how the literal meaning of a classical text can change once uttered by a black performer, and how Brewster afforded black actors the opportunity to work within a genre they would not ordinarily be considered for.

Finally, Chapter 7, 'Don't tell massa', sums up Brewster's contribution to the genre of black British theatre she was instrumental in creating. It also explains her departure from the company and her final efforts to establish a second home for Talawa specifically and for black British theatre generally.

CHAPTER 2
POST-TRAUMATIC SLAVERY DISORDER

Talawa's theatrical roots are tripartite. Its lineage began in West Africa with the performance forms of ritual and storytelling. It continued in Jamaica throughout and after the transatlantic slave trade with significant periods of continuous theatrical activity between the 1700s and the 1980s. It finally came to Britain with the post-war contributions of black British artists, who began what would later be termed black British theatre.

Ritual: A survival technique

Ritual was part of West African daily life and served to highlight communal beliefs as well as preserve cultural history.[1] This was exemplified in African religion and extended into African performance, where such work was often based on real life. Even in performance, ritual acts were believed to be real and were worked through with an audience who knew how to respond to their development. Due to this, performers saw themselves as taking part in a ritual event rather than acting a role.

African drama ritual can be divided into sacred and profane rituals. The former was for spectators only, the latter allowed participants. Much of the revelry seen during the slave years which was later reproduced in West Indian and black British theatre incorporated elements of the profane. Ritual revelry in the Caribbean that has African roots include Jonkonnu (Jamaica), Crop-over (Barbados), Carnival (Leeward/Windward islands; Trinidad and Tobago), Papa Diable Mask, La Rose and La Marguerite (St Lucia).[2]

---

[1] Helen Gilbert and Joanne Tompkins, *Post-Colonial Drama: Theory, Practice, Politics* (London and New York: Routledge, 1996), 57.
[2] Kole Omotoso, *The Theatrical into Theatre: A Study of Drama and Theatre in the English Speaking Caribbean* (London and Port of Spain: New Beacon Books, 1982), 33.

It was on the slave ships that the first incidents of African ritual were seen by the West. Although the slaves had been stripped of life as they knew it, they maintained a strong sense of self. This was illustrated by their 'names of gods, ancestors and self, language, social constructs of community, oral traditions, communal traditions; gestures, tales, games, humour, music, dance, riddles, food and folklore'.[3] As they were all black, the basis of their identity was their communal practices and not their skin colour. The fact that they were stolen from different tribes meant that ancient traditions were mixed with new ones which created an African slave identity where 'The decks of these ships became the first ritualized spaces for forced performance'.[4]

Some of the new and newly practiced rituals were survival techniques in the most hostile of environments. These included suicide and the killing of newborns to escape the horrors of slavery. Isert, a slave ship doctor, did not understand why the Africans preferred death to a life of enslavement. He wrote to his father from St Croix in 1787, of slaves who had thrown themselves overboard, 'Some faced death with such stubbornness that they pushed the rescue ropes away and drowned of their own free will.'[5]

The majority who did not take their lives were kept fit in the Middle Passage by forced limbo and other dancing. A surgeon on a slave ship in 1788 recognized that the slaves' singing and dancing expressed their sadness whilst ritual body rocking developed for those who were determined to keep their spirit alive.[6] For those who made it to the plantations, African rituals had to be both functional and 'non-threatening to the slavocracy'.[7] This is not unlike contemporary black British life when allowed into the mainstream.

The slaves developed profane welcome rituals for new arrivals. In 1761 the Moravian scholar Christian Georg Andreas Oldendorp interpreted what he saw: 'These newly-arrived ones were paraded, made to form circles, and

---

[3]Beverly J. Robinson, 'The Sense of Self in Ritualizing New Performance Spaces for Survival', in *Black Theatre: Ritual Performance in the African Diaspora*, ed. Paul Carter Harrison, Victor Leo Walker II and Gus Edwards (Philadelphia: Temple University Press, 2002), 332.
[4]Ibid.
[5]Isidor Paiewonsky, *Eyewitness Accounts of Slavery in the Danish West Indies also Graphic Tales of Other Slave Happenings on Ships and Plantations* (New York: Ford University Press, 1989), 26.
[6]Robinson, 'The Sense of Self in Ritualizing New Performance Spaces for Survival', 333–4.
[7]Katrina Hazzard-Gordon, *Jookin': The Rise of Social Dance Formations in African American Culture* (Philadelphia: Temple University Press, 1990), 13.

chanted over in the Congo tongue. They were then given several symbolic lashes across the back and shoulders to atone for their evil doings in the African countries from whence they came.'[8] Oldendorp's interpretation fails to recognize that the ritual symbolized the slaves' determination that whilst their bodies had been stolen, their spirits could never be broken. Oldendorp also describes a profane birth ritual in which the father sets up a vigil until midnight on the eighth day of his newborn's life. This is to prevent an evil spirit putting 'his toothless gums to the full breast of the mother and suck it dry!' The evil spirit was also thought to leave a poison on the mother's breast that would quickly kill the child.[9]

Following the welcome and birth rituals were the profane rituals associated with music and dance. The slavers experienced elements of these with trepidation. In 1758 Richard Haagensen, a Danish observer, wrote about slaves drumming in St Croix: 'Here something was happening which the white people did not understand . . . but deep down they feared that this recreated jungle atmosphere might create rebellion . . . so they passed numerous laws forbidding these dances.'[10] What was this fear based on? The knowledge that the enslavement of another was wrong? Or was it that the enslaved were stronger in every conceivable way, would one day be free and retaliate against those who had forced them into a life of servitude? There was only one thing for it: keep the slaves in place with laws designed to destroy their culture whilst legalizing every aspect of their suffering.

The slavocracy across the Caribbean also saw African drumming along with 'violent' dancing as rebellious and similarly outlawed both. Jorge de Juan's November 2018 version of Lorca's *Yerma* at London's Cervantes Theatre featured a profane fertility ritual which incorporated both of these performance elements. As this black Yerma, played by Nansi Nsue, writhed, the white audience became visibly uncomfortable as the ritual went on and on and on. This real-time technique illustrated Yerma's desperation and presented the audience with a blackness it might prefer to avoid even today. The fear that led to the slavers' bans, and which made de Juan's audience fidget nervously, is matched in equal measure by both the slavocracy's and contemporary society's ability to marvel at black people dancing.

---

[8] Paiewonsky, *Eyewitness Accounts*, 92.
[9] Ibid., 99.
[10] Ibid., 152.

It was with a mixture of wonderment and jealousy that the slavocracy viewed the varying West African dance traditions the slaves brought with them. This is exemplified in the Bamboula, from the coast of Guinea, and the 'lunatic balls'. The Bamboula was particularly popular with Danish West Indian slavers and was performed as a treat for them as they could not do it. They took pride when their children, taught by slaves, learnt to perform the 'wild rhythms and body contortions of the African slave'.[11] Edwards outlines how the 'lunatic balls' featured both music and dance and allowed the slaves a free reign with the imaginative characters they created, dressed and gave a performance setting to.[12] This was a forerunner to contemporary Caribbean and black British Carnival. Although music and dance were outlawed at times, it was a ritual occurrence that came from within the individual and collective spirit of the slaves. Also from within was the slaves' belief, equally necessary for their survival, in powers stronger than mortal men. This was shown in sacred witchcraft rituals.

The slavocracy was particularly fascinated by slave witchcraft. This once again stemmed from fear. If they did not understand it, it could be used against them. Their interest meant they would observe and write about slave witchcraft events, which the slaves would pass on orally, ensuring intentionally or not that they were officially documented. When French priest Pere Labat visited St Thomas in 1701, he was told how an Obeah man was to be burnt alive for allegedly making a pot speak. The man boasted he would make a walking stick speak in response to its owner's queries about a vessel on its way from Denmark to St Thomas. The Obeah man was executed both because and in spite of having made the stick speak. The details the stick provided proved to be exact when the vessel arrived three days later.[13]

Similarly, Johan Lorentz Carstens, writing about life amongst slaves in St Thomas and St John in 1742, describes equivalent feats: 'They [witch-masters] can put into people a lump of twisted hair, cut-off nails, or sharp thin pieces of rusted iron and in a short time their victim dies. Some of these witch-masters have been known to shrink people in size. Others have

---

[11]Ibid., 153.
[12]Gus Edwards, 'Caribbean Narrative: Carnival Characters - In Life and in the Mind', in *Black Theatre: Ritual Performance in the African Diaspora*, ed. Paul Carter Harrison, Victor Leo Walker II and Gus Edwards (Philadelphia, Temple University Press, 2002), 108.
[13]Paiewonsky, *Eyewitness Accounts*, 139.

been known to turn away bullets fired directly at them.'[14] Bryan Edwards's 1807 study of West Indian slavery explains that the Obeah man is feared yet turned to for all matters, including health, predicting the future and exacting revenge on thieves and adulterers. The slavocracy controlled this practice, which was hidden from them, by spreading fear with the routine hanging of the Obeah man in his regalia.[15] This was faster than creating a law and would end the problem immediately.

In spite of these murders, British author Mrs Carmichael in her 1834 study of customs and superstitions of West Indian slaves highlights the proliferation and secrecy surrounding Obeah: 'There is not a single West Indian estate upon which there is not one or more Obeah men or women. The Negroes know who they are, but it is very difficult for white people to find them out.'[16] This practice still continues across the Caribbean. In Jamaica in 1991, my brother complained of stomach pains and my niece of headaches. One Sunday morning my brother drove the three of us to a church in Portland to see an Obeah woman. I watched as, after much massaging and coaxing, the Obeah woman took a nail from my niece's head. I then stood over my brother as she removed a nail from his stomach. I know what I saw, but I still do not know what it was.

As with life, death, whether by hanging the problem or by natural causes, also brought profane ritual amongst the slaves. In 1761 Oldendorp believed slavery did to slaves what death does to everyone: 'it flattened them to a common level, kings, queens, children of princes, nobles, tradesmen. Slavery had set them in a kind of rigid equality.'[17] Slaves then suffered death twice. In their physical death, however, profane ritual separated the living slaves from their captors. This was because the passing of one of their own awakened their African past. The slavocracy could only ponder the spirituality it witnessed.

Those attending a funeral gathered hours before the funeral began, barefooted and dressed in white. If the dead person was old or respected the lead pallbearer discussed the route to be taken with the corpse. Corpses were known to refuse to pass the houses of old enemies or leap from the shoulders of the pallbearers, along with the coffin, if it objected to the

---

[14]Ibid., 124.
[15]Ibid., 135.
[16]Ibid., 133.
[17]Ibid., 92.

route. Funeral processions halted when they passed a large silk cotton tree to give the spirit of the deceased a chance to look for the spirits of loved ones already passed. It was believed the dead would join the procession to welcome the new spirit.[18]

Some foresaw death, as Hans Nielsen did in 1747 when he saw a carriage with four black horses, a black coachman and black footman at the same time as his estate owner died.[19] Others prevented death coming at all. In the 1830s the West African Mongo Maud, renowned for her knowledge of medicinal herbs and ability to preserve the dead, was asked to prepare the corpse of a landowner's wife. She went one better and brought her back to life.[20]

Whilst the slavocracy witnessed the rituals of the slaves, it had rituals of its own: the unchaining of a dead slave from a live one with no regard for the survivor other than his monetary value; the lack of recognition for the bones of captured Africans which, if the Atlantic ocean dried up, would line the path from the slave coast of Africa to America; the ritual humiliation of black life that has led to black self-hatred centuries on; the hanging of male slaves in front of their pregnant wives; the ritual rape of both male and female slaves; the admiration of the Africans' powerful physicality and jealousy of their sensuality, sexual prowess, spirituality and freedom in spite of captivity.

Black rituals were further developed in the churches of the new world. Preachers, unable to read, became master storytellers and connected with their congregations through powerful speaking voices, movement, music and the ritual call and response that was a normal part of their services. Black church was not a passive experience. In the early black Caribbean and American churches the preacher was like the elder in a traditional African society who cured all the problems of his community.[21]

When Prince Harry married Meghan Markle on 19 May 2018 at Windsor Castle, the ceremony that was broadcast live worldwide showed how the American Bishop Michael Curry exemplified the above. Black audiences internationally were instantly familiar. This was a black idiom in language, style, form, presentation and content. Much of the white audience in the church appeared uncomfortable, as if afraid they might be asked to join in. Some giggled nervously.

---

[18]Ibid., 125.
[19]Ibid., 117.
[20]Ibid., 129–30.
[21]Robinson, 'The Sense of Self in Ritualizing New Performance Spaces for Survival', 338.

Whilst we are wittingly or otherwise experiencing ritual that stems from Africa in contemporary daily life, it is in Teer's work that a clear line from African ritual to present-day performance is intentionally made. Teer based her performance theory for black performers on African, and specifically Yoruba, rituals and the Pentecostal churches in Harlem. This was for her the black performers' being and background and they should unashamedly live it: 'In a ritual you mend and heal the mental wounds in the minds of your people. You attempt to get your people out of the box that Western civilisation placed us in, inhibiting us, keeping us from being natural.'[22]

Teer created the five cycles of blackness as part of her classes. The categories were to be used as a guideline and a way of creating her black theatre standard.[23] They were:

The Nigger. He is the most free, creative and colourful but has strong material and individualistic values.

The Negro. He is also materialistic and individualistic. He accepts and imitates white cultural standards.

The Militant. He is still materialistic and individualistic. He hates whites but is not for real change. His anger comes from not being allowed to be part of the system.

The Nationalist. He is non-material. He is for the collective. He has real love for his people.

The Revolutionary. This is the highest spiritual level of blackness. He knows who he is, what he has to do, and goes about it quietly.[24]

This is the intentional creation of a performance standard that would be considered political. Whenever black people seek to understand themselves, raise the level of consciousness of their communities or simply wish to be treated equally, wider white society regards this as a political act. Teer was more concerned with what she could create than how it could be perceived by those it was not intended for: 'Every ritual has a function,' she states. 'Ours is to open up, liberate, regain and reclaim our spiritual freedom. If we are successful, then people watching will feel this.'[25]

---

[22]Charlie L. Russell, 'Barbara Ann Teer: We Are Liberators Not Actors', *Essence*, March 1971, 50.
[23]Russell, 'Barbara Ann Teer', 49.
[24]Thomas, 'Barbara Ann Teer: From Holistic Training to Liberating Rituals', 358.
[25]Ibid., 361. The source for this interview is Thomas Johnson, 'On Harlem Stage', *New York Times*, 11 May 1971, E44.

Perhaps it is because of the brutality and length of the American slave trade and the continued overtly racially segregated American society that black American artists are able to articulate themselves with a clear reference to African ritual. For black Britons the journey has been from Africa to the Caribbean and then to Britain. With each step there is a watering down, a readapting, a chance to become a local and appear to erase the most relevant aspects of who you are. Except you cannot forget. Wider British society would not let you, even if you could and wanted to.

The tradition of African ritual as further developed in the Caribbean provided a legacy for the work, hundreds of years later, of black Caribbean artists that used ritual as a major element of their work. These include Marina Omowale Maxwell, Lennox Brown and Zeno Constance from Trinidad, and Henk Tjon from Surinam.[26] Jamaican Sylvia Wynter presents the theatrical legacy of Jonkonnu in her play *Maskarade* (1973).

Jonkunnu was the most popular masquerade in Jamaica prior to emancipation and saw the Jonkonnu, jester, dancing in the streets accompanied by a band of musicians and followers. From the 1950s Jonkunnu was recognized with the new status of a Jamaican art form and has become part of the performance repertoire of the Jamaican National Dance Company. Similarly, fellow Jamaican Dennis Scott's *An Echo in the Bone* (1974) displays the inheritance of African religious profane ritual through its presentation of the Nine Nights ceremony where the body of a dead person is watched over by relatives and friends for nine days and nights.[27]

Black ritual, whether from Africa, the Caribbean, the USA, Britain, or anywhere black people live, is central to black life. It is survival both at home and in any environment made home: 'our stories are in our flesh in our genetic memories in our ancestral callings and responses.'[28] And so black rituals adapt and continue because they must, from fathers and brothers taking their sons to the barber for as long as they have hair, to the peeling of an orange in one single continuous movement on the promise of

---

[26]Judy S. J. Stone, *Studies in West Indian Literature: Theatre* (London and Basingstoke: Macmillan Caribbean, 1994), 155–6.
[27]At the time of writing, Natasha Gordon's *Nine Night*, of the same theme, was being performed at the National Theatre, London.
[28]Keith Antar Mason, 'From Hip-Hop to Hittite: Part X', in *Black Theatre: Ritual Performance in The African Diaspora*, ed. Paul Carter Harrison, Victor Leo Walker II and Gus Edwards (Philadelphia: Temple University Press, 2002), 382–7, 382.

new clothes. Rituals structure and bind us; they are an ancestral gift to be lived and performed.

Storytelling

> 'We create rituals and tell myths . . . we come from a culture that believes the universe is made up of stories and that is how you can tell where you are in the universe.'[29]

The importance of West African and plantation storytelling lay in its dual aim to tell the history of the community and to entertain. The story was not fixed and neither then was history. The storytellers' gift was in making the tale their own by adding local colour through carefully chosen themes, characters and popular situations. The artists would also perform multiple characters and incorporate music and dance into their work.[30] Storytellers performed in their native tongue. This display of overt language behaviour has remained a fundamental feature of Caribbean folk tales across the centuries as the tradition has evolved.

The fact that women played a central role in West African tradition is reflected in the number of storytellers who were female. For Europeans, the historical accounts of these women were dubious on account of their gender, and sometimes seen as no more than 'Little fictitious histories.'[31] The 'fictitious histories' impacted not only the slaves but also the children of the slavocracy who were being raised and nurtured by their black nurses who shared their stories with them. Carmichael's 1834 study points to the love, 'unbounded affection' and respect the children of the slavocracy had towards those who were really looking after them.[32]

Similarly, Paiewonsky explains that 'One of the links of affection between planters' children and their Negro nurses might be traced directly to storytelling.'[33] He tells us that Nana Bela, a Bantu tribeswoman from Angola and a domestic at the Sprat Hall Estate in St Croix, circa 1787, was the most

---

[29]Ibid., 383.
[30]Gilbert and Tompkins, *Post-Colonial Drama*, 126–31.
[31]Errol Hill, *The Jamaican Stage 1655–1900: Profile of a Colonial Theatre* (Amherst: University of Massachusetts Press, 1992), 226.
[32]Paiewonsky, *Eyewitness Accounts,* 154.
[33]Ibid.

renowned of storytellers: 'Nana Bela's variety of tales, her ability to express them, to convert African folklore into a West Indian setting earned her a wide reputation. She was in great demand for garden parties for children which were well attended by grownups as well.'[34]

Nana Bela arrived in St Croix as a young woman in a cargo of slaves. She grew up and spent her entire adult life at Sprat Hall estate. Becoming part of the Sprat Hall establishment by her late fifties, when the estate was sold in 1833, there was a precondition that Nana Bela remain on the estate. Such was her storytelling notoriety in later years that requests were made for her to tell her stories at events on estates across the island.[35]

Nana Bela's stories have the type of ritual call and response that vastly predates the Pentecostal traditions that Teer works with. The use of moral message and the written phonetic form of the oral language is strikingly similar to later written forms of the work of subsequent storytellers across the Caribbean: 'Pickaninnies, tis you who tief me? Eat me peas soup and grief me?/ And the children answered/ No, Mamy Luna, we no tief you!/ Belly bawl, but we no grief you!'[36]

Paiewonsky points further to groups of children leaving school and rushing to hear the Bru Nansi stories of Nana Mini. Always expecting children to visit her, if she suddenly had to leave before their arrival, she would leave messages such as: 'Nana Mini say if you cum to tell you/ that Mr Holst (the local banker), sen a/ bile [automobile], to take her to his/ house to tell him stories.'[37]

Here, the adults appreciated her stories with or without children present. Mini's Bru Nansi was an adapted form of the African word *Anansi*. Although the literal meaning is that of a big black daddy long legs spider, the symbolic meaning is much deeper. The spider represents trickery and dishonest cleverness. Anansi started in Africa and became Bru Nansi in parts of the Caribbean throughout the eighteenth and nineteenth centuries, before becoming Brer Anancy across the Caribbean from the twentieth century to the present.

This West African storytelling tradition continued and later produced a wealth of male and female Caribbean storytellers. Amongst the best

---

[34] Ibid., 156.
[35] Ibid.
[36] Ibid., 157.
[37] Ibid., 158.

known are Derek Burrows from the Bahamas, Paul Keens Douglas from Trinidad, Shake Keane from Saint Vincent, Bill Trotman from Guyana and Louise Bennett from Jamaica. Continuing the tradition to date in Jamaica, amongst others, are Amina Blackwood Meeks, Joan Andrea Hutchinson, Mutabaruka, Yasus Afari and Mervyn Morris.

Artists working in this genre, prior to and during Bennett's era, produced their work in spite of the common notion that the voice in which they expressed themselves was considered to be unsophisticated and inadequate. It was the sound of the poor and uneducated who need not be heard. They could expect to gain low artistic status for their efforts. Those who followed Bennett have been acknowledged for what they are aiming to achieve because of the barriers she broke down.

The notion that storytelling in a native voice stemming from West African tradition is inferior comes from Western ideas of African drama. Biodun Jeyifo argues that this is due to three such views in particular. Firstly, that there are no native drama traditions. Secondly, that Africa's theatrical tradition does not compare to that of Europe and Asia. And finally, that what exists in Africa comes from Western sources.[38]

Throughout slavery and colonization it was difficult for black artists to alter the above perceptions. Since emancipation and despite the successes of those mentioned above, these ideas have been well ingrained not only into the Western psyche, but also into that of black people. The success of this brainwashing is unsurprising when the performance work that emerged in Jamaican theatre between the 1700s and the 1980s is considered. This also marks the second stage in Talawa's theatrical roots.

Jamaican theatre 1700s–1980s

When Jamaica became a British colony in 1655 all public theatre performance was banned ensuring that theatrical styles developed under Spanish rule were erased. In 1682 when theatre spaces were established to bring British theatre to the Jamaican expatriate community there were three main groups of performers: touring professionals from Britain and

---

[38]Biodun Jeyifo, 'The Reinvention of Theatrical Tradition', in *The Intercultural Performance Reader*, ed. Patrice Pavis (London and New York: Routledge, 1996), 153–4.

the North American colonies that later became the United States; resident amateurs; and actors from the Jamaican working classes.[39]

The first group brought the most theatrically respected work to the island, including the latest work from home. This was imitated by rich locals. 'Real' theatre, then, meant British work, especially Shakespeare. The Creole actors, local whites, could not reach this British ideal so produced work depicting their own expatriate life. This explored living apart from other islanders, material gain and luxury, making fun of island-born Creoles, plantation life, historical figures and politics.

For more than thirty years from the 1750s, the Hallam Theatre Company provided a large part of the theatrical entertainment on the island. During 1783 the company performed two favourite pieces that focused on expatriate life and simultaneously revealed the low regard with which simply being black or Creole was held. The first of these was Bickerstaffe's *The Padlock* (1770). The picture of West Indian life is presented from a privileged white land-owning perspective. Much of what is gleaned about expatriate life however is through the black character Mungo.

Bickerstaffe's depiction of Mungo demonstrates the period's notions of slavery based on colour. His blackness automatically acquires him the lowest position in society as a slave. His language is distinguished from the other characters as it is written in pidgin. This serves to illustrate that he lacks the intelligence of the white people around him and justifies their perceived superiority and enslavement of him. Similarly, his later drunkenness is presented as a sign of his projected backwardness.[40] The play demonstrates that the white West Indians are superior in every way. Following the abolition of slavery in 1834 the play was no longer performed.

The second piece was Richard Cumberland's melodrama *The West Indian*, performed in 1771. It satirizes the cultural problems of a wealthy Creole male in England. Despite his physical whiteness the West Indian protagonist Belcour is shown to be inferior to the Englishman. He arrives in England with inappropriate luggage from Jamaica including 'grey parrots, a Jamaica sow and pigs, and a mongrove dog'.[41] Belcour sums up, and

---

[39] Hill, *The Jamaican Stage*, 4.
[40] Isaac Bickerstaffe, *The Padlock* (Cork: Anon, 1770), 26.
[41] Richard Cumberland, *The West Indian* (Perth: Morison and Son, 1771), 4.

seemingly accepts, the English idea of a West Indian at the time: 'I am an idle dissipated, unthinking fellow, not worth your notice: in short, I am a West Indian.'[42]

Some years later the cultural dilemmas of Creoles were highlighted by the response to Margaret Cheer Cameron's *A West Indian Lady's Arrival in London* (1781). The play offended Jamaican society as the 'lady' used dialect speech. The author argued that her protagonist 'for a time lay aside the elegance of her character and assumed an awkwardness'.[43] Jamaican society's response served to ensure and perpetuate the idea that any form of black speech was inferior and childlike.

In addition to the above, Jamaican theatre continued to produce European classics. With time, however, the emergence of black performers was seen. What follows highlights the significant developments in Jamaican theatrical activity between 1781 and 1912:

1781: Reciters and the single performer were introduced.[44]

1802: Designated seating was introduced for people of colour in Kingston Theatre.[45]

1813: John Anderson Costello, Guyanese actor, came to the fore on the Jamaican stage.

1824: French operatic society performed at Kingston Theatre for five months.

1827: Mr and Mrs Castells's Company performed English work only.

1829: The English company performed twice weekly.

1841: The Italian Opera visited Jamaica.

1842: The Monier family performed their work from America including Jamaica's first production of Othello.

1847–50: At Kingston's Theatre Royal, the following black groups performed: the Kingston Amateur Association, the Philo-Dramatic Association, the Amateur Thespian Association, an amateur French troupe, the Ethiopian Amateur Society and the Numidian Amateur

---

[42]Ibid., 44–5.
[43]Hill, *The Jamaican Stage*, 161.
[44]The work of the reciters is detailed further in the discussion of Louise Bennett's lineage and legacy.
[45]Richardson Wright, *Revels in Jamaica* (New York and London: Benjamin Blom, 1937), 305.

Association. These groups performed the same style of work as their white counterparts.

1850s onwards: Black artists were creating their own theatre with Bruckins and Tea Meetings.

1862: Obi, or Three Fingered Jack, appeared: the true story of the runaway slave who waged war on Jamaican plantation society.

1865: The first quartet of Minstrels performed in Jamaica.[46]

1873: Charles Rampini published Letters from Jamaica with Negro proverbs, demonstrating white academic interest in native Jamaican speech.

1890: Reverend D.J. Reynolds wrote the article 'Jamaica Proverbial Philosophy' for *Timehri*, the Demerera journal.

1900: Old Theatre Royal in Kingston was torn down, rebuilt, then destroyed once more by the 1907 earthquake.

1912: The Ward Theatre was built in Kingston, and would later become the home of the annual Christmas pantomime which from 1943 and Louise Bennett's initial performance in *Soliday and the Wicked Bird* would incorporate more and more black talent.

The first part of the 1900s also saw two artistic movements that centred on the development of black performance. The first was the 1920s Harlem Renaissance that produced black writers and performers who placed their blackness at the forefront of their work. Though based in America the movement gained international attention and produced artists such as Josephine Baker, Langston Hughes, Zora Neal Hurston and the Jamaican Claude McKay. Additionally Jamaica had its anticolonial champion and political figure in Marcus Garvey (1887–1940), who also played a key role in the Harlem Renaissance.

Garvey had dedicated his life to the development of the black race and in the 1920s formed the Universal Negro Improvement Association (UNIA) based in Harlem. He played a fundamental role in the development of Jamaican theatre and the wider West Indies by demonstrating that theatre

---

[46]Their work encouraged a tradition amongst black and white performers that produced the double acts of Cupes and Abe, Ike and Mike, Harold and Trim, and Racca and Sandy. Minstrel work remained successful throughout the 1950s and 1960s in Jamaica with the work of Bim and Bam.

should have a social responsibility. Stone celebrates Garvey as being the first West Indian to break the stereotype of blacks as mammy types in subservient roles.[47] In 1930 Garvey's plays *The Coronation of an African King*, *Roaming Jamaicans* and *Slavery from Hut to Mansion* were performed in Kingston.

Garvey's plays were accompanied on a literary level by the novels being written by Jamaican artists in the 1930s that were writing about the West Indies from a black perspective. These included Herbert George De Lisser's *Susan Proudleigh*, *The White Witch of Rose Hall* and *Jane's Career*, and G. Ogilvie's *Ethelred Marlow* and *One Soja Man*. The West Indies was also producing other political artists including Norman Cameron of British Guiana, and Trinidad's C. L. R. James.

Importantly the mood of the Harlem Renaissance was echoed in Europe by the 1930s with the rise of Negritude heralded by Martinique's Aimé Césaire. He encouraged a rejection of French colonialism and embraced his African heritage through theatre. His work was to prove long-lasting and in 1948 Léopold Sédar Senghor published *New Negro and Malagasy Poetry*, featuring excerpts from Césaire's 1930s *Return to my Native Land*. In the 1960s Césaire himself launched a resurgence of his Negritude theme in theatre to advance his politics of black consciousness. All of this would provide an artistic, political and sometimes overlapping backdrop for developing West Indian theatre and the work of Jamaica's Louise Bennett. This would in turn influence the development of black theatre in Britain decades later.

Louise Bennett's lineage and legacy

In the 1930s, Jamaica saw the emergence of one of its most celebrated contemporary artists in writer and performer Louise Bennett (1919–2006), known affectionately as Miss Lou. The impact of Bennett's work came from her physical presence and the fact that her work was epitomized by her overt use of Jamaican language. This choice was in stark contrast to her British colonial education and the mainly British literary influences she had grown up with. Her determination to work in her chosen style ultimately

---

[47]Errol Hill, *The Pioneers of West Indian Theatre 1900-1950*, as quoted by Stone in *Studies in West Indian Literature*, 17.

brought her considerable recognition in the shape of many awards. These include an MBE in 1960, the Order of Jamaica in 1974 and two honorary D. Litt. degrees from the University of the West Indies in 1983 and from York University, Toronto in 1998.

Bennett is part of a line of Jamaican artists who chose to use the working class language of people as the main medium of their work. Morris comments, 'Louise Bennett was not the first West Indian, nor even the first Jamaican poet to make extensive use of dialect. Her best known predecessor in Jamaican dialect verse was Claude McKay.'[48] McKay (1890-1948) started his literary career in Jamaica in 1912 with two volumes of poetry, *Songs of Jamaica* and *Constab Balldads*.[49] Both Bennett and McKay have, however, a Jamaican theatrical history that begins a century prior to the latter's work.

In 1781, a new style of acting was introduced to the Jamaican stage when the Hallam's Company began recitals, led by readers. The recitals featured a single performer who recited known and new poetry in multiple characters. The earliest recitals were based on George Alexander Stevens's satirical monologue *The Lecture on Heads*. Papier mâché busts represented characters who were satirized in turn.

Of the many expatriate, Creole and foreign performers who visited Jamaica to recite, the work of Rafael J. de Cordova, whom Hill describes as a 'humorous reader',[50] has a similar content to that of Louise Bennett. De Cordova, a wealthy white Jamaican who wrote in the 'standard English' of the period, may be seen as Bennett's cultural polar opposite, yet they wrote on the same subjects.

De Cordova wrote 'Broadway', the story of an omnibus ride. Bennett's first dialect poem was *On a Tramcar*. She wrote further on the same subject, *Rough Riding Tram*, *Tan-Up Seat*, *Buy a Tram*, *Bear Up* and *Ole-Time Tram*.[51] Additionally, both de Cordova and Bennett wrote extensively on royal visits.

De Cordova wrote a poem to celebrate the 1860 royal visit to America of the British Prince of Wales, Albert Edward. Some eighty-five years later and for the next thirty years, Bennett produced works on royal visits. Both

---

[48]Louise Bennett, *Selected Poems* (Kingston: Sangster's Book Stores Ltd., 1982), xiv.
[49]Wayne F. Cooper, Claude McKay: *Rebel Sojourner of the Harlem Renaissance* (New York: Schocken Books, 1987), 35.
[50]Hill, *The Jamaican Stage*, 191.
[51]All of the poems appear in Louise Bennett's *Jamaica Labrish* (Kingston: Sangster's Book Store Ltd., 1966), 47, 48, 51, 52 and 53 respectively.

Victory and *De Victory Parade* written in 1945 celebrated the end of the Second World War and the British victory.[52] Bennett's poem *Ben Dung* deals with the visit of Princess Margaret and the Earl of Snowdon to Jamaica's Independence celebrations.[53] In 1973 on her Jamaican Broadcasting Company (JBC) radio show *Miss Lou's Views*, Bennett delivered a piece entitled *Dear Princess*, on the honeymoon visit of Princess Anne and Captain Mark Phillips to Jamaica in the same year.[54]

Further similarities exist with both writers and their poetry commenting on social situations. Hill states, 'During the war years he [de Cordova] produced some of his most enduring pieces such as *Courtship and Marriage*, and its sequel *Our First Baby*.'[55] Bennett produced similar works as observations in response to the Second World War including *Married, Solja Work* and *White Pickney*.[56] Like her predecessor her comment on social institutions and behaviour was not limited to wartime. She also wrote *Mass Wedding, Registration, Colour Bar* and *Pass Fe White*.[57]

Similarities between the work of de Cordova and Bennett are not limited to subject matter alone but can also be seen in their style: 'In the tradition of the solo performer de Cordova peopled the stage with a cast of imagined characters "with whom he laughed, and talked and pleaded, and remonstrated, never for a moment losing his identity, or making confusion among his lively motley company".'[58] In the same way Bennett presented multiple characters in her work as seen in her poem *Cus Cus*.[59] The popularity of the single performer from de Cordova's time led to the emergence of readers who unlike de Cordova worked in the patois of the people and hence can be seen to provide a more direct theatrical history to Bennett's work.

Three performers of this kind are Henry Garland Murray (d. 1877) and his two sons Andrew C. Murray and William Coleman Murray. Like Bennett they were black, wrote about Jamaica in the language of the people and

---

[52] Ibid., 106–10.
[53] Ibid., 172.
[54] This show ran from 1965 to 1982. Some fifty of these 'views' are presented in Louise Bennett's *Aunty Roachy Seh* (Kingston: Sangster's Book Stores Ltd., 1993), *Dear Princess*, 20.
[55] Hill, *The Jamaican Stage*, 195.
[56] Bennett, *Jamaica Labrish*, 90–1, 97–8 and 111–12 respectively.
[57] Ibid., 30–1, 42–3, 211–12 and 212–13 respectively.
[58] Hill, *The Jamaican Stage*, 195 quoting the *Colonial Standard*, March 1877.
[59] Bennett, *Jamaica Labrish*, 188–9

displayed overt language behaviour. The elder Murray also used proverbs and Anancy tales in his work, as Bennett was to do later. Their success was enhanced by the fact that they were performing when white intellectuals and leaders of the Kingstonian Presbyterian community were taking an interest in Jamaican language. The case for dialect being carried forward by white intellectuals meant that in 1866 dialect writing occurred in the press for the first time starting a legacy of scribal overt language behaviour.

A century later, Bennett had her own column in the local press writing in patois. This in turn paved the way for later patois writers to continue her legacy. This is seen in Dr Carolyn Cooper's weekly *Zig Zag Talk*, in the *Jamaican Weekly Gleaner* and Dr Jennifer Kean-Dawes's weekly *Dear Jamaica* in *Outlook Magazine*. Both continue to write for the *Jamaican Weekly Gleaner* and other local and international publications.

Bennett's use of patois took on a political dimension particularly as she used it in the Jamaican theatrical white space where 'standard English' was the norm. For those who supported her work she was seen as 'helping Jamaicans to express their identity and cultural heritage through drama'.[60] This was more than overt language behaviour; it was antilanguage speech as it was used to rebel publicly against the expected standard. Those who did not support her use of patois found it difficult to appreciate her work. This lack of support came generally from the middle classes that had the power to choose to leave her out of published anthologies of West Indian literature despite all printed evidence of her work.[61] She was seen as 'a local joke; a good, high-spirited joke, but, in the end, only a joke'.[62]

By the time Bennett no longer travelled to her audience, they were able to access her work through a variety of forms, including written stories, readers and records. Her work was also televised principally through her children's programme, *Ring Ding* (1969–80). It was via the medium of radio however that Bennett's talent would be best transmitted to her audience in the early years. Her radio show *Aunty Roachy Seh* was aired from 1965 to 1982. Bennett became so popular on radio that when JBC celebrated thirty-

---

[60] Barbara Gloudon, 'The Hon.Louise Bennett, O.J. Fifty Years of Laughter', *Jamaica Journal* 19, no. 3 (August/October 1986), 10.
[61] Mervyn Morris, 'On Reading Louise Bennett Seriously', *Jamaica Journal* 1, no.1 (December 1967), 69–74.
[62] Ibid., 69.

five years in business, the Lou and Ranny show was aired live from the Carib Theatre.[63]

Once Bennett became fashionable, the criticism she had had to accept for many years was put behind her. By the 1970s she was widely accepted as a heroine of Jamaican folklore and culture. Praise for her work also focused on the ill-treatment and lack of recognition she had received in the early days. Morris points out that her work was not included in the *Jamaican Anthology Focus* for 1943, 1948, 1956 and 1960, and she was not welcomed as part of the Jamaica Poetry League.[64] Morris describes her as the 'only poet who has really hit the truth about her society through its own language', and as an important contributor to her country of 'valid social documents reflecting the ways Jamaicans think and feel and live.'[65]

Influenced by Bennett, Jamaican theatre saw various attempts to promote patois in the 1950s and 1960s. This came in the shape of the Yard Plays that discussed the harsh realities of Caribbean life. The plays produced throughout and beyond the pre-independence era included Douglas Archibald's *Junction Village* and *The Rose Slip* (Trinidad 1954 and 1962), Barry Reckord's *Della* (Jamaica 1954), Samuel Hillary's *Departure in the Dark* (Jamaica 1960), Errol Hill's *The Ping Pong* (Trinidad 1966), Eric Roach's *Belle Fanto* (Trinidad 1966) and Slade Hopkinson's *A Spawning of Eels* (Guyana 1968).

In addition to the Yard Plays, two theatre companies became prominent in Jamaica in the 1960s and 1970s whose work exemplified the range of activity that was being produced by a new generation of artists who continued to use Jamaican patois in performance. Yvonne Clarke and Trevor Rhone set up The Barn in 1965 as discussed further in Chapter 3, 'A Stranger in Non-Paradise'. This was followed by the emergence of the all-female group Sistren Theatre Collective which formed in 1977.

Sistren was unique on two grounds: firstly, they were an all-female group and secondly, they used Jamaican patois as the exclusive linguistic mode of their performance work. Their choice of language was both political and strategic. Politically, they sought to return to black women the voice that had been denied them during slavery, whilst they strategically aimed to attract

---

[63] Anon, 'JBC – Thirty-five years of Broadcasting', *Outlook Magazine*, 10 July 1994, 14.
[64] Bennett, *Selected Poems*, viii, Introduction by Mervyn Morris.
[65] Morris as quoted by Nettleford in his introduction to Bennett's *Jamaica Labrish*, 9 and 10.

a predominantly working class audience.⁶⁶ They created *Downpression Get a Blow* under the dramatist Honor Ford-Smith, using the technique of collective creation, based on actual experiences, to explore exploitation of factory workers. The Collective continues to perform today.

Jamaican patois-speaking theatre further developed from the late 1970s to include various specialized groups including those for children and prisoners.⁶⁷ By the early 1980s the Jamaican School of Drama set up the Caribbean Lab, which Barbadian Earl Warner ran for three years with the aim of developing indigenous theatrical techniques.⁶⁸ Without the work of Bennett and those that went before her, this proliferation of Jamaican patois theatrical work may not have expanded in Jamaica, or found itself in Britain.

Bennett's influence on the development of present-day language use in black British theatre is seen in the performance work of fellow Jamaicans Linton Kwesi Johnson and Dr Yvonne Brewster OBE. Johnson's use of Jamaican patois in performance, and Brewster's direction of it, form part of the linguistic heritage of black British performers following in their footsteps.

Johnson came to Britain from Jamaica in 1963, aged eleven. He would form part of a new generation of black people in Britain, those Caribbean immigrants who were less than a generation older than the first generation of blacks born here, all of whom would later be termed, along with ensuing generations, as black Britons. Johnson is now recognized in Britain and Jamaica alike as a prolific dub poet, using his native Jamaican patois as the language of his poetry. Johnson acknowledges Bennett's poetry in the BBC Arena documentary *Upon Westminster Bridge*, describing her as revolutionary for her chosen form of language, and as 'The mother of Jamaican poets which I think is responsible for all of us'.⁶⁹

Bennett considered Brewster her protégé. Brewster's vast contribution in providing British audiences with performances in many of the voices of the Caribbean since the early 1970s is in part due to Bennett's legacy.⁷⁰ Like

---

⁶⁶Gilbert and Tompkins, *Post-Colonial Drama*, 186.
⁶⁷Omotoso, *The Theatrical into Theatre*, 85.
⁶⁸Stone, *Studies in West Indian Literature*, 143.
⁶⁹*Arena: Upon Westminster Bridge: A Tribute to Jamaica's Dub Poet Mikey Smith* (1982) [TV programme], BBC 2, 23 November 1982.
⁷⁰Yvonne Brewster, Personal Interview David Johnson, London, 9 January 1997.

Bennett, Brewster used patois uncompromisingly in her work. Far from only attracting the dispossessed, Brewster's work in patois also appealed to her British middle class audience. This strategic use of language in performance was a purposeful sign of non-conformity to British linguistic performance standards and acted as a refusal to be dominated by British colonial attitudes past and present. It simultaneously placed patois speakers at the centre of their Caribbean stories. This speech in performance was an echo of the initial development of the language, born out of repression and used as a code to confuse the slavocracy, before it became the native language of millions of people.[71] Brewster's intentional use of it on stage aimed at attracting those for whom the message within the overt language and antilanguage was intended; those that British theatre very often ignored.[72]

As British theatre largely continues to avoid any meaningful interpretation of black lives, it also disregards the many battles fought by the post-Second World War black British theatre pioneers and their contributions to the British stage. It is vastly due to Brewster and her efforts to document the lives of these artists that a comprehensive record exits today. Their stories complete Talawa's theatrical roots.

Lest we forget: Black British theatre and the post-war pioneers

Blackgrounds is Talawa's first oral history project. It documents the achievements of black theatre practitioners on the British stage from the 1940s to the 1960s. The project was launched in 1997 with the collaboration of the Arts Council of England. It culminated in the production of five video interviews between myself and Earl Cameron, Cy Gant, Barry Reckord, Pearl Connor and Alaknanda Samarth. In 2002, the project entered a second phase entitled *Blackstages*. The end result was six video interviews between Tara Mack and the following pioneering black performers who worked on the British stage between the 1950s and the 1970s: Thomas Baptiste, Corinne Skinner Carter, Frank Cousins, Mona Hammond, Ram John Holder and Rudolph Walker. The seventh video interview for *Blackstages* was between myself and Yvonne Brewster. As

---

[71]G. llewellyn Watson, *Jamaican Sayings: With Notes on Folklore, Aesthetics, and Social Control* (Tallahassee: Florida A&M University Press, 1991), 6–7.
[72]Gilbert and Tompkins, *Post-Colonial Drama*, 168–70.

with *Blackgrounds,* the *Blackstages* artists told their performance histories in their own words. Whilst the central focus here is on the four Caribbean *Blackgrounds* contributors, they serve as an illustration of the many others whose stories are yet to be told.[73]

In December 1994 Brewster was in Ghana giving a paper. It was here that she heard that Norman Beaton had died 'as he lived, very dramatically'.[74] He had got off the plane in his native Guyana and died on the tarmac. Brewster explains the impact of his death:

> I thought, I want to see a recording of Norman, in his words... Nobody seemed to have a recording of Norman, in *Desmond's* yes, but none of Norman speaking. I thought, we'll never get him in his flamboyance, his drunken elegance, his illness, his coughs, his brilliance and yet still his despair. So in honour of Norman, I thought we should grab those people that are in their 70s and 80s and have them at least on tape before they died. That was why *Blackgrounds* happened.[75]

By happenstance: Earl Cameron, 1917–2020

Cameron was born and raised in Bermuda. His desire to act was inspired by the vast amount of theatre that existed on Bermuda, including a regular company that came to perform straight plays from Britain annually. In spite of this influencing the local population, Cameron's shyness stopped him performing until he arrived in Britain in 1939.[76]

Cameron found his way to Britain by doing menial jobs on a ship that sailed between Bermuda and New York. He then transferred to *The Eastern Prince* which sailed to South America. On his second South American trip from Montevideo to Buenos Aires the Second World War started.

---

[73] Rodreguez King-Dorset has accepted that the interviews I conducted with Earl Cameron, Pearl Connor, Cy Grant and Barry Reckord for *Blackgrounds* and my interview with Yvonne Brewster for *Blackstages* were plagiarised by him in 'his' text *Black British Theatre Pioneers: Yvonne Brewster and the First Generation of Actors, Playwrights and Other Practitioners* (McFarland & Co., 2014). Rodreguez King-Dorset has since admitted his plagiarism and the book has subsequently been made unavailable.
[74] Yvonne Brewster, *Blackstages* Interview by Tara Mack, London, 17 July 2002.
[75] Brewster Interview, 26 November 2018. *Desmond's*, in which Norman Beaton played the lead role of Desmond, a barbershop owner, aired on Channel 4 for six seasons between 1989 and 1994. There were seventy-one episodes.
[76] Earl Cameron, *Blackgrounds* Interview by David Johnson, London, 29 May 1997.

When one of the ship's engines broke down, unrelated to the war, it was abandoned. The British Admiralty told all British subjects to sail to London on the *War Head*. Cameron was happy to be going to London in spite of the war. Once in London, the difficulty he had in getting any job took the young Cameron by surprise 'from a racial point of view'.[77] 'Reluctantly' taken on as a dishwasher at the Charing Cross Hotel, fate dealt him a difficult blow when he contracted pneumonia as he came out of the kitchen one night.

In despair in St Pancras Hospital, Cameron had a life-changing experience. Having refused to take food, a night nurse told him it was his job to eat to avoid his parents getting a telegram saying he had died. Unable to stand the thought of his mother crying, he ate. When a new nurse came the following night, Cameron asked for the previous one only to be told there was no other nurse the night before, just her. Whether illusion or reality, the experience had strengthened him. Reluctant to spend any more winters in London hungry and broke, Cameron decided to return to Bermuda. From Liverpool, he got a job on an Egyptian ship on a five-month trip to Calcutta. Unable to save the money he needed to get back home, he returned to London, somehow feeling he had fallen in love with the place.[78]

Determined to make his way, Cameron did the jobs he could get in hotels. In 1941 whilst working he met Harry Crossman. Crossman was in *Chu Chin Chow* and gave Cameron tickets for the show. His reaction after seeing it was, 'Hell, I can do what you guys are doing' and he went backstage to ask for work in the production. A couple of weeks later, Crossman told him that the director, Robert Atkins, wanted someone new. After looking Cameron up and down Atkins said, 'Yeah Harry, I think he'll do.' Cameron found himself on stage for the first time that night at the Palace Theatre in Cambridge Circus, London. He worked on the show in a non-speaking role both in London and then touring for a total of nine months through much of 1942.[79]

Cameron's professional career developed in 1943 whilst in *The Petrified Forest* at the Globe Theatre. He was grateful for his one line, 'Is it alright Mr Chisholm?', both because it was his first speaking part and because he was on stage with big names of West End theatre at the time: Owen Aires, Constance Cummings, Robert Beatty and Hartley Power. In 1944, Cameron found himself again with lines, this time in *All God's Children* at the Colchester Repertory Theatre.

---

[77]Ibid.
[78]Ibid.
[79]Ibid.

During the early part of his career, Cameron performed regularly on the London stage, developing his craft. In 1945 he embarked on a three-month tour to India with the Entertainments National Service Association (ENSA), performing in *The Duchess and the Two Dukes*. The racism that Cameron experienced which resulted in his initial joblessness in London was equally rife in India. The first class accommodation as per the group's contract was inexplicably unavailable when they arrived until the band leader Lesley Hutchinson threatened to return to London with the whole group. They were equally inexplicably 'fit in' at the Grand Hotel. Cameron is measured in his explanation: 'that type of stupid racism follows one around, it's annoying but anyhow we dealt with it very well.'[80]

In 1947 Cameron's earlier work in *The Petrified Forest* saw him invited by H.I. Tennant, who had produced the show, to be the understudy to Gordon Heath in *Deeper the Roots*. Cameron realized how bad he was when in a rehearsal for the pre-West End tour the stage manager told him he couldn't understand a word he was saying from the fifth row. This encouraged him to develop his diction with Miss Amanda Ira Aldridge (daughter of the actor Ira Aldrige), Cicely Berry and Iris Warren. Due to his efforts, Cameron worked on the show for five years in repertory and credits it with giving him a good living.

In 1950 Cameron worked on the stage play *13 Death Street Harlem*: 'I hated every minute of it, but like everything else in the theatre you do it.' Whilst in the show Cameron made a call about another film that was being cast, *The Pool of London*. Basil Dreardon, who was casting it, thought Cameron was too old for the part. Although he was thirty-two years old, Cameron said he was twenty-six and argued that his moustache, which was making him look older, could be shaved off. Despite originally testing badly, he got better as time went on as he was tested with lots of actresses. Finally, he was offered the kind of part 'most actors are longing for'. Cameron had secured his first film. When it was released in 1951, it was the first of thirty-two films he would make over the next twenty years.[81]

In 1952 Cameron was in *Fox Hole Parlour* with Dirk Bogarde at the New Lindsay Theatre. Most recently his film appearances have included playing a lead role as the fictitious dictator Edmond Zuwanie in *The Interpreter* (2005) starring Nicole Kidman and Sean Penn. For his efforts he was referred to in

---

[80]Ibid.
[81]Ibid.

The Observer as 'That fine Caribbean actor'.⁸² The following year, 2006, he appeared in *The Queen* starring Helen Mirren, and in 2010 he appeared in *Inception*. Cameron's chance opportunity of seeing *Chu Chin Chow* showed him what he knew he wanted to do with this life. He remained dedicated to performance until his death, one month short of his 103rd birthday, in 2020.

A black trap: Cy Grant, 1919–2010

Grant was born and grew up in Guyana when it was still a British colony. This, coupled with the fact that his father was a church minister, meant that his moral and academic education was British in every way. After secondary school he worked as an administrative clerk both in the department for agriculture and the law courts. This allowed him to travel around the country with a magistrate and develop a taste for law. He is clear about how in Guyana the British intentionally divided the population by race and colour. 'You see in Guyana I would never have considered myself as being black; I was coloured and then the lower classes were black, and then there were the Indians and Portuguese.'⁸³

In 1941 the Royal Air Force (RAF), which previously did not accept black men, started advertising for new recruits as air crew; although Grant thought the sudden lack of colour bar strange, he was attracted to the opportunity. He wanted to get out of Guyana: 'the thought of losing my life never entered the picture.'⁸⁴ Grant arrived in Britain in 1941 and joined the RAF where he trained as a navigator. Shot down on his third operational trip over the Ruhr in Gilzenbury, Germany, Grant became a prisoner of war for two years. It was at this point that he started to fully realize his sense of self: 'what was I doing here a West Indian, fighting this war, I didn't feel any clear sense of patriotism.'⁸⁵

When first captured, Grant was placed in solitary confinement and repeatedly photographed. In shock, his only concern was what was going to happen to him. Months later and once settled in the prisoner of war camp, he was shown his photo in the German newspaper *Volkischer*

---

⁸²https://en.wikipedia.org/wiki/Earl_Cameron_(actor), accessed 13 May 2019.
⁸³Cy Grant, *Blackgrounds* Interview by David Johnson, London, 7 May 1997.
⁸⁴Ibid.
⁸⁵Ibid.

Beobachter. The caption below read 'A Member Of The Royal Air Force Of Unknown Race'. Grant saw being a prisoner of war as his university. Being in the officers' camp he learnt from 'the cream of the country': intellectuals, scientists and artists. Already thinking about what he wanted to do with his life, he realized he could be a successful barrister and go into politics in Guyana, where he wanted to fight for independence. This was a battle he wanted.[86]

After the war, Grant worked as a liaison officer for a West Indian air crew that had been recruited towards the end of the war. Due to what Grant understood to be racism against them, they were 'always getting into trouble'. He sat in courts either as an officer of the Court Marshal or as a defence lawyer for his fellow West Indians. This experience served him well as he joined Middle Temple and qualified as a barrister in 1951. Despite being qualified and experienced, Grant did not get a single response to applications made for any post requiring a legal qualification. Nobody would take him on once they discovered his place of birth. Grant explains, 'It was OK having black officers in the RAF during the war, but after the war the kind of racism which is under the surface surfaced very much.'[87] Grant never worked in law and was forced to seek another career path.

In his first acting role, Grant took over from Cameron in *13 Death Street Harlem*, set in Harlem; he remembers it as 'a terrible play' but headed off around the country with Moss Empire Tours performing the play twice nightly for a year. Playing a leading role as Duke the night club manager, it was here, in 1950, that Grant learnt the tricks of the trade. The following year, in 1951, whilst Laurence Olivier was casting for his festival of Britain Company, he told Grant that although he was leading man material, he had no parts for him. Acknowledging that he did not have the experience of the established actors in the company, Grant accepted when Olivier said he could carry a spear for £10 per week. Walk-on parts earned £8 weekly at the time. Grant began his time with the Olivier Company at London's St James Theatre, prior to going to the Sequel Theatre in New York for six months.

Olivier was reluctant to take Grant to America due to concerns he may experience racism. 'You're being very naïve,' the young Grant told him. Olivier's reticence stemmed from Grant and fellow black actor Eddie Craft having recently been beaten up by Teddy Boys one evening as they

---

[86]Ibid.
[87]Ibid.

left the theatre with co-actress Elspeth Marsh. Marsh's leg was broken for being in the company of black men and she was unable to make the tour to America. Olivier allowed Grant to go on the tour after Grant argued that the difference between racism in America and Britain was that the British variety was neatly swept under the carpet. The tour took place during the 1951 Tallulah Bankhead trial. The company was surprised to see the judge was black and agreed this would not have been in the case in Britain.[88] Grant felt vindicated.

Grant's career, like that of Cameron, saw him working with major artists including co-starring with Joan Collins and Richard Burton in *Seawife*, 1956. In the same year he appeared in the television play *The Man From the Sun* with Errol John and Nadia Cattouse. In spite of these successes, Grant was aware that there was not enough work for black actors. He had to diversify. Whilst filming *Home of the Brave* for Granada TV in 1957, he also sang and played guitar at the society club Esmeralda's Barn. It was here that he was approached to sing regularly on the BBC's *Tonight* show. Grant soon became a household name presenting aspects of the news in calypso from 1957 to 1960.

Grant's career was both made and perhaps broken by his appearances on *Tonight*. Grant explains:

> By staying on *Tonight* for that long period of time people just saw me as a calypso singer. It interfered with my acting career quite considerably. I had made two films either side of 1956. In 1958 I'd been in two very big television plays, so my career as an actor had been quite established, but I found that people saw me purely and simply as a calypso singer. At the time I resented it very much, it kind of devalued what I was.[89]

Grant went on to work in theatre, films, television and radio continuously throughout the following decades. The contributions that stand out for him include *Freedom Road* (1961), a musical documentary on civil rights with Cleo Laine, Madeline Bell, Paul Prescott and Nadia Cattouse, and a production of *Cindy-Ella*, with Cleo Laine, Elizabeth Welch and George Ban (1962). He also saw playing Othello in 1965 at the Phoenix Theatre in

---

[88]Ibid.
[89]Ibid.

Leicester as a highlight. Grant, however, was more than a performer; he had a social conscience which saw him creating work that was deeply connected to his identity.

It is unusual to hear a black man speak in positive terms about Enoch Powell whilst acknowledging that he stirred up racial hatred with his 'Rivers of Blood' speech in 1968: 'Powell did this country a great service in a sense because he brought racism out into the open and I think that indirectly it was a very good thing.'[90] Grant's reaction was to aim to develop a black arts project. In the early 1970s he knew that the Arts Council saw such endeavours as crazy and so he approached Olivier to be a patron, to help the project along. Olivier did not want to be associated with Grant's initiative. He accused him of being 'separatist': 'You fellas have to be like us, that's what he was saying, you don't have any culture.'[91]

Grant's response to Olivier became the articles for The Case For A Black Theatre Workshop. This in turn saw Grant set up the Drum Arts Centre in 1974. Writer Steve Carter was brought from the Negro Ensemble Company in America to London. They ran a six week workshop at Morley College, which led to Mustapha Matura writing his play *Bread*. This was performed at the Young Vic Theatre in 1976, and as a result the National Theatre held a workshop with black actors and National Theatre actors the following year. In spite of these successes, there was little forthcoming from funding bodies and Grant was forced to abandon his project.

Grant appreciated the process: 'I felt it was very important, as far as black identity [is concerned] to assert one's "negritude", as Aimé Césaire would say, but then you can get caught in another trap, I call it a black trap because it's black people wanting to have the things that Western society appreciates and they forget about their own cultures, community, their language.'[92] Heavily influenced by Aimé Césaire, Grant was aware that the only aspect of Césaire's voice the mainstream could hear was his pride in his blackness.

Later agreeing with Wole Soyinka's notion that 'A tiger doesn't talk about its tigritude', Grant came to feel that only talking about one's blackness creates division. In what he describes as his 'farewell to negritude, his transition from Drum and his final black statement', he performed Césaire's *Return To My Native Land* at both the National Theatre and the Royal Court

---

[90]Ibid.
[91]Ibid.
[92]Ibid.

Theatre for over two years between 1977 and 1979. Grant knew the piece was much bigger than the blackness it would be seen to be about. It was also anticolonialist.[93]

Whilst Grant had put Drum and a fixed image of blackness behind him, he had not given up on the idea of multicultural performance. In 1981 the Race Relations Board and Commonwealth Institute invited Grant to direct a programme of cultural diversity before an invited audience of members of parliament. The success of the event led Grant to set up the multicultural performance festival he called Concorde. Conducting a feasibility study over a six-month period with a £1,000 bank-funded budget, Grant travelled the country speaking to theatre companies about creating work to celebrate inclusivity.

Later in 1981 Grant did the second Concorde at the Birmingham repertory theatre. He put the opposition from the local black activists down to jealousy at someone from London working at venues they could not get into. Grant structured the events so that the first half was local talent with the second being groups that he had booked in. His aim was to celebrate minorities by putting them on stage, and avoid casting them purely by the colour of their skin. Grant clarifies: 'At that time, black actors were only playing roles that specified a black person. In society a black person could be a doctor, he could be a bus driver, his blackness should not be the issue.'[94] Grant used Concorde to show in quantity and style where he felt performance should be headed:

> Sometimes we had four or five Concordes in a year. I went for the main venues in the major cities like the Nottingham Playhouse. I did twenty inner city Concorde festivals in four years. One in Devon lasted for four months. In Gloucestershire we did a five month long festival. I was very happy that I moved from the black situation. I'm disgusted at the kind of black comedy shows that they put on television because it just seems that it's all they will permit.[95]

Grant is referring here to Channel 4's television series *Desmond's*. He saw this work as debasing, unrepresentative of black people and black artists,

---

[93] Ibid.
[94] Ibid.
[95] Ibid.

and allowed by Channel 4 to ensure that modern day minstrelsy was kept alive. Due to his experiences, Grant came to conclude that 'theatre is theatre' with no need for the 'black': 'If you're pushing your black identity as your only identity, I think that is wrong. I found a lot of difficulty within the black community. I was not getting support from my own peers. The black actors who had made it were not supportive. There was a lot of infighting.'[96]

Grant told me that in 1997. Decades later, with some of the 'infighting' having dissipated, there is only appreciation for what he did amongst the black artists of his era and his singular contribution to contemporary black British theatre. Brewster explains:

> It's important for young people to realize there were the Cy Grants of this world. Cy Grant was the most elegant, best educated, erudite, brave man I'd ever met. He started Drum, the first sort of approach to having black people in theatre. If he was in this room right now Cy Grant could do *Return To My Native Land*. He was on top of that; really rather beautiful; and what is he remembered for? Singing calypsos on *Tonight*. However there was more to the man because he aided and abetted people like me saying, 'Don't give up. Don't give in.'[97]

The main obstacle that both Cameron and Grant faced at the height of their careers was in the fact that their colour would generally have made them unsuitable for parts in traditional British theatre. Material written for black performers was limited, and where it did exist was confined to minor roles. This would change by the late 1950s with, amongst others, the work of Barry Reckord.

Bottom of the pile: Barry Reckord, 1926–2011

Born in Jamaica, Reckord grew up taking his family's love for granted. This love shrouded the not knowing where the next meal was going to come from, his father suffering with tuberculosis and the constant worry of medical bills. The money troubles followed the four break-ins to his father's

---
[96]Ibid.
[97]Yvonne Brewster, Personal Interview by Ben Thomas, London, 31 October 2014.

business which drove the family into debt. This, coupled with the violent physical attacks Reckord witnessed from the Chinese man in the shop next door, along with watching a man get stoned to death in Denham Town, was unlike the life of the other middle class kids he knew. It was, however, the background which developed Reckord's view on unnecessary suffering.[98]

Reckord read English at Cambridge University in spite of his interest in politics. Describing his time at Cambridge as 'background music', he was there in body only as his mind was sorting out Jamaican problems. He wrote *Della* at Cambridge, which was sent to the Royal Court by a friend. The name was changed to *Flesh to a Tiger* when directed by Tony Richardson in 1958. The production sold out for the three-day run. At the opening night, Gregory Poke ran his hand through Reckord's hair, stating, 'I love this stuff.' Offended by Reckord's 'Yes my barber tells me that', he asked, 'Did you know I paid your fare to come here?' Reckord promptly found himself and his 'stuff' permanently uninvited to Poke's Sunday breakfasts for Royal Court writers.[99] After the Royal Court production, Reckord did the play at The Ward Theatre in Kingston, Jamaica. He describes the play as expressing his political interest in religion: 'I think the court did it because it was exotic and the language was poetic. That is what they expect of black people.'[100]

In Jamaica post-university, Reckord decided to go into politics. He did not want Jamaica to become owned by America like Puerto Rico and aspired to do something about it. There was no intention to write. Reckord describes the very successful beginning of his playwriting as 'purely accidental' and his subsequent career as 'out of the blue'. He saw life for black people both in Jamaica and in Britain as identical. Black people were not making progress and this bothered him. His political aspirations were halted in Jamaica when he realized he was unable to be crafty. It was because of this that he took the decision to use theatre as a vehicle to get his ideas across. He was introduced to the reality of being a playwright in Jamaica when a Chinese man walked out of a play he wrote in the 1960s saying, 'Me cum ya fi laugh me noh cum ya fi tink.'[101] Reckord used the sentiment to guide the future writing of his many successful plays.[102]

---

[98]Barry Reckord, *Blackgrounds* Interview David Johnson, London, 22 April 1997.
[99]Ibid.
[100]Ibid.
[101]Ibid., 'I didn't come here to think, I came here to laugh'.
[102]Ibid.

Seven of Reckord's plays were performed at the Royal Court Theatre between 1958 and 1974: these were *Flesh to a Tiger* (1958), *You in Your Small Corner* (1960), Skyvers (1963 and 1971), *Don't Gas the Blacks* (1969), *Liberated Woman* (1970), *Give the Gaffa Time to Love You* (1973) and *X* (1974). *Skyvers* transferred to the Roundhouse. It had an all-white cast as there were apparently no black actors. Although unthinkable now, this was not controversial at the time. Reckord confirms, 'I wanted to cast it for five or six black youngsters, but we couldn't find any. It was impossible to find at that stage; now you could find five hundred probably.'[103]

Despite his success, Reckord shines a sobering light on the harsh realities of being a black writer in Britain in the late 1950s and early 1960s. Having returned to London from Jamaica for a six week run of *Flesh to a Tiger*, he was quickly reminded of the double-edged career and racial helter-skelter he was on: 'When my play was on at the Court they were saying, "Let's find you a flat, you're going to be rich." So we walked along the King's Road and saw these new estate agents saying, "No blacks, no dogs, no children." . . . The play flopped and I was living in a boarding house.'[104] Those who had pursued him when he was on top now ignored him. This however prepared him for the ups and downs to come.

Of Reckord's seven plays at the Royal Court, three transferred. *You In Your Small Corner* was the first to make the transition and went to the Arts Theatre in 1961. During rehearsals one of Reckord's black actors left the show. The actor's agent, Pearl Connor, had got him a part in Tony Richardson's 1961 film version of Sheila Delaney's *A Taste of Honey*. Echoing Grant's comment above, Reckord explains how being left stranded was not that surprising to him: 'I'm afraid this happens quite a lot in black theatre. People have more than two eyes, they have two in the back of the heads as well. There is an enormous amount of screwing up that goes on.'[105] Is this any different to mainstream theatre, or were black artists holding themselves to an impossibly high standard? Whatever the answer, *You in Your Small Corner* went on to make history when the 1962 televised version featured the first interracial kiss on British television, between Reckord and his co-star Elizabeth MacLennan.

---

[103]Ibid.
[104]Ibid.
[105]Ibid.

Whilst Reckord achieved personal success, he attributes the general lack of it in black British theatre to backstabbing amongst black British artists.[106] He expresses these sentiments in spite of the huge contribution that his writing has made to the genre. His thoughts on the future of black British theatre highlight, as Grant did, his despair with Channel 4's black television shows *Porkpie* and *Desmond's*:[107] Reckord is unambiguous:

> I think Channel 4 should be put in front of the firing squad for putting on this stuff. White people put on the same sort of things but they have other things, we don't. Young black writers are looking at this crucifyingly boring embarrassment and thinking this is West Indian, and in fact that is what it's become. It's the kind of embarrassment that makes you angry.[108]

Conversely and importantly, because black artists' views must be allowed the space to differ, Ram John Holder describes *Desmond's* as:

> One of the greatest pieces of television comedy in this country ever. It ranks alongside *Fools and Horses*, *Dad's Army*, *Black Adder*, *Fawlty Towers* and *Steptoe and Son*. I'm very pleased to work at the top level of British television, the very highest level you could work at. *Desmond's* showcased the leads but was also a school for black British Talent.[109]

Reckord's opposing view is couched in the belief that this type of work existed so programme makers could perpetuate their belief that both in theatre and television 'blacks can't hack it, they don't have the talent, we give them every chance and they can't write it'. It is in part because of this kind of treatment that Reckord formulated a single question he feels black people have to address: 'Why are we at the bottom of every pile?' Reckord's own answer lies in the historical fact that black people are the only people who

---

[106]Ibid.
[107]*Porkpie*, in which Ram John Holder played the lead role of Porkpie, a former Ford Motor Company employee turned lollipop man, who wins £10 million on the lottery and finds himself working out who he can and cannot trust now that he is rich, aired on Channel 4 for two seasons between 1995 and 1996. There were twelve episodes. This was a spin-off from *Desmond's* in which Holder also played Porkpie.
[108]Reckord, *Blackgrounds* Interview, April 1997.
[109]Ram John Holder, *Blackstages* Interview by Tara Mack, London, 21 August 2002.

were legally enslaved for 400 years, then lived in slums, then were afflicted with drugs, and so no real chance for development has been had.[110]

In the 1980s, Reckord's brother Lloyd appeared in a Jamaican television advertisement for skin bleaching cream with the tagline, 'Is darkness clouding your life?' This reinforces Reckord's conviction that white people take black people's subordinate position for granted and that especially young black people must think through and answer his question on black status. This would mean writing about what it is to be black in Britain as well as being black and British.[111]

These discussions took place in 1997. Reckord did not feel such writing was for him to do. This was partly because of a combination of his seniority, lack of desire to write and his relationship with Britain. He explains: 'I don't think of myself as living in England. I think of myself as living on Primrose Hill. I am in England but not of it.' Once again Holder and Reckord hold contrasting views as the former explains his, and by extension Reckord's, legal nationality: 'I was born British. I've never known anything else. All British West Indians were British. We weren't immigrants. I didn't come here as an immigrant. I just came home to the capital of Guyana, which is London.'[112]

Reckord never felt this attachment, but rather a sense that something less welcoming was bubbling under the surface: 'I expect this society in twenty years to be racist. I have fantasies of walking down the street and people I have known all my life putting their head out of the window and singing, "We don't want to lose you but we think you ought to go".'[113]

Without putting a name to it, Reckord predicted a Brexit-like situation for precisely when the process started. In *The Strange Death of Europe*, Douglas Murray explains, 'It would be an unsustainable position for the political and media elites to continue to pretend that the views of the majority of the public are unacceptable whilst the pro mass migration views of a comparatively small and extreme fringe are the only legitimate views for the mainstream in European politics.'[114] Reckord knew, almost precisely, when time would run out.

---

[110]Reckord, *Blackgrounds* Interview, April 1997.
[111]Ibid.
[112]Holder, *Blackstages* Interview, August 2002.
[113]Reckord, *Blackgrounds* Interview, April 1997.
[114]Douglas Murray, *The Strange Death of Europe: Immigration, Identity, Islam* (London: Bloomsbury, 2017), 304.

As with Grant, Brewster is grateful to Reckord: 'He has done more for black British theatre than anyone.' Brewster recalls his play *Flesh to a Tiger* was on at the Royal Court when she arrived in London as a seventeen-year-old. Reckord's was the only black play on and she was the only black student at Rose Bruford at the time. Determined to meet him, Brewster hung about 'like a groupie'. 'He was considered to be eminence grise at the Royal Court at that time. That did me the world of good and gave me a sense of purpose.'[115]

Reckord gifted Brewster his personal copy of Osborne's *Look Back in Anger* with the original notes that Osborne had asked him for. Decades later when Brewster realized Reckord's plays had not been published she set about finding them. Reckord's friend, Diana Athill, explained 'he chucked his plays out on the heath'. After unearthing three full plays and eventually finding *Flesh to a Tiger* archived under the name of the director Tony Richardson, Brewster approached Oberon who published the compilation which she called *For the Reckord* (2010). The BBC then optioned one of the plays. Reckord thanked Brewster for the plays she 'had the temerity to publish' and described the £4,000 fee as 'the first cheque I have earned from my writing in over twenty years'.[116]

Brewster was able to create the setting for Reckord to relive some of the acclaim he had earned in his earlier years, whilst simultaneously ensuring his work was permanently documented in print. Reckord has since passed on and his bottom-of-the-pile question remains unanswered, or perhaps, more shamefully, unasked.

Unequal opportunities: Pearl Connor, 1924–2005

Born and raised in Trinidad in a mixed race, educated family, Connor was exposed to the arts and British education. Growing up in a British colony, Connor was influenced by Beryl McBurnie, founder of Trinidad's Little Carib Theatre. McBurnie developed her students' national consciousness through the folk dancing and [black] history she taught them. 'We needed to have some idea about who we were, or where we were going, and she did that for me.' Additionally, involved in the youth movement, Connor

---

[115] Brewster Interview, 26 November 2018.
[116] Ibid.

interviewed leaders in favour of Trinidadian independence.[117] She was inspired by Captain Andrew Cirpriani (1875–1945), Mayor of Port of Spain, leader of Trinidad Workingmen's Association, and founder of the Trinidad Labour Party.[118]

Connor came to London to study Law in 1948. She met and married Edric Connor in the same year. The couple had crossed paths months earlier at the Little Carib Theatre in Trinidad, but meeting Edric in London now changed Connor's trajectory: 'I was led straight into theatrical things because of him.' Edric had come to London from Trinidad on an engineering scholarship, but as an actor and singer he brought his experience of making films on folk dances, a portfolio of music, 'his voice and his personality and he slotted immediately into the BBC'. Connor saw Edric's type of welcome as the British government thanking Caribbean islanders for their war effort.[119]

Connor became acquainted with Edric's contacts at the BBC West Indian Service. This later became the Caribbean Service where writers such as Kamau Braithwaite (Barbados), Jan Carew (Guyana), C. L. R. James and Vidia Naipaul (Trinidad), Andrew Salkey (Jamaica) and Derek Walcott (Trinidad) were broadcasting their work. Their work also heralded the wider advancement of West Indian language-based theatrical activity in Britain through BBC Radio's Caribbean Voices and the first publication of the Caribbean Plays Series edited by Errol John. The introduction of the series into British and Caribbean literature signalled the beginnings of such work being taken as worthy literature on an international level and by extension afforded the work the possibility of being seen as 'serious' performance material. Whilst this was all a welcome step in the right direction, Connor's intentions were political: 'When I came to England, everything was a colony, we were all beginning to emerge: Nigeria, Ghana, the Caribbean, we all had the same kind of inspiration and aim of independence, freedom and to get our culture known in the world.'[120]

Although Connor did not perform in her own right, she became an important port of call for black performers in Britain throughout the 1950s and 1960s. Having set up the Edric Connor Agency in 1956 with her husband, Connor represented African-Caribbean and Asian artists at a time when

---

[117]Trinidad became independent in 1962.
[118]Pearl Connor, *Blackgrounds* Interview David Johnson, London, 25 June 1997.
[119]Ibid.
[120]Ibid.

black artists had neither representation nor an adequate performance niche. The agency did the actors' CVs and hosted spotlight evenings for directors to meet artists. Any training the performers had outside of Britain was not recognized. Artists included Patti Boulaye (Nigeria), Nina Baden Semper (Trinidad), Nadia Cattouse (British Honduras, Belize), Mona Hammond (Jamaica), Ram John Holder (Guyana), Horace James (Trinidad), Lloyd and Barry Reckord (Jamaica), Coreen Skinner (Trinidad) and Nancy Kwan (Hong Kong). After Kwan played Suzy Wong in the 1960 film and play of *Suzy Wong*, she kept her character's name.

Connor supplied Indian actors in *North West Frontier* (1959) and two boys from Trinidad in *Two Little Indians* (1953). For Burton and Taylor's *Antony and Cleopatra* (1963), she provided dancers. Connor serviced the industry with African-Caribbean performers: 'They just had to perform the lines, they already had the right appearance.'[121] With so few openings for non-white performers, Connor felt her artists had to prove themselves with each new job, even though much of the work was stereotypically singing and dancing in clubs.

Whilst Connor held the fort, Edric became 'the first black actor to play at Stratford-upon-Avon', where he played Gower in *Pericles*, directed by Tony Richardson in 1958. Robeson played Othello at Stratford the following year. These were exceptions to the general rule that it was difficult for black actors to find work. Edric's opportunity came as he was taken under the wing of a group of avant-garde actors at the Royal Court at the time including Sean Connery and Rex Harrison.

Connor notes the reviews of Edric's Gower fixated on: 'Ah, black man with a spear leaping about. What is he doing in that outfit posing in Shakespeare?' She continues, 'They didn't quite accept our people, black people, on the stage, performing in a Shakespeare play or production. This has now become commonplace, I mean people walk on and off like it's Christmas and you'd think it was always happening and of course, it never was.'[122] The notion of the spear-carrying black man had not moved on since Olivier paid Grant to do the same in 1951. Spears or not, many of the artists who came through the agency form part of what is now increasingly recognized as a black British theatre legacy.

---

[121]Ibid.
[122]Ibid.

In addition to securing her artists work, Connor also took on Equity and succeeded in obtaining rights for her artists. One of her wins was in getting Equity to agree that overseas performers would have a time-limited contract of six months. They would then have to be replaced. She also fought for proper Equity fees when her artists were treated like extras with no billing: 'We were very unequal. We had unequal opportunities not equal.' Connor describes the battle:

> We tried very hard with Equity. We paraded up down with banners, we carried on really alarmingly. Now there is an African section, a black section, people on the committee, trustees that are black, it's a wonderful change. The generations today have no idea what was happening because it hasn't been documented. People haven't been told what was going on. Every day was a struggle, every day was a fight for every penny an artist got.[123]

Connor also fought for repeat fees when Unilever used her artists in advertisements to sell soap or flour on the African continent. Once informed by people who had seen the adverts she approached Unilever directly. This put an end to single fees being paid at that time. Furthermore, Connor continually scouted for new talent because she knew it was both there and unrepresented. Working with her personal assistant June Baden Semper, Connor advertised in *The Stage* and *Melody Maker* and travelled the country holding auditions. This is how the original cast members for the West End productions of *Hair* (1968) and *Jesus Christ Superstar* (1972) were found. Joan Armatrading (St Kitts and Nevis) and Floella Benjamin (Trinidad and Tobago) both went into *Hair* and became Equity members because of it.

In addition to running the agency, the couple co-founded the Negro Theatre Workshop (Workshop) in 1961. Connor was the driving force behind this innovation which attempted to combat the lack of working opportunities black artists faced. Performing in churches and town halls around the country, the Workshop was invited to the first Black and Third World Festival of Arts and Culture in Senegal in 1966. The Workshop's performance of the *Saint Luke Passion* resulted in Equity membership for those in the thirty-strong cast who did not previously have it.

---

[123]Ibid.

Connor's Workshop became a hub for black performers. Rudolph Walker believes Connor was instrumental in helping black British theatre get to where it is today because of her Workshop, along with the fact that new arrivals from the Caribbean or Africa with an interest in theatre went straight to her. She provided them with a platform for performance, along with a place to bond.[124] Similarly, Ram John Holder did his first play with Connor's Workshop, touring the country with the musical *The Dark Disciples* (1965). Holder then gained more work when the play was commissioned by the BBC. Holder believes himself to be 'The only negro that ever appeared on stage with Olivier' whilst he [Holder] worked for a year at the National Theatre in *The Bacchae* and *The Party* (1973), the latter being Olivier's final stage play. Holder recognized the exposure, experience and work Connor's Workshop allowed black actors in an era that held few opportunities for them. He offers his explanation for the lack of work: 'I don't think it had anything to do with race. It had to do with demographic factors. If you have a small population that can't support a commercial theatre, you can't have a commercial theatre, but you can do things like the Negro Theatre Workshop.'[125]

It was through sheer will that Connor provided her Workshop with opportunities. The only funding the group ever received was a grant of £300 from the Arts Council for 1965 to 1966. The same was granted for the period 1966 to 1967. Chambers details the Workshop's problem as the 'want of suitable material, working in a vacuum without a supportive context, and, above all, lack of resources'.[126] None of this, however, was going to stop Connor from trying to promote black arts and culture.

In 1966 black theatre developed further in Britain when Barbados's Edward Kamau Brathwaite, Trinidad's John La Rose, and Jamaica's Andrew Salkey founded The Caribbean Artist's Movement (CAM). The work of the Movement from 1966 to 1972 is detailed in Walmsley's *The Caribbean Artist's Movement* and illustrates the Movement's commitment and determination to developing West Indian theatre and literature in Britain.[127] CAM's first public reading was held on 3 March 1967 at London's Jeanetta Cochrane Theatre. The meeting at which Braithwaite read *Rights of Passage* was to

---

[124]Rudolph Walker, *Blackstages* Interview by Tara Mack, London, 5 August 2002.
[125]Holder, *Blackstages* Interview, August 2002.
[126]Chambers, *Black and Asian Theatre in Britain*, 133.
[127]Anne Walmsley, *The Caribbean Artist's Movement 1966-1972: A Literary and Cultural History* (London: New Beacon Press, 1972).

be the first of monthly reunions to take place over the next three years. By the second meeting the group was already discussing the importance of West Indian language-based work, particularly that of Louise Bennett and calypsonian, Sparrow.[128] This marked the beginnings of their quest for appropriate cultural representation.

Eight months later, the Movement held a conference at the University of Kent on 10 November 1967. Amongst the group were Lloyd Reckord, Marina Maxwell, Evan Jones, Ram John Holder, Celia Robinson and Pearl Connor. Whilst some members saw black people as living in the ghettos of the world and as the world's true proletariat, Connor's message was concerned with theatre standards. Her request to those assembled was, 'We must have a critical faculty about ourselves. We can't just be submerged in self-love for our own peoples' sake, we must give them a standard . . . let us present this thing properly.'[129]

Connor's plea was twofold: as performers they should aim high, whilst seeking, as West Indians, to give the fairest impression of themselves and their cultural identity. Having made themselves responsible for the theatrical representation of West Indian culture in Britain, they could not afford to do bad work. Connor nurtured her artists with this view in mind and two of her early performers later made significant inroads in the 1970s.

Firstly was Rudolph Walker playing Bill Reynolds in the ITV sitcom *Love Thy Neighbour*. The seven series and fifty-four episodes which ran from 1972 to 1976 showed a white working class couple, Joan and Eddie Booth, played by Kate Williams and Jack Smethurst, adjusting to having black neighbours in Walker's Bill and Nina Baden Semper's Barbie Reynolds.

Walker's Reynolds was far more sophisticated than his white neighbour who called him 'nig nog', 'choc ice', 'sambo' and 'King Kong'. His equally racist retorts included 'honky', 'snowflake', 'pale-face' and 'Big White Chief'. This was the first time that comedy had been used to show a black man giving as good as he got in a British television sitcom and was a precondition of Walker accepting the role.[130] The show was a phenomenal success making Walker and Baden Semper household names both in Britain and internationally.

Walker was not offended when a make-up artist was asked to make him lighter so that he 'looked more West Indian'. He was told, 'Nina is lighter and

---

[128]Ibid., 68.
[129]Ibid., 117.
[130]Walker, *Blackstages* Interview, August 2002.

she looks West Indian.' In those days black people in Britain were judged to be either Jamaican or African. There was no in between.[131] The fact that he was West Indian was irrelevant. He had to look like the white programme makers' vision of a West Indian. This was until he explained the reality.

The sitcom was pure comedy: 'it was never meant to solve racial problems.'[132] Whilst the content is racist and unacceptable in modern Britain, Walker defends the show in today's climate: 'I became a household name as a result of that, so there is no way that I am going to knock it.' His view is the same towards Americans in the 1920s and 1930s who played the black mammy, subservient roles: 'they did what they had to do for that period and it's because of them that I am here today.'[133]

Connor saw the work strategically. Whilst it was popular it also meant that there was a chance for black artists to build their reputation. She wanted more from this exposure. She wanted 'stories about our real lives, not just send-ups. A send-up is good for amusement but you need something else to stabilize your whole community, to make you feel proud of who you are and also so they could respect us, and this would avoid racism.'[134]

Secondly was Corinne Skinner Carter, playing Hortense in the BBC sitcom *Empire Road* alongside on-screen husband Everett Bennett, played by Norman Beaton. The show ran for two series between 1978 and 1979. Connor thought it put 'a mirror on lives, showing something of the lives of people here which was unknown'.[135] Carter also points to some of the reasons Connor approved of the show:

> [It] was written by blacks for blacks . . . the main characters were all black. Normally if you see a black person on television or on stage they are always just the teeth, or the robber or the drug dealer or the whatever. And for a change a black person owned a shop. And everything was based around that shop.[136]

For all the good it did, Carter felt sure the show was intentionally time-limited to two seasons.[137] A stark reminder of where the power was and of

---

[131] Ibid.
[132] Ibid.
[133] Ibid.
[134] Connor, *Blackgrounds* Interview, June 1997.
[135] Ibid.
[136] Corinne Skinner Carter, *Blackstages* Interview by Tara Mack, London, 29 August 2002.
[137] Ibid.

black British vulnerability in mainstream performance and beyond. It was precisely because of the precariousness of black life in the arts that Connor and Edric dedicated themselves to theatre in the way they did; they loved it, believed in it and thought it was worthwhile. This was not just about creating work for them, but also 'about presenting an image of our people to the world that will show us as real people'.[138] Connor further clarifies her clear political aim in theatre: 'I am committed to the liberation of our people, bringing us into the world, getting us self-respect, getting people to know who we are and to treat us as equals.'[139]

Connor's fervent commitment is mirrored by her contemporaries, some of whom are mentioned in passing, or not at all, in this book. They make up the very many others whose black British theatre experience confirms and adds to that of their fellow pioneers detailed above. These include Thomas Baptiste, Carmen Manley, Mona Hammond, Nadia Cattouse and Errol John. They and their experiences are also a central part of the fabric of contemporary black British theatre that illustrates their fortitude and dissolution in an environment that often sought to belittle and simultaneously erratically include them.

For Thomas Baptiste, Guyanese opera singer, others' use of his blackness was a tacit tradable currency. He comments, 'People would ask me to their homes to show me off to their friends.'[140] He was prepared to withstand the patronizing attitude to his blackness and his desire to be an opera singer by the white upper middle class circles he moved in, if being 'shown off' also meant he avoided playing stereotypes and unemployment.

Whilst Baptiste had found his method of getting by, others in the 1960s felt the wrath and confusion of white directors who claimed to know more about black people, their appearance and talents than they did themselves. When Carmen Manley was cast in a show because it was assumed her blackness meant she could sing, although she had explained she could not, her director shouted when she sang out of tune: 'Sing you bitch, sing!' Sadly, 'the bitch couldn't sing!'[141]

Similarly when Mona Hammond auditioned for *Black Girl in Search of God* (1968), she was deemed not to be black enough until she put dark

---

[138]Connor, *Blackgrounds* Interview, June 1997.
[139]Ibid.
[140]Thomas Baptiste, *Blackstages* Interview by Tara Mack, London, 2 September 2002.
[141]Reckord, *Blackgrounds* Interview, April 1997.

make-up on. Hammond reminded herself that nobody had a problem recognizing she was black in the street.[142] It was just creative theatrical eyes that viewed her differently. Once she got the part, Dame Edith Evans, who was in the show, advised, 'Mona, if you actually get into trouble with this part, I can help you out because I have played the black girl in search of God.'[143] As it turned out, undermining black British artists' ability to create authentic blackness in their work, if that was ever really wanted, was not the preserve of white British theatre practitioners.

Errol John won the Observer Prize for his play *Moon on a Rainbow Shawl* in 1957. This was then published and performed at the Royal Court in 1958. John was also a Hollywood ghost screenwriter. His work included *Ice Cold in Alex* (1958). When John returned to London in 1986, it was to direct *Moon on a Rainbow Shawl* at the Theatre Royal Stratford East. This was the second time that Brewster met him. The first was decades earlier in Jamaica when she was sent to interview him and was mesmerized by his sexy voice. This time, John was struggling to direct his play successfully and dismayed that Britain did not receive him for the accomplished writer he was.[144]

In 1988 when Maya Angelou directed *Moon on a Rainbow Shawl* at the Almeida, John was banned from the rehearsals. In casting a white character as black, Angelou had shattered John's perception of his work. Brewster comments, 'And that was the end of Errol.' At this time, John visited Brewster at the Arts Council. Whilst his voice was the same, 'He looked like hell. He looked like a real down and out.' John explained, 'It's not good. I'm nobody.' He was distressed by Angelou's direction: 'the black consciousness in the play has been reviled and revoked.'[145]

Noting his despair, Brewster held a dinner for him at her home. He was depressed but happy amongst friends. Looking at an umbrella as he left, he asked, 'may I borrow it? It will give me an excuse to come back.' John headed off with the umbrella and his sexy voice and died the next day. Decades later, Brewster realized that the cold reception John received in London in 1986 had crushed him.[146] Rooted in its tripartite theatrical lineage, this was also the year that Talawa emerged.

---

[142] Mona Hammond, *Blackstages* Interview by Tara Mack, London, 6 August 2002.
[143] Ibid.
[144] Brewster Interview, 26 November 2018.
[145] Ibid.
[146] Ibid.

CHAPTER 3
A STRANGER IN NON-PARADISE

In order to understand Talawa's performance work under Brewster's direction from 1986 to 2001, Brewster's early personal and professional biographies are presented. The development of black British theatre between the 1970s and the 1990s is then analysed. Finally, Talawa's residency at the Cochrane Theatre is discussed.

Brewster's beginnings

Yvonne Brewster, née Clarke, was born into an upper-middle-class family in Kingston, Jamaica. She credits her Polish grandfather, Samuel Abraham Issacs, originally Lejinsky, with awakening her creativity. Issacs, unable to practice law in Jamaica, turned to funeral directing as he realized 'black people like funerals'. This 'big blind creature' shaved quoting Shakespeare generally and Macbeth specifically when keeping the young Brewster in check, with: 'Vaulting ambition which o'er leaps itself and falls and falls and falls on the other side.' It was from Ba, then, as she called him, that Brewster developed her love of Shakespeare, along with the notion that his plays 'had more messages for people who suffer than for people who rule'. Additionally, Ba made his granddaughter scat to Ella Fitzgerald, read his complete library of Dickens and listen to Chopin.[1]

Brewster attended St Hilda's boarding school for girls in St Ann, Jamaica. Her pioneering spirit showed in the fourth form, when she directed a performance of a Louise Bennett song in Jamaican patois. The only black teacher in the school, Miss Iris Johnson, who commented that the work was 'excellent', opened Brewster's eyes to just how forbidden dialect performance was in the school.

---

[1] Yvonne Brewster, Personal Interview by David Johnson, 16 January 1997; Brewster Interview, 31 October 2014.

Efforts to expel Brewster were exercised on more than one occasion: once for disguising her Daphne Du Maurier's *Frenchman's Creek* as *The Bible* and again for translating the school's Latin motto into Jamaican patois. The Latin original read *Re servera verum gaudium est*. The 'standard English' translation was 'Great endeavour brings true rewards'. Brewster's patois translation, with its intended connotations, read 'And a hard, hard thing is a true, true, joy'.[2] Surviving expulsion due to her father's interventions, it was at St Hilda's that she developed what was to become a lifelong passion for European and British theatre.[3] Added to this was her love of the BBC reel-to-reel radio plays that made her want to do radio in the UK.

At seventeen, Brewster was admitted to Rose Bruford Training College of Speech and Drama.[4] Her ability was vouched for by a man at the British Council in Kingston, as Sidcup was deemed too far for her to travel to, to attend an audition. Brewster promptly set sail for Britain on the *Queen Mary* in 1956. Making the most of her voyage, her chaperone only discovered she had been sneaking out at night when pictures of her appeared in the ship's lounge of her winning a fancy dress parade. On arrival in Britain, Brewster stayed at the Cumberland Hotel in London and wondered, 'How many loaves of bread do these people need?' when she noted the multitudinous smoking chimneys before being driven to Rose Bruford in a Rolls Royce by her father's friend. Mistakenly, Brewster thought this latter experience was a taste of what life in Britain was going to be like.[5]

Studying in Britain was a family tradition. Brewster was following in the footsteps of her mother, an accountant, and her father, a land surveyor. This British influence did not make her feel less Jamaican: 'I'm not at all English, I love England and I love being here, but I am never anything other than a Jamaican'. As a young Jamaican woman in London, Brewster was aware of her perceived exoticism. This was expressed by white people wanting to touch her skin and hair, whilst men in bowler hats on buses tried to touch more. Her response to the latter was to scream loudly, 'He's touching me up!' In spite of feeling forced to develop strategies for others' behaviour,

---

[2] Brewster, *Blackstages* Interview, July 2002.
[3] Roy Bartholemew, 'Homeless, but Not Rootless', *Independent*, 1 November 1995, 10.
[4] The college became Rose Bruford College of Theatre and Performance in 2016.
[5] Brewster, *Blackstages* Interview, July 2002.

Brewster is certain that had she been a black man, life would have been even harder. They were seen as a threat to the status quo and not sexy, as they are now.[6]

Less sexy, but in line with the everyday racism Brewster had to contend with, was her lack of Christmas dinner during her first year in Britain. Invited to celebrate Christmas with her landlord, Mr Alexander and his family, Brewster was quizzed by an invited father-in-law as to why she had not dressed in her national costume. He found her modern 1956 outfit an insult to his intelligence: 'Your address in Jamaica is Half Way Tree, that means you live half way up the tree and so therefore you're middle class. You go and put on your grass skirt!' Brewster comments, 'So I never had any Christmas dinner because I didn't have a grass skirt.'[7] Brewster moved out and continued to live her permanent negotiation of British racism.

Brewster became Britain's first black female drama student at Rose Bruford where she studied speech, drama and mime. On entry, she was warned, 'You'll never work. Your father has paid for you for three years. We'll take your money but you'll never work, you do know this don't you?'[8] Decades on and whilst being made a Fellow of the College by Bruford in front of a graduating class, Brewster told them, 'Never believe what they tell you in this place because they said I'd never work and I was the first person to get a job in my year.'[9] That job, the Fairy of the Ring in *Aladdin* at Colchester Repertory, also got Brewster her Equity card whilst she was still a student.

Brewster's drama school training familiarized her with the work of European international writers and theatre practitioners including Brecht, Chekhov, Ibsen, Shakespeare and Strindberg. She did not expect her Jamaican roots to feature in her work but saw the opportunity to use non-'standard English' when performing poetry. Although she argued that poetry is personal and has its own voice, she knew that her decision to work in this way meant that she could be threatened with course failure. She had to think of something to avoid running the risk of returning to Jamaica without the certification she was expected to have

---

[6]Brewster Interview, 31 October 2014.
[7]Ibid.
[8]Ibid.
[9]Ibid.

earned. Having been told in mime class 'there was too much passion in her elbows', she suspected she would also fail this course.[10] Brewster took precautionary courses in mime and voice and speech at the Royal Academy of Music. She passed both with distinction having kept the whole plan secret.

It was also at Rose Brufrord that Brewster took to directing. 'There were no parts for me and that's why I went into directing.' Her directorial debut was a production of Shaw's *St Joan* with Tom Baker as the dauphin. Through this experience, Brewster began to discover her later developed notion that directing is a form of manipulation, where the director must have the clearest idea of the end result, in a cast-led process. She explains, 'In fact you step back further and further and it's sometimes very upsetting that the things you'd planned are not going to happen because the cast, by the end, know more than you do. At the beginning you're in charge. At the end they're in charge.'[11]

For Brewster, drama school was a three-year experience during which she refused to be demoralised.[12] Simultaneously, she adapted to being called 'lazy' because she walked slowly, along with learning the British customs of one bath per week and burning her legs in front of the single bar electric heater.[13] By the end of her course, Brewster was ready to return home. She initially taught drama and worked as a radio DJ and newsreader, finally producing and presenting her own TV show for the Jamaican Broadcasting Corporation (JBC). It was not long, however, before she recognized the need for a national theatre in Jamaica and set up The Barn.

The Barn

The Barn, established in 1965 as Jamaica's first professional theatre company, was designed by Brewster's father. The theatre, seating 144, was built in the garage of the family's Kingston home at 5 Oxford Road. The Barn was named after the practice theatre at Rose Bruford and also after Spanish

---

[10] Ibid.
[11] Ibid.
[12] Brewster, 'A Short Autobiographical Essay Focusing on My Work in the Theatre', 391.
[13] Brewster Interview, 31 October 2014.

playwright Federico Garcia Lorca's (1899–1936) theatre, La Barraca, which translates as The Barn.

The idea for The Barn was developed by Brewster and her contemporaries who had been studying theatre abroad: Trevor Rhone had also studied at Rose Bruford, Leonie Forbes had been at the Royal Academy of Dramatic Art (RADA) in London and Sydney Hibbert had studied in America. They had expected to return home to Jamaica and 'set the world on fire'.[14] What they found, however, was a theatre setup that continued to be dominated by expatriates.

Brewster auditioned for a 1965 production of *South Pacific* for the Jamaican Operatic Society. Although she was British trained and could sing, she was cast as a tree, 'and they cast this woman who couldn't sing the part, why? Because she was white.'[15] The rampant white expatriate theatrical domination led to what Brewster calls 'one of the most exciting times of my life'.[16]

With Jamaica newly independent in 1965, the attitude to local innovation was: 'Oh these jumped up people with their woolly heads.'[17] Brewster credits Hibbert with initiating the creation of The Barn and wanting to call it Theatre 77. She explains his thinking: 'It is now 1965 and will take us twelve years to become professionally adept.'[18] The Barn members soon turned to creating their own work. Having all been black international students, returning home to Jamaica to find there was no work for them they decided to base their plays on their experiences. These included being regarded as spoilt because of their privilege and suffering ridicule because their Jamaican English was now peppered with words and intonation from either Britain or America.

For their first show Theatre 77, as the group was initially called, produced a double bill of Strindberg's *Miss Julie* (1888) and Albee's *The Zoo Story* (1958). This was performed at the Old Theatre at the University College of the West Indies, as it was then. In the cast were Yvonne Brewster, Sidney Hibbert, Patricia Priestly, Trevor Rhone, Billy Woung and Munair Zacca. The entire run received an audience of four, in spite of the 2,000 programmes Hibbert had printed.

---

[14]Brewster Interview, 9 January 1997.
[15]Brewster Interview, 31 October 2014.
[16]Ibid.
[17]Brewster Interview, 26 November 2018.
[18]Ibid.

Theatre 77 then restructured to become The Barn and set up permanent theatrical shop in Brewster's redesigned family garage. As there were no chairs, the audience brought their own cushions. The company then devised *It's Not My Fault Baby: A Play in Dialect* (1966). As most of the group wanted to act, Rhone wrote the play, from their devised tape recordings, and Brewster directed. This marked the beginning of their respective professional careers.[19] Whilst performance work in dialect was not new to the island, The Barn presented a new forum for this kind of initiative to thrive in. It did this without excluding middle class Jamaicans who were also accustomed to attending the expatriate style performance work. Discussing The Barn in 2006, Brewster comments:

> The idea was to give young irreverent Jamaican actors, directors and playwrights a chance to test their wings and wits in a safe place. To see themselves and the society they lived in reflected on the stage. . . . Thus in the tiny space of the Barn Theatre: 144 seats, stage 24' wide and 19' deep, and no headroom to speak of, my directing skills were honed.[20]

In The Barn they were free to do the work they wanted to. At the time, performing modern classics and creating their own plays was new to the island's theatrical traditions of pantomime and some Shakespeare. The latter was largely produced by the expatriate Paul Methuen who ran the Garden Theatre. As The Barn grew in popularity, the audience included the chauffeurs who had previously taken their employers there and stood at the back. The work increasingly related to working class life and so the ordinary man would dress up to see himself performed on a Sunday. At its height, Rhone wrote *Smile Orange* and the show ran and ran. Once Brewster returned to London in 1972, she no longer worked at The Barn except to direct Rhone's *Bellas Gate Boy* in 2003. The sex comedies that proliferated from the 1970s were not what Brewster wanted to see there.[21]

---

[19]Brewster, *Blackstages* Interview, July 2002.
[20]Brewster, 'A Short Autobiographical Essay Focusing on My Work in the Theatre', 391.
[21]Brewster Interview, 26 November 2018.

Fifty-four years on, The Barn presents four plays each year. As it is non-profit-making, this ensures Jamaicans can access cheap theatre. Groups are not permitted to stay for longer than three months to guarantee that profits are not made. Although there is no artistic policy, the work shown must have a black perspective and/or be written and directed by a black artist. Brewster further expresses her specific commitment to writers: 'Young Jamaican artists, especially playwrights, must have a place where they can put their work on without too much expense and know that they will get an audience. My wish is that we produce more playwrights and the only way we can do this is if they can get a chance to put their work on, so I subsidize.'[22]

Brewster's return to Jamaica from Rose Bruford was productive for more than her major project of The Barn. There were three other noteworthy projects that allowed her to place her unique mark on them. Firstly, Brewster was the director for the Jamaica Festival Commission for a year in 1968. This post took her to Cuba for training and culminated in a show with 30,000 participants across Jamaica's twelve parishes. High-profile participants included the prime minister of the day, Michael Manley, and artists Jimmy Cliff and Jean Binta Breeze. For Brewster, this kind of work allows Jamaicans to be seen for more than just reggae and ganja.[23]

Secondly, she was instrumental in helping to secure the status of arts teachers as 'proper teachers' in Jamaica. Whilst working at Excelsior College under Wesley Powell, she willingly received an untrained teacher's salary whilst the political point was made to the government that arts teachers should be paid the same as other subject specialists. Six months later arts teachers were granted equal pay in a change that has remained in place ever since.

Finally, Brewster hosted her own radio show, *Open House*, on JBC. She played requests, read the news, received a weekly gift of a cake from one listener, and at Christmas fans sent her gungo peas and even a live turkey. Although returning to Britain would be equally busy, the cultural and racial climate would be very different to the Jamaica Brewster was about to leave behind.

---

[22]Brewster Interview, 9 January 1997.
[23]Brewster, *Blackstages* Interview, July 2002.

Talawa Theatre Company

The making of contemporary black British theatre: Brewster's role

During the 'angry decade' of the 1950s in British theatre, the question of immigration was entirely ignored.[24] Two decades on, however, the work of Roland Rees and Clive Barker with Interaction opened a theatrical door to black artists. This gave voice to some black artists who were visible, but who had often been effectively silenced through the lack of exposure of their work. In 1970 Roland Rees directed Trinidad's Mustapha Matura's *Black Pieces* at the Institute of Contemporary Arts (ICA). In 1971 he directed Matura's *As Time Goes By*. The latter was performed both in Edinburgh and at London's Royal Court. Twenty years later, in 1991, Matura's play *The Coup* was the first Caribbean play to be performed at London's National Theatre.[25] Brewster acknowledges Interaction's work: 'It was a platform because there was no other platform as black people were not going to be given any money to do things like that.'[26]

Whilst Rees developed Interaction in the early 1970s, Brewster moved permanently back to Britain and began her British professional directing career. Her first foray was *Lippo the New Noah* at the ICA (1971). She then directed Jamal Ali's *Black Feet in the Snow* at the Commonwealth Institute, the Roundhouse (1972), and then for television (BBC2 1974). The piece exposed the racism that black people experience daily.[27]

In 1972, the Jamaican High Commission asked Brewster to do a twelve-stop tour of Rhone's *Smile Orange*, to celebrate Jamaica's tenth independence anniversary. The cast included Mona Hammond, Stefan Khalifa, Trevor Thomas and Charlie Hyatt. Reminiscent of The Barn's opening night, the first show in Acton Town Hall had four people in attendance. At the end of the tour they did three nights at Anson Hall in Cricklewood. The first night was full, the second attracted long queues, and on the third there were as many people outside the hall as inside it. Post-Rose Bruford, Brewster's intention in Jamaica was to 'set the world on fire'. Now back in Britain, the people of Cricklewood had similar thoughts:

---

[24]Jatinder Verma, 'Cultural Transformations', in *Contemporary British Theatre*, ed. Theodore Shank (London: Macmillan, 1994), 55.
[25]Stone gives an account of Matura's success, *Studies in West Indian Literature*, 167–73.
[26]Yvonne Brewster, Personal Interview by David Johnson, London, 2 October 1998.
[27]Brewster, 'A Short Autobiographical Essay Focusing on My Work in the Theatre', 392.

It was a matter of supply and demand. There was no supply and there was a lot of demand. Well, the good citizens of Cricklewood saw an audience of almost exclusively black people turning up in *their* neighbourhood, which wasn't black at all in those days, and they burnt the place down. So that's how the tour ended. Everything went up in flames. It was accepted as arson. You know, trying to work in black theatre in Britain is quite hard.[28]

Mona Hammond also remembers the event and questions whether the fire was connected to the long queues of black people in the area.[29] More positively, Chambers credits the tour as 'probably the first such tour of a play by a black playwright with a black cast directed by a black director'.[30]

Brewster's career from the 1970s also saw her displaying film-making talents as a production manager and assistant director on *The Harder They Come* (1970), *Smile Orange* (1975), and *The Marijuana Affair* (1976). As a filmmaker she also produced and cast for BBC television *The Fight Against Slavery* (1975), *My Father Sun Sun Johnson* (1976) and later *Romeo and Juliet* (1997). Additionally she produced *The Gods Are Not To Blame* (1995) for BBC radio and in 1977 directed Harold Pinter's *The Lover* (1997) in Florence. Her renown was now as an international director.

Alongside Brewster's early work, the wider voice of black theatre developed throughout the 1970s due to the efforts of her fellow black artists, as well as available funding. The Greater London Council (GLC), under a Labour government, offered financial support to black theatre and other 'minority' projects. As the political climate changed, so did interest in the development of such projects and the people that benefited from them. On 31 January 1978, Margaret Thatcher, as Leader of the Opposition, was quoted in the *Daily Mirror*:

> People are really rather afraid that this country might be rather swamped by people with a different culture... the British character has done so much for democracy, for law, and done so much throughout the world, that if there is any fear that it might be swamped, people are going to react and be rather hostile to those coming in.[31]

---

[28]Brewster, *Blackstages* Interview, July 2002.
[29]Mona Hammond, *Blackstages* Interview, August 2002.
[30]Chambers, *Black and Asian Theatre in Britain,* 189.
[31]Dahl, 'Postcolonial British Theatre: Black Voices at the Center', 46.

Talawa Theatre Company

With Thatcher's victory in 1979, the major source of funding for 'minority' arts was cut by the early 1980s due to the abolition of the GLC. This, however, did not immediately stop either the black theatre companies that already existed, or the proliferation of new ones that surfaced in the same period. These companies often took names that rejected the historical negation of words preceded by 'black' and their rise stemmed partly from the theatrical inroads that first generation Caribbean theatre practitioners had made.[32] This was coupled with the coming of age of black Britons who realized they had no stake in British society and who were expressing themselves theatrically. Existing and emerging groups included Temba (1972–93), Black Theatre Co-op (1978–96), Theatre of Black Women (1982), Black Theatre Forum (1983–90), Carib Theatre (1983–2011), Umoja (1984–6), Black Mime Theatre (1984–97) and Talawa (1986–present). Most of these companies used African theatrical ritual forms and non-'standard English' speech. As a by-product, they illustrated the multiplicity of what black theatre offered.

Mainstream efforts to marginalize the developing genre came via the dangling of the ever-elusive funding carrot. Despite the companies' desires to create their individual identities, funding bodies required black groups to do work that they categorized as black. This meant having black performers and writers who produced work that came from an African-Caribbean perspective, as defined by white funding bodies. To 'help', in 1986 the Arts Council of Great Britain introduced an Ethnic Minority Arts Policy. This gave 4 per cent of any subsidy offered to a theatre company to the development of work for black artists within the company.[33] Black artists automatically became 'political' because of this and were consequently denied the full possibility of exploring creatively, as criteria had to be met.

Carlson points out that regardless of the wishes of black theatre practitioners their work is highlighted by contemporary theatre because of what makes it different.[34] This perceived difference, mostly based on colour, also helps exclude them from the mainstream. In spite of the 1986 subsidy, however, the steady loss of funding throughout the 1980s meant that many

---

[32]See discussion of the language of the British stage in Chapter 6.
[33]Elizabeth Clarke, 'Black Theatre in England: A Perspective', *Banja: A Magazine of Barbadian Life and Culture*, no. 2 (1988), 63.
[34]Marvin Carlson, *Performance: A Critical Introduction* (London: Routledge, 1986), 144–64.

companies were forced to close. For those that survived funding cuts the future looked bleak. They rapidly became the black fringe companies seen as catering to a 'minority' audience.

Apart from the individual success in the mid-1980s and early 1990s of Brewster directing Lorca's *Blood Wedding* at the National Theatre (1991), and the general success of Talawa and Matura's work, much of the black theatre to emerge in this period came from black British artists. Their issues, experiences, attitudes and expectations differed from their Caribbean theatrical forebears.[35] Only they, as insiders, could tell their stories. It was, after all, only they that in spite of having been born and raised in Britain still had to deal with racism in every aspect of their lives. It was also only they that were able to communicate the complexities of their existence to their group and others.[36] Their black stories, told in their black voices, were seen as a political act of revolt against the status quo.

The all-female BiBi Crew (1980s–present) and the all-male The Posse (1992–4) started at the Theatre Royal Stratford East. Their devised work discussed black British identity and topical issues in a mixture of West Indian speech forms, 'standard English' and black British speech. This period also saw new comedy artists such as Llewella Gideon, Angie La Mar and Felicity Ethnic, whose issues and stance paralleled those of their performance ancestor Louise Bennett. In the male role was Felix Dexter, along with the comedy duos of Jefferson and Whitfield, and Curtis and Ishmael.

Black British playwrights at this time also produced work that gave black actors new and challenging roles conceived from a contemporary black British perspective. This included Caryl Phillips's *Strange Fruit* (1988) and *Where There Is Darkness* (1990), Killian Gideon's *England Is De Place For Me* (1985), Winsome Pinnock's *Rock in the Water* (1989) and *A Hero's Welcome* (1990), Trish Cook's *Back Street Mammy* (1991) and *Running Dream* (1992), and Edgar White's *Redemption Song* (1993).

These black Britons felt it was their right to define themselves on the British stage. Interviewed by Rees, Pauline Black demonstrates their stance: 'If you, in the RSC and National, won't cast us, then we will do that work

---

[35]The difference in attitude of these two groups is demonstrated in Roland Rees's *Fringe First: Pioneers of Fringe Theatre on Record* (London: Oberon, 1992).
[36]Deborah Wood Holton, 'The Dramaturg's Way: Meditations on the Cartographer at the Crossroads', in *Black Theatre: Ritual Performance in the African Diaspora*, ed. Paul Carter Harrison, Victor Leo Walker II and Gus Edwards (Philadelphia: Temple University Press, 2002), 253.

ourselves and cast all the parts with black actors.'[37] This echoes Brewster's belief that black theatre practitioners should define themselves through their original work. A lack of self-definition will lead to being categorized as 'Culturally diverse theatre. The term used by the London Arts Board for all minority theatre to mean: when the black people come and muddy up the water.'[38]

This 'muddy water' theatre is perceived as inferior by the mainstream and sometimes by those involved in creating it: 'People don't even want to say that they are in black theatre. They don't want to be associated with something that is always on the fringes.'[39] This attitude is unsurprising given that it stems from the mainstream notion that black theatre is at best a subgenre in a lower strata of performance in which black cultural forms, where it is acknowledged that they exist at all, are regarded as inferior in every technical and historical way.[40] The irony of course is that there would be no history, in theatre or any other arena, if there were no black history.[41]

Without specifying it as such, each black British theatre group above gave black African-Caribbean and black British performers the type of forum for artistic freedom and creation that Teer's Negro Theatre of Harlem, Connor's Negro Theatre, Grant's Drum and Brewster's The Barn had done for their artists. Teer specified she wanted her performers to 'stop denying and start identifying.'[42] She explains, 'as a subculture in a dominant culture, we were not included. We inherited a legacy of "less-than-ness".'[43] The creation of all the black theatre groups above gave black artists the chance to be themselves in a predominantly white space without feeling 'less-than'. Teer saw this process as 'rehabilitating black people's ability to love themselves.'[44] This is a vital component in any environment where black performers and black people generally are expected to adopt standards that are not African-centric.

---

[37]Rees, *Fringe First*, 143.
[38]Brewster Interview, 2 October 1998.
[39]Ibid.
[40]Tejumola Olaniyan, 'Agones: The Constitution of a Practice', in *Black Theatre: Ritual Performance in the African Diaspora*, ed. Paul Carter Harrison, Victor Leo Walker II and Gus Edwards (Philadelphia, Temple University Press, 2002), 65.
[41]Antar Mason, 'From Hip-Hop to Hittite: Part X', 385.
[42]Barbara Ann Teer, 'The Great White Way Is Not Our Way - Not Yet', *Negro Digest*, April 1968, 25.
[43]Gary Schoichet, 'Barabara Ann Teer', *Other Stage*, 17 April 1980, 2.
[44]Sandy Satterwhite, 'Black Actress Shares Her Soul', *New York Post*, 6 February, 1976, 21.

A Stranger in Non-paradise

In the process of becoming Western and white, blacks are weakened.[45] Just how damaging Western acting theory is to black people is shown in the consequences of black actors using Stanislavsky's 'magic if'. Their 'ifs' may include 'If there had not been slavery', 'If I were white', 'If there were no racism' and 'If I could get a good job'.[46] This underpins why Teer aimed to create a black theory of acting and liberating, where actors are forced to study both themselves and their roots.[47]

The black British theatre companies were doing this by allowing themselves to create work about themselves in their unique performance voice. The aim here was not to define black British culture but rather to give examples of its varying parts. Brewster's direct contribution to these diverse elements is seen in the work she did with some of these, and other, black British theatre companies.

Dark and Light

In 1971 the Dark and Light Theatre Company, which operated until 1977, was founded by Jamaican Frank Cousins (b. 1940). Although the company name was assumed to mean multicultural, it was chosen to reflect the light on the stage and the darkness in the audience. When Cousins formed Dark and Light, it was the only black theatre in Britain to have its own theatre building. This was at Longfield Hall, London. Brewster notes that it was 'one of the first buildings in London to be aided by the funding bodies to produce "black" work'.[48] From the outset Cousins had the central tenet, 'If you don't know anything about my culture, what do you know about me?' He wanted the wider population to be more aware of both his roots and of the problems Caribbean immigrants living in Britain faced.[49]

The company used Caribbean and African English language forms in its work. It produced *Evolution of the Blues* by Jon Hendricks, *Kataki* by Shiman Wincalbert, *The Slave* by Amiri Baraka, *The Tenant* by Richard

---

[45]Thomas, 'Barbara Ann Teer: From Holistic Training to Liberating Rituals', 352. Thomas discusses Teer's intention to create an alternate system of values to the Western concept.
[46]Ibid., 353.
[47]Ibid.
[48]Brewster, 'A Short Autobiographical Essay Focusing on My Work in the Theatre', 392.
[49]Frank Cousins, *Blackstages* Interview by Tara Mack, London, 18 August 2002.

Cron, *Raas* by Robert Lamb, *Anansi and Brer Englishman* by Manley Young, *Twisted Knots, Dark Days and Light Nights* and *Jericho* by Jamal Ali, *Jumbie Street March* by T. Bone Wilson and *Seduced* by Jimi Rand.

Appearing extensively on British television and on the London stage before he founded Dark and Light, Cousins viewed racism as par for the course whilst acting. Performing in *Jack of Spades* in Liverpool (1965–6), the cast and director Terry Hands needed police protection from gangs wanting to beat up the black performers. Similarly, whilst acting in *The Blacks* for the UK-touring Oxford Players Company, the cast was welcomed in Oxford with the graffiti 'Blacks are coming, lock up your daughters'.[50]

When *The Blacks* toured to Antwerp, the black cast had trouble getting back into Britain because they all had different passports. Cousins explains, 'Nobody wanted to change their passport, they didn't think it was important then. They all considered themselves as British, from the colonies. The Caribbean passport still said British passport.'[51] In order to be allowed back into the country, Equity had to vouch that they had been representing Britain in a festival.

Brewster became connected with Dark and Light when Cousins contacted her in 1971 to direct the Jamaican pantomime *Brer Nancy*.[52] This was Brewster's first professional show in Britain.[53] To avoid losing Arts Council funding, Cousins needed to do something that would bring an audience. Jason Rose was loaned from the Royal Shakespeare Company (RSC) to star in the show and Gloria Cameron played the female lead. To conform with Jamaican tradition the show started on Boxing Day. It was sold out for the whole run. Brewster describes this as black British theatre history because the show introduced the Jamaican pantomime tradition to post-Windrush generations who had never been to Jamaica.[54] The work translated to the black British audience because they understood the language and it finished with the Jamaican getting the better of the Englishman, 'who by the end was eating rice an' pea an' dumplin' an' plantain'.[55] Brewster credits Dark and

---

[50]Ibid.
[51]Ibid.
[52]Brewster Interview, 20 November 2018.
[53]Brewster, *Blackstages* Interview, July 2002.
[54]Brewster Interview, 20 November 2018.
[55]Ibid.

Light with being 'the first black theatre in Britain that was defined through the eyes of a Caribbean person'.[56]

The pantomime's success saw it repeated the following year, with Brewster directing. As Cousins had to go to Jamaica the production was managed by Norman Beaton. Cousins's departure warning was that the show could not go over budget. On his return he discovered the company was in huge debt. The Arts Council wasted no time in asking him to resign as artistic director. It was at this point that the company became the Black Theatre of Brixton with Norman Beaton (Guyana), Jamal Ali (Guyana) and Rufus Collins (America) at the helm. In search of something more 'radical', 'within six months they lost everything'.[57] With no building or Arts Council support they had to shut down. Brewster is left with the impression that despite everything Cousins had done for the company, he was ousted by those who took over from him. The same people who presided over the collapse of what was Britain's first black theatre company, with its own home and Arts Council funding.[58]

Cousins's legacy lives on, however, both in the wealth of black British theatre it preceded but also with both Lambeth and Southwark Councils adding Cousins's Dark and Light theatre home to their Black History Walks. With the next groups Brewster directed, their black British identity and experience would be at the forefront of their performance expression.

Theatre of Black Women

The Theatre of Black Women was started in 1982 by Bernadine Evaristo, Patricia Hilaire, Pauline Randall and Joan Williams, whilst they were in their third year at Rose Bruford. Brewster had been invited to work with the four women who were fed up with being directed by people who did not understand them. Together they devised a show which dealt with the types of situations they found themselves in as women.

The women contributed their experiences. Brewster explained how she had a terrible time fighting off Nigerian men: 'They love brown women, well in those days; I don't know about now, they probably don't.' Evaristo

---

[56]Brewster, *Blackstages* Interview, July 2002.
[57]Cousins, *Blackstages* Interview, August 2002.
[58]Brewster Interview, 20 November 2018.

talked about how her Nigerian father's friend would always say, 'I know your fada (father).' They explored the meaning and every connotation of that phrase. The question arose, 'If this man knows your father, then what is it he knows about you?' They called the piece *Coping*, to mean coping with unwanted male attention. Brewster recalls the college was embarrassed by the work. 'It was these black people shining a light on these black people, as if they had the right to do that.'[59] The women had created work that spoke to them as it was about their lived experiences.

It was when they went to perform the show at a women's support group in Stockwell that they had to come up with a name for themselves. They decided on the Theatre of Black Women. In spite of the success of the show and the requests they were getting to perform it, there were two problems. Firstly, Brewster had taken the students to perform outside of Rose Bruford without permission. Secondly, the students were not permitted to work whilst at college. Brewster was called in and they had to stop the show, as 'It was giving the college a bad name and making it political.'[60] That old 'political' chestnut. Although the show was forced to end, the Rose Bruford connection continued.

Carib Theatre

In 1983 Brewster was a co-founder of the Carib Theatre (1983–2011), along with Anton and Judy Philips. All three were graduates of Rose Bruford and their aim was to develop high-quality theatre by and for young black people, through their theatre in education workshops and productions. Brewster directed much of Carib's early musical work and comments, 'We were able to bring a black perspective into schools, where these inner city kids had never heard that they had a perspective, or that any aspect of their lives was worthy of being shown.'[61]

Despite struggling for, and often not getting, funding, they all worked hard touring the country. Brewster hated touring. One night, having returned home from Bristol at 3.00 am following the company's performance of a musical version of Reckord's *Sykvers* renamed *Streetwise*, Brewster found

---

[59]Brewster Interview, London, 26 November 2018.
[60]Ibid.
[61]Ibid.

herself alone in the tour van.⁶² Surrounded by set and props and unable to find a parking space, she became clear. She no longer wanted to do all the directing and rehearsing as well as the booking, driving, travelling, packing and unpacking. 'It was all too pyah pyah and beggy beggy for me.'⁶³ Brewster took unconventional action: 'so I left it [the van] in the middle of the road with the keys in it and thought sod it, I hope somebody drives it away and teef it.'⁶⁴

By morning, the van had been parked and the keys returned to Brewster. The parking culprit was Ken Chubb, then director of the Tricycle Theatre. In addition to saving the van, Chubb advised Brewster that if she wanted to get out of small-scale touring, she needed to find out how the funding system worked. Chubb then played a key role in encouraging and when that failed, daring Brewster to apply for the role of drama officer at the Arts Council. At the interview Brewster was impressed by the then drama director, John Falconer. It was his shiny shoes that drew her to him. Once Brewster was offered the job, Chubb advised her that she would be entering a great department with John Falconer and Jean Bullwinkle. He also felt the Arts Council would benefit from Brewster's ability to energize companies.⁶⁵ Brewster became the Arts Council's first black female drama officer and held the post from 1 November 1982 to 31 October 1984. Whilst this new post temporarily closed Brewster's work with Carib, it marked the beginning of her political and administrative astuteness.

Brewster saw first-hand that the Arts Council staff was dedicated to working for the theatre companies: 'I loved it because you could see theatre working from the heart of the engine.'⁶⁶ In addition to the love was the reality, as the usual racism reared its ever-present head, when on entering an Arts Council meeting it was assumed Brewster was there to serve the coffee.⁶⁷

Post-Arts Council, the advantage Brewster had was that she knew how theatre funding worked. From the inside, she saw that black theatre companies were not applying to the Arts Council or the London Arts Board for grants. When she contacted Carib with this information, she

---

⁶²Brewster, 'A Short Autobiographical Essay Focusing on My Work in the Theatre', 393.
⁶³Brewster Interview, 26 November 2018. Brewster found the set up too poor (pyah pyah) and reliant on borrowing and favours (beggy beggy).
⁶⁴Ibid. Brewster hoped the van would be stolen.
⁶⁵Ibid.
⁶⁶Brewster Interview, 31 October 2014.
⁶⁷Ibid.

was told that whilst she was at the Arts Council, it was decided she was no longer needed.⁶⁸ Brewster continued to work nonetheless, but now there was a pattern emerging in black British theatre. Whether intended or not, the genre was becoming increasingly political. This is seen in Brewster's experiences with both the Black Theatre Cooperative (BTC) and the Black Theatre Forum (BTF).

Black Theatre Cooperative

BTC was co-founded by Mustapha Matura and Charlie Hanson in 1978.⁶⁹ The freshness of this group was based on its 'authentic street expression' founded in its black Britishness.⁷⁰ This would force audiences to see who they were as people and performers, as borne out of the relationship that Britain had had with the Caribbean. They did not feel the need to be polite; they were at home after all. Brewster explains, 'I love those people because they were facety, that's a Jamaican word, they were fas[t], that's a Jamaican word, and they were forward.'⁷¹ Brewster continues:

> Lovely young people who didn't give two flying feathers for what anybody thought. Politically they were right on the button and they were led in the beginning by Farrukh Dhondy, Mustapha Matura and Charlie Hanson. I must have made a mistake, who was the black guy? I can't remember, it can't have been two Asians and a white man?! Good God in heaven, what does that say? I've just realized this now after all these years.⁷²

By 1984 BTC got its first Arts Council annual grant and did four shows a year in its first five years.⁷³ In 1988 it was again awarded funds under a three-year Arts Council revenue funding scheme.⁷⁴ Brewster sums up BTC's winning structure in the people who ran it: 'Hanson was political

---

⁶⁸Brewster Interview, 26 November 2018.
⁶⁹Between 1996 and 2015 BTC became Nitro under Felix Cross. Since 2015 it has been Nitrobeat under Diane Morgan.
⁷⁰Rees, *Fringe First*, 126–8.
⁷¹Brewster Interview, 26 November 2018. 'Facety', 'fast' means 'cheeky', 'meddling'.
⁷²Ibid.
⁷³Chambers, *Black and Asian Theatre in Britain*, 176.
⁷⁴Graham Saunders, *British Theatre Companies 1980–1984* (London: Bloomsbury, 2015), 84.

and could get funding, Matura wrote the plays and Dhondy had television and clout behind him. In addition to the high quality of BTC's work, they had black political beliefs: Victor Romero Evans, Malcolm Frederick, Janet Kay and Judith Jacob were absolutely devoted to the cultural impact of their outward looking work.[75]

Knowing that the group was political, Brewster was surprised when she was asked to direct its 1985 production of *Raisin in the Sun*. Whilst touring, Brewster was aware of the group's political energy and the positive impact it had on her: 'it brought out my fist in a way.'[76] This influence helped Brewster to sack her leading man for lateness in the middle of the run. He had also not wished to rehearse on the grounds that he did not need to, as he was performing his own black American culture.

Brewster found black American actor Doyle Richmond as a replacement and rehearsed with him for two nights. She announced the change to the audience and the timeframe Richmond had had to learn the part. When he used the script at the end, the audience gasped. They had forgotten he was new to the role. He did the rest of the tour. In reference to her decision and Richmond's willingness, Brewster explains, 'That's what you need to do, you need to have balls.'[77]

BTC, like all other black theatre groups and individual black performers, had the burden of being the spokespeople for all kinds of 'black'. The performers however wanted to do the work that best spoke for them. They would not be able to 'represent both diasporic experience and contemporary life in Britain'.[78] Whilst the group's work was popular, Norman Beaton felt they had 'fallen into the trap of ghettoizing every social issue [giving us] pimps, prostitutes, tired reluctant old West Indian men and their long suffering wives, sons on the dole or in prison, an entire society at war with the forces of law and order . . . and [which] therefore reinforces the white man's prejudice'.[79] Beaton's comment gives no credence to the fact that BTC's chosen subject matter came directly from the black British experience its performers were witnessing and living. Their sentiment was however echoed in the work of the BTF.

---

[75] Brewster Interview, 26 November 2018.
[76] Ibid.
[77] Ibid.
[78] Saunders, *British Theatre Companies*, 83.
[79] Ibid., with reference given as Norman Beaton, 'Origins, Aims and Objectives of Company', 19 August 1983, ACGB, 41/9/13.

Talawa Theatre Company

Black Theatre Forum

Anton Philips started the BTF in 1983 from his premise that black and Asian theatre companies should unite and approach the GLC's Ethnic Arts Subcommittee with a policy for their work.[80] He also applied to them for funds to stage a season of black plays in the West End.[81] A grant of £26,000 was awarded and the BTF's first season took place at the Arts Theatre, London in 1983. This would be the venue for the first four seasons.

For season one, Brewster directed *Fishing* by Paulette Randall for Black Woman Time Theatre. For Terracciano, Brewster's production 'echoed the feminist concerns of the time. It also represented one of the early attempts to portray black British women's life on stage from a black woman's perspective, revealing, in the words of the reviewer Nicholas de Jongh, "the gulf between black women of two generations, and their angry, despairing submission to men"'.[82]

Brewster recalls the production thirty-five years on and how the protagonists, Ellen Thomas, Corinne Skinner Carter and Peggy Phango, were fishing for a life and for men from their high-rise tower block homes. Brewster's memory is of artists telling their stories truthfully, with no overt political aim. Did they see themselves as the feminists they were deemed to be, or were they simply not rejecting the political labelling of the mainstream? The reality of course is that, as black women in Britain, they were much more than the singular definition of feminist. Adding to the storytelling was Lubaina Himid's set design. In this, her first professional job, she represented the tower blocks with tea chests. In 2017, aged sixty-three, Himid became the oldest woman to win the Turner Prize.

For the second season in 1985, Brewster directed Lovelace's *The New Hardware Store*. This represented a preview of what was to come. The theatrical and political devices of Carnival, calypso and Calvary Hill would re-emerge five years later when she directed Lovelace's *The Dragon Can't Dance* at Talawa, in the kind of Caribbean work that came to epitomize black British theatre in Talawa's early years. Due to her commitments with

---

[80]Chambers, *Black and Asian Theatre in Britain*, 186.
[81]Alda Terracciano, 'Mainstreaming African, Asian and Caribbean Theatre: The Experiments of the Black Theatre Forum', in *Alternatives Within the Mainstream British Black and Asian Theatres*, ed. Dimple Godiwala (Newcastle: Cambridge Scholars Press, 2006), 23.
[82]Ibid., 25. Also, Nicholas de Jongh, 'Fishing', *Guardian*, 9 December 1983. No page number available.

Talawa, Brewster did not participate in the Forum's 1986 third season. For the fourth season in 1987, the Greater London Arts Association (GLAA) provided £165,000 in funding. Having had a resounding success with Talawa's first production in 1986, C. L. R. James's *The Black Jacobins*, Brewster was back directing Edgar White's *Moon Dance Night* for the BTF. The play focused specifically on ritual which Brewster knew to be 'culturally and conceptually very important to people of African descent'.[83]

White attended the rehearsal process and ritually played his flute at the back. Brewster worked with the distraction. The production offered the chance to work with a great cast including Jean Binta Breeze and Jason Rose, on a show that believed in the Caribbean. Additionally, there were the nightly pre-performance off-stage rum sprinkling rituals that Brewster went through with 'the brilliant Breeze'.[84] This was much more than a directing process but rather a love for the Caribbean and its people: a love of self. Brewster acknowledges that Prince Edward's enthusiasm at the Royal Gala performance on 21 October 1987 did Talawa more good than the BTF.[85] Nonetheless, Brewster sees the BTF generally as:

> One of the instances in which people in black theatre actually did work well together, it was fabulous. At one stage there were thirty-two members mixed with Indian, Pakistani, African and Caribbean companies, with the London Arts board and other funding bodies happy with this. I always thought, if they have us all in one place, they can bomb us out with one bomb.[86]

This realism is mirrored by some dissatisfaction from within the BTF. Derek Blackwood wanted the performances to be in venues that black people were more likely to attend.[87] Brewster remembers Blackwood 'used to ask uncomfortable questions and he was totally right'.[88] Questions were also raised regarding the unspoken hierarchy which meant that the more accepted companies with a profile – Carib, Talawa, Tara, Temba and Umoja

---

[83]Terracciano, 'Mainstreaming African, Asian and Caribbean Theatre', 43. The reference given is Brewster, Yvonne (15 December 1999), interview with Aldo Terracciano.
[84]Brewster Interview, 26 November 2018.
[85]Ibid.
[86]Ibid.
[87]Terracciano, 'Mainstreaming African, Asian and Caribbean Theatre', 44.
[88]Brewster Interview, 26 November 2018.

– would direct the shows.[89] Younger directors with a lesser prominence did not do well in this structure. Additionally, there were cultural difficulties as expressed in the 'tension' between the African-Caribbean and Asian strands over policy.[90]

Whilst the white mainstream kept its theatrical pie, it had locked all non-white practitioners, with very little in common other than their perceived immigrant outsider status to unite them, into one 'political' underclass group. Despite the political designation given to the BTF, Brewster adopts my phrase in describing it as 'political after the fact' and adds, 'The black theatre forum was non-political. Perhaps the aim was just the aims of the various people who founded it to get a show on. In retrospect, it became a very big political affair, but just for my money, it wasn't that political. Others may not see it this way.'[91]

The BTF's fifth season in 1989 was at the Shaw Theatre, London. Once again the GLAA supplied funding to the tune of £165,000. Brewster did not participate but returned for the sixth and final season in 1990 at the Riverside Studios, London. She directed *Blood, Sweat and Fears* by visually impaired playwright Maria Oshodi. Whilst the 26 April 1990 gala performance was not appreciated by all those in the BTF, Brewster used the event to provide a solid community link by fundraising for sickle cell.[92]

Due to the BTF's successful work, discussions were held with a view to creating a home for black theatre at the Roundhouse, London. The plan involved Camden Council buying the building, the GLC paying the running costs and the Arts Council contributing to project budgets.[93] The project's failure was announced in the *Daily Telegraph*: 'the limited company set up to run the project is to go into voluntary liquidation after the Arts Council refused to release £900,000 allocated for the scheme, deeming it unrealistic.'[94]

The Roundhouse was refurbished and reopened in 2006, with no indication that its new performance space was aimed at black arts. The BTF faced further challenges when the GLA became the London Arts Board and funds previously allocated to the BTF theatre season were reallocated to

---

[89] Ibid.
[90] Chambers, *Black and Asian Theatre in Britain*, 186.
[91] Brewster Interview, 26 November 2018.
[92] Terracciano, 'Mainstreaming African, Asian and Caribbean Theatre', 47.
[93] Chambers, *Black and Asian Theatre in Britain*, 183–4.
[94] Terracciano, 'Mainstreaming African, Asian and Caribbean Theatre', 47.

'other diasporic work.'[95] Any long-term planning for the BTF and its artists was now made impossible.

Actual reasons for stopping such work have included the companies' lack of ability to manage themselves and the poor quality of work. Jane Milling highlights further reasons for the scarcity of mainstream support in this genre: 'theatre did not trust that there was a large enough black audience, or one they could attract, nor that their current audience constituency could find black playwrights' work "accessible", or a reflection of "universal" human experience.'[96] Such notions reflect a mainstream refusal to acknowledge black life as worthy on stage.

None of this would stop Brewster forging ahead. By the time the BTF closed, Talawa had been running for four years. When she started Talawa Brewster was trained, well established and an experienced performer, director and administrator. She was seasoned in the precarious nature of working in black British theatre and knew that from one day to the next a praised artistic director could be 'thrown to the dogs' and 'become a person of little consequence'.[97] She also knew the challenges, pitfalls, expectations, burden of representation and the racism that went with the job. How would this serve her in starting Talawa and in steering the company through its three-year residency in the West End?

Talawa

In 1985 Lord Birkett contacted Brewster to let her know that the GLC's Race Equality Unit's Black Experience Arts Programme was offering production funding as part of a season to celebrate the life and work of Trinidadian writer and activist C. L. R. James. Encouraged to apply, Brewster stayed up for the next two nights preparing her proposal for James's play *The Black Jacobins*.[98]

Brewster knew the show had been done in 1936 with Paul Robeson, black doctors and lawyers, and 'roles designated for black actors played by white

---

[95]Chambers, *Black and Asian Theatre in Britain*, 188.
[96]Jane Milling, *Modern British Playwriting, the 1980s, Voices, Documents, New Interpretations* (London: Methuen, 2012), 81.
[97]Brewster Interview, 20 November 2018.
[98]Brewster Interview, 31 October 2014.

Englishmen blacked up'.[99] Her 1986 production would require £80,000 and have Norman Beaton in the lead role of Toussaint L'Ouverture. It would celebrate fifty years since the earlier production and have the advantage of the natural hue of the twenty-three-strong cast, none of whom would need to black up.

One day after submitting the application, it was confirmed that Brewster had been awarded the full amount for her show. Saunders offers an explanation for this speedy response: 'Talawa in many ways were in the right place at the right time, able to benefit from the GLC's largesse who, earmarked for abolition, seemed to have gone on a final spending spree knowing it had nothing to lose'.[100] In testament to years well spent at the Arts Council, Brewster should also be given credit for her ability to get the application right with breakneck speed, as well as for having the guts to make the uncompromising proposal she did. She would now be able to do her show exactly as she wished.

Next, Brewster needed a company name. Whilst Mona Hammond stipulated it should be 'Something Jamaican' and Carmen Monroe that it should be something 'round', Brewster searched the Jamaican dictionary starting from the back. 'Zuzuwap' sounded too African. 'Talawa' brought back the memory of how often the phrase 'She Likkle but she Talawa' was used in Jamaica. It described Brewster and the other women involved; small but feisty. Brewster explains, 'I'm still quite proud of that name because I think it means something about asserting what you know you have, which others might want to tell you you don't'.[101]

Two more nights were spent setting the company up. The founding members of Talawa, along with Brewster, were Inigo Espejel, Mona Hammond and Carmen Munroe. The secure GLC funding was accompanied by GLC expectations for Brewster's show. Her request for a reasonable preparation period for the work was met with: 'What do you want with six weeks of rehearsals? Black plays don't need more than three'.[102] Despite this challenge, Brewster went ahead with the production, because of the strength

---

[99]Yvonne Brewster, 'Talawa Theatre Company 1985–2002', in *Staging New Britain: Aspects of Black and South Asian British Theatre Practice*, ed. G. V. Davis and A. Fuchs (Brussels: Peter Lang, 2006), 87.
[100]Saunders, *British Theatre Companies*, 44.
[101]Brewster Interview, 31 October 2014.
[102]Lyn Gardener, Interview with Yvonne Brewster, *City Limits*, 21–27 February 1986, 75.

of her belief that 'Theatrically speaking, England is the most receptive place in the world'.[103]

Brewster had assumed her production of *The Black Jacobins* would be a one-off project. It was unimaginable at that time that she was staging the first show by what would become Britain's longest running black theatre company. The fact that this debut production was funded in the way it was and that it put black revolution centre stage meant the company could not avoid the politically black branding the press would view it with. This was not an issue for Brewster:

> I don't see anything wrong with having a political reason for wanting to do something artistic, but what particularly pleases me about this production is that I began by wanting to revive it because I thought that the politics of CLR James was so immensely important to black people in this country today. Then I realized that not only are the politics correct, but it is also a smashing play.[104]

Talawa then, without Teer-type defined criteria, and whether it was intended or not, was destined to have a political edge. This notion continued throughout Brewster's era and beyond. Igweonu explains, 'Talawa provided a political platform for black people to ask questions about what it meant to be black and British.'[105] This politicization also came from Talawa's audience, who 'saw their patronage of Talawa as a "political act"'.[106]

Twenty-one years on from *The Black Jacobins*, Ukaegbu describes Talawa's body of work as entirely political and intentionally showing different races in opposition to each other, to 'reveal prejudices that surround race relations and the perception of people of minority backgrounds. Whatever the source and setting of their performance texts, the company tends towards politicized if not overtly political productions'.[107]

Since its initial funding from the GLC, Talawa has received continuous support from the Arts Council of England for the past thirty-three years.

---

[103] Ibid.
[104] Ibid.
[105] Igweonu, 'Talawa', 238.
[106] Claire Allfree, 'The Big Interview: Talawa Theatre Company, from Feisty to Philosophical', *Metro*, 13 October 2011, 53–4.
[107] Ukaegbu, 'Talawa Theatre Company: The "Likkle" Matter of Black Creativity and Representation on the British Stage', 131.

Talawa Theatre Company

As Talawa's work and range of projects evolved during Brewster's era, the company enjoyed further funding from a wide body of organizations between 1993 and 2001:[108] quite remarkable for a company that came into existence as a result of Brewster identifying and seizing an opportunity in what she regards as a 'happy accident'.[109] A 'happy accident' which between 1986 and 2001 saw Talawa produce twenty-nine productions in a range of genres including African, American, Caribbean and British classical works. This was the beginning of a legacy that to date has produced eighty-nine productions and that has ensured black British theatre's place in the contemporary theatrical mainstream.

When the time is right: Talawa's residency at the Cochrane

Whilst at the Arts Council in 1984, Brewster reported, 'there are regrettably no building-based ethnic minority theatre companies in receipt of annual subsidy from the Council.'[110] She would change this in 1992 with a new stage in Talawa's development. Discussions with The London Institute and Central St Martin's School of Art and Design led to Talawa's successful bid for development funds from The London Institute and the Arts Council. Additionally, Talawa received a three-year lease to work at the newly named and refurbished Cochrane Theatre, owned by The London Institute.[111] The theatre space, designed by architect Abiodun Odedina, aimed at creating a theatrical adventure, in addition to providing a performance area. To this end, the front-of-house design used African-Caribbean images that

---

[108] During this period Talawa received funding from Baring Foundation, British Council, British Telecom, Calouste Gulbenkian Foundation, Cilntec, Contact Theatre, Department for the Environment, Esmee Fairbairn, John Lewis Partnership, John Lyons, LAB Women Writers, Lionel Rogosin, London Hispanic Foundation, London Weekend Television, Paul Hamlyn Foundation, Prince's Trust, Stoll Moss Theatres, The London Institute, The Festival Theatre, Ward Theatre Foundation and the Wates Foundation.
[109] Brewster Interview, 31 October 2014.
[110] Saunders, *British Theatre Companies*, 100. The reference on 265 is (1984l), Yvonne Brewster, 'Paper for Inclusion in Council Paper: One Step Forward - Developing Support by the Arts Council and RAAs of Ethnic Minority Arts', 28 September, ACGB 38/32/4).
[111] Brewster Interview, 31 October 2014. Brewster credits, amongst others, MP Mo Mowlam (1949–2005), performer Floella Benjamin, former director of the London Arts Board Pat Abrahams, consultant Judith Strong and designer Ellen Cairns with being instrumental in securing the Cochrane.

highlighted the cultural identity of the work that would take place at the Cochrane.

Brewster obtained the Arts Council funding she needed by employing a clear strategy. The Arts Council had a total of £300,000 to be divided between ten black theatre companies. In order to get its potential £30,000 share, each company had to present its case to the Arts Council's board. Brewster's then administrator David Hoare suggested that she should apply for the full £300,000. He found a Victorian leaflet with the wording 'When the time is right' and asked Ben Thomas to make a short video that would serve as Talawa's application. Knowing that the Cochrane was empty and unused, Brewster was filmed in front of it, with a message in the background which read, 'When the time is right'. Aware that Lord Palumbo sat on the decision making Arts Council board, Hoare then acquired Palumbo's signature cufflinks and an Arts Council blank cheque from Palumbo's secretary. These props were used to film a scene which showed Palumbo's hand and cufflinks signing a cheque to Talawa for £300,000.[112]

Talawa was the last company to present its case. Brewster introduced the film, and it ran for four minutes and thirty seconds, after which 'There was so much laughter in the room. When they saw Palumbo's hand signing the cheque, he roared with laughter.'[113] Talawa was awarded £250,000. The remaining £50,000 was divided amongst the other companies. Brewster is frank: 'And there began the hate campaign.'[114] She continues, 'The people that supported us the least were our own black people. After the event it's not so painful now but it was almost terminal and that's why I got sick.'[115]

The lack of support was accompanied by 'vicious letters' to the Arts Council.[116] These were shown to Brewster and verified that her attackers offered a plethora of reasons to explain why Talawa was undeserving of this support, 'but never because we had a good case. We'd even identified the theatre and what we were going to do with it and the budget and the lot, and the reaction was terrible. They slagged us off for the rest of our lives. Now they're all gone.'[117]

---

[112]Brewster Interview, 26 November 2018.
[113]Ibid.
[114]Brewster Interview, 31 October 2014.
[115]Ibid.
[116]Ibid.
[117]Brewster Interview, 26 November 2018.

Talawa Theatre Company

In a new high-profile home with a £350,000 refurbishment, Talawa's status was raised. This move was symbolic both for itself but also for the wider black arts community. Connor explains, 'we were finally going to have a headquarters for black theatre in Britain because we had all gone on and on and on and borrowed and rented places, and been on the doorstep with the begging bowl. What a great breakthrough. It became a Mecca, it was a centre for all of us.'[118]

During its residency at the Cochrane, Talawa's contractual remit was to produce an annual performance programme of three to four productions that would run for periods of four to five weeks. By the end of the residency, Talawa had produced a total of ten productions in the following genres:

- three African plays[119]
- two American plays[120]
- four Caribbean plays[121]
- one British classical play[122]

With this programming, Talawa was both meeting the needs of its varied community, as well as widening the scope of what West End theatre had to offer. Audience attendance figures rose from 12 per cent at the beginning of the residency to almost 60 per cent by the end.[123] In addition to the annual productions, Talawa devised an education programme aimed at serving the wider community. This included collaborations with the Theatre Design degree at Central St Martin's which offered students practical set design experience on Talawa's productions.

---

[118]Connor, *Blackgrounds* Interview, June 1997.

[119]*The Road*, Wole Soyinka, 26 February to 28 March 1992, Director Yvonne Brewster. *Mooi Street Moves*, Paul Slabolepszy, 6 September to 17 September 1994, Director Paul Slabolepszy. *Resurrections*, Biyi Bandele-Thomas, 28 September to 29 October 1994, Director Yvonne Brewster.

[120]*The Love Space Demand*, Ntozake Shange, 1 October to 31 October 1992, Director Yvonne Brewster. *From the Mississippi Delta*, Dr Endesha Ida Mae Holland, 1 April to 1 May 1993, Director Annie Castledine.

[121]*Smile Orange*, Trevor Rhone, 28 April to 30 May 1992, Director Trevor Rhone. *Arawak Gold*, Carmen Tipling and Ted Dwyer, 9 December 1992 to 16 January 1993, Director Yvonne Brewster. *The Lion*, Michael Abbensetts, 30 September to 30 October 1993, Director Horace Ove. *Maskarade*, Sylvia Wynter, 9 December 1994 to 14 January 1995, Director Yvonne Brewster.

[122]*King Lear*, William Shakespeare, 16 March to 16 April 1994, Director Yvonne Brewster.

[123]Brewster, *Blackstages* Interview, July 2002.

Talawa's new audience was mixed both in terms of race and age. Despite her programming success, a man told Brewster, 'Oh, I don't think that's what black theatre should be doing at the moment. I know about black theatre.'[124] Whilst his whiteness did not exclude him from knowing about this genre, he was incapable of recognizing that Brewster's blackness and her years producing black British theatre might mean she knew something about it too. In addition to dealing with this inevitable arrogant racism, Talawa faced further difficulties from the outset of the residency. These stemmed both from the mainstream view of Talawa's performance work and the relationship between Talawa and the Cochrane's resident staff.

Brewster acknowledges that taking Walcott's advice to open the Cochrane with Wole Soyinka's *The Road* was a mistake. Following her 1991 production of *Antony and Cleopatra*, he told her to avoid the opening night comedy that he felt most black people would do. Brewster agreed on the choice because the play 'brought Yoruba culture with a colonial hint and in Jamaica we are at the colonial end of the Yoruba culture'.[125] The reviews of the production suggest the work was both misunderstood and underappreciated. McSherry's letter to Moffatt regarding the reviews also points to Talawa's tacit philosophy under Brewster that ensured the company kept its edge: 'not quite what we would have wished for, but of no consequence to our commitment to providing our audience with work that is representative of the classics of black culture, rather than the diluted "feel good" offerings which prevail in the West End.'[126]

Whilst some reviewers found Soyinka's play too difficult to understand and questioned Brewster's choice, others predictably swiped at the company's West End worthiness: 'Talawa will have to do better if they are not to be challenged by other ethnic minority companies with an equal or better claim to a roof over their heads.'[127] Wardle's comment is qualified by his preconceived notion that Talawa's work will be disappointing: 'The Cochrane Theatre, long lost to the general public, reopened last week,

---

[124]Ibid.
[125]Brewster Interview, 26 November 2018.
[126]Letter from Angela McSherry, Talawa's administrator, to Richard Moffatt, lighting designer for *The Road*, 16 March 1992. Talawa's production archives for *The Road,* personnel file.
[127]Irving Wardle, 'Further Scenes from the Execution of Culture', *Independent on Sunday*, 8 March 1992, 18.

stunningly redesigned by Abiodun Odedina as a permanent home of Talawa Company – at which point my enthusiasm cools.'[128]

For Igweonu, this period 'reflected the pressures of the singularity of Talawa's position and the eruption of expectation which descended upon the Company and its new building based status.'[129] A step in a direction that was not popular with the mainstream and eviction loomed. The mainstream critics offered Talawa no support by omitting to highlight individual performances or aspects of Brewster's direction that worked well. Only Armistead's review sought to highlight the positive aspects of the show with her appreciation of the set design as 'the best feature of Yvonne Brewster's production.'[130]

The black production that prevailed in the West End at the time was the Cameron Mackintosh and the Theatre Royal Stratford East's musical production of *Five Guys Named Mo* at the Lyric Theatre, Shaftesbury Avenue. Was Talawa expected to use its West End venue to fall in line and only produce the kind of musical work that black artists had been expected to do on the British stage since the 1940s? Was seeing black actors in carefully crafted black classics, discussing aspects of African life, too uncomfortable for the mainstream? Ukaegbu explains Talawa's production from a black perspective:

> It explores complex existential issues and metaphysical concerns that African and black people everywhere are familiar with . . . Talawa's intention for the production was clear; it was not necessarily contesting the tragic and social visions of Western audiences but presenting another set of traditions and values that if not applying fully to black sections of UK society, are at least implicated in the world view of some of them.[131]

Whilst being professionally misunderstood may be part and parcel of a general black experience in Britain, archival correspondence points to Talawa company members feeling they were personally ill-treated by the Cochrane's established staff, both during the rehearsal period and the run

---

[128]Ibid.
[129]Igweonu, 'Talawa', 251. The reference on 287 is Yvonne Brewster, 'Projections and Options January 1995 - December 1997', 18 June, TTC, 1/2/1.
[130]Claire Armistead, 'Twisty Road', *Guardian*, 4 March 1992, 36.
[131]Ukaegbu, 'Talawa Theatre Company: The "Likkle" Matter of Black Creativity and Representation on the British Stage', 136–7.

of the debut production. In a letter to Ms Teerth Chungh, general manager of the Cochrane Theatre, from Diane Wilmott, Talawa's company stage manager for *The Road*, Ms Wilmott complains of the abusive behaviour of a cleaner to her company.[132] Talawa's archival records also demonstrate that further challenges were made regarding perceived hostility from established Cochrane staff to Talawa staff. None of these issues were brought to a conclusion.

The stay at the Cochrane lasted for two and a half years, ending in January 1995. Although Talawa's residency at the Cochrane made British theatre history, the experience that held so much promise for Talawa specifically and black theatre practitioners generally had by the end of the process not been entirely positive. The period of three years for which the Cochrane had been leased was seen, from the outset, by Brewster and the company's board of directors as a formality. They imagined that the lease would automatically be renewed.[133] This view had come in part from the contents of a welcome letter from the chairman of the Arts Council:

> Dear Ms Brewster,
>
> I am delighted to welcome the establishment of Talawa Theatre at the Cochrane Theatre, London. This marks a major step forward in the progress of Black Theatre in this country.
>
> The development of the company has been consistently supported by the Arts Council. This year an increased level of funding has been given, which includes a special enhancement grant, in order to facilitate Talawa's move into a permanent theatre base.
>
> My very best wishes go with the company for the future.
>
> Lord Palumbo.[134]

When Talawa's lease was not extended and the company had no home to go to, the negative events of the previous two and a half years made the conclusion seem like an inevitability which those at Talawa were powerless to control.[135] In spite of this, Brewster regards the process of her longevity

---

[132]Letter dated 21 February 92 - Talawa's production archives for *The Road* - personnel file.
[133]Yvonne Brewster, Personal Interview by David Johnson, London, 21 February 1998.
[134]The letter was used in Talawa's debut publicity campaign to mark the company's arrival at the Cochrane.
[135]Brewster Interview, 21 February 1998.

at the Cochrane as her biggest achievement: 'It is almost an achievement to recognize when you are being undermined and to walk away. It was hell, because it wasn't only me, it was a whole group. To take a whole group of people and keep them together was an achievement.'[136]

This ability to 'recognize' is not new in the diaspora. Harry Belafonte's truth on how whites show blacks on television is fitting to Brewster's Cochrane experience: 'It's a difficult journey . . . and unless you're of colour you'll not truly understand the depth of what I'm saying because it's not something you can intellectually speak of. You had to be black in order to know what the subtleties are of the fact.'[137] Black artists have the words to express these sentiments articulately because this is the unsolicited backbone of their existence. They understand that the intention behind the racism is more than simply to keep the 'other' away, but rather to cause irreversible harm. Teer explains, 'it [racism] goes to the very core of that person's being, to his very soul: he is rejected not for a mere "offense", he is rejected for what he is.'[138]

Having a home for black theatre then symbolized more than the running of a performance space. It was intended as a home, with all the positive connotations that having a home brings. Brewster explains:

> The idea came out of the need that most humans have for shelter, shelter which even if you don't own it outright, you can call upon to protect you, and to allow you to make mistakes, welcome people in, as well as throw them out. So it was a home, that was the idea . . . we got the place, we found pretty non-savvy people, when they got savvy they threw us out.[139]

The relatively sudden removal from the Cochrane served to highlight that 'artists of colour are welcome to visit the mainstream, but it is not their "home".'[140] Talawa's Cochrane ejection can be likened to the arson attack on Cricklewood's Anson Hall on the final night of *Smile Orange* in 1972. In Cricklewood, illegal steps were taken to show that black productions

---

[136] Brewster Interview, 16 January 1997.
[137] *Black Hollywood*, BBC1, 13 October 2018.
[138] Thomas, 'Barbara Ann Teer: From Holistic Training to Liberating Rituals', 360.
[139] Brewster Interview, 31 October 2014.
[140] Mahone, 'Moon Marked and Touched by Sun', 260.

and their audiences were unwelcome. A more legal approach was employed to achieve the same thing with Talawa at the Cochrane. In contemporary democratic British society, it seems unthinkable that blatantly aggressive tactics can be employed to lessen the visibility or entirely remove groups of black performers from mainstream British theatre. This is, of course, until undeniable slip-ups are made in public. Inchley explains such an error on the BBC's *Newsnight*: 'Mark Lawson admits to being "terrified" of meeting the actors from *Sing* outside the "safety of the theatre". He comments, "If it gets to the West End, you would want to exclude certain people because of the wrong people coming in."'[141]

Lawson's 'terror' of the 'wrong' people would be comical if it were not for the prevailing fact that black theatre practitioners have no power in the mainstream. Whilst, as Inchley explains, Lawson's prejudices are based on class and not race, this distinction is of no comfort to black people as mainstream society invariably, at first sight, assumes black skin colour is a marker of belonging to the lowest echelons of society.[142] In the case of black people in Britain, then, class and colour are so inextricably linked by the mainstream as to make them indistinguishable.

Brewster commends two board members, Dr Marie Stewart and Alan Smith, for seeing the writing was on the wall before the lease ended. Stewart advised Brewster to leave as the working conditions narrowed drastically. Initially Talawa was given carte blanche with its use of the theatre. The only exception was August, when the theatre could not be used. This changed to exclude theatre use during Easter, Christmas and all of summer, thus effectively reducing theatre time from forty to twelve weeks. This was followed by the 'request' for Talawa to leave the Cochrane offices.

Although Talawa was made homeless, the company still had funding and shows to put on. This put Brewster back in the position of having to secure venues. When, in 1996, Brewster took her proposal for *Flyin' West* to Nick Kent at the Tricycle, she was told, 'He didn't think that was the sort of thing that black people wanted to see.'[143] The play ran at the Drill Hall

---

[141] Inchley, *Voice and New Writing*, 100. The reference cited is Mark Lawson, discussion of *Fallout*, on Newsnight Review (BBC 2), 9 May 2002, http://news.bbc.co.uk/1/hi/programs/newsnight/review/1976889.stm, accessed 25 January 2007.
[142] Ibid.
[143] Brewster Interview, 31 October 2014.

Talawa Theatre Company

'because the Drill Hall understood what is was like to be in the minority [Brewster laughs]'.[144]

With no fixed abode Talawa became a middle-scale touring company, with the fact remaining that under Brewster, the company achieved a three-year West End residency. More than two decades on, Talawa is still the only black British theatre company to have achieved this accolade.

---

[144] Ibid.

CHAPTER 4
THE ISLAND PLAYS

Contextualizing Talawa's Caribbean genre with *An Echo in the Bone* and *Maskarade*

Talawa's performance of Caribbean work allowed the company to build on black British theatre history. Additionally, the company was providing British audiences with the work of established Caribbean writers and writers of Caribbean descent that perhaps remained little known in Britain. Working within this genre also enabled the company to use theatre to demonstrate aspects of African-Caribbean cultural history to the British audience. Talawa's 1986 performance of Dennis Scot's *An Echo in the Bone* and its 1994 performance of Sylvia Wynter's *Maskarade* illustrate this.

An Echo in the Bone premiered in Britain as Talawa's second production. It was performed at the Drill Hall, London between 24 June and 19 July 1986. Scot's play is set in Jamaica in 1937. It highlights the importance of African ritual in death as it deals with the Nine Nights tradition. As part of this tradition the living friends and relatives of a recently departed loved one watch over the deceased's body, which is believed to return to its home nine nights after dying. The gathering of family and friends at the deceased's home is believed to protect the deceased's soul from evil during its journey into the afterlife. Their rejoicing allows the deceased's soul to pass over peacefully into its new life after death. Ukaegbu believes Brewster's direction intentionally frames 'the Nine Night ritual as the setting for collective and individual soul searching'.[1] He explains:

> Talawa questioned ritual retreat as a viable solution to contemporary problems... Nine Night made Crew's unjustified death and unproved guilt acceptable without contesting the injustice done to him, his

---

[1] Ukaegbu, 'Talawa Theatre Company: The "Likkle" Matter of Black Creativity and Presentation on the British Stage', 142.

family and entire black race. As far as the production was concerned, such rituals should frame collective political action.[2]

The newness of Talawa's work prompted a positive response from sections of the black press in Britain who welcomed seeing aspects of their cultural history displayed in a theatrical forum: 'This play is a beautiful blend of history, folk tradition, superstition, social commentary, Caribbean rhythms and Jamaican dialect.'[3] Comments from factions of the mainstream focused on an alternative view of what the play offered culturally: 'After centuries of blacking up it is something of a novelty to watch black actors playing at being white.'[4] Edwardes is referring to the fact that the black actors also play white characters. Her phrase may also suggest that the act of blacks working in theatre, despite the Caribbean nature of the play, was mimicry of an historically 'white pursuit' in Britain.

Brewster presented more African-Caribbean cultural history in Talawa's eighth Caribbean work and eighteenth production in total, with Wynter's musical *Maskarade*. Performed at the Cochrane between 9 December 1994 and 14 January 1995, this Jamaican tale is of the ritual Jamaican Christmas street parade known as Jonkunnu. The festival started in Africa before coming to the Caribbean. It was an occasion when slaves were permitted to drum and dance. Talawa's production enabled British audiences to learn about the Jonkunnu celebrations with its Actor Boys and Set Girls.[5]

The play's overt use of Jamaican patois speech elicited comments from sections of the mainstream press that suggest the cultural subject matter had not been fully appreciated as the language could not be fully understood: 'there is a certain intelligibility problem with the Jamaican dialect, but that rather enhances the exotic charm of the piece.'[6] The passing of time did nothing to resolve the mainstream's 'intelligibility problem' and presumably its notions of 'exotic charm'. This is seen in the media response to Kwame Kwei-Armah's *Elmina's Kitchen*, performed in 2003.

---

[2]Ibid.
[3]Laurel B. Ince, 'An Echo in the Bone by Dennis Scott', *Caribbean Times*, 4 July 1986, 31.
[4]Jane Edwardes, 'An Echo in the Bone', *Time Out*, 2–8 July 1986, 38.
[5]Hill, *The Jamaican* Stage, 229–53.
[6]David Murray, 'Caribbean Carnival', *Financial Times*, 17 December 1984, 16.

Inchley points out that 'Reviews of *Elmina's Kitchen* contained a very high frequency of comments on the challenge the voices of the play posed to auditory expectations of "white" space'.[7] Georgina Brown, in her review of the production, comments, 'the thickness of the dialect often got the better of me'.[8] Similarly, Charles Spencer uses his review to explain, 'the West Indian street-talk means that for whities like me it is sometimes hard to follow'.[9]

Kwei-Armah's play was for everyone, including the black audience, for whom much of contemporary British theatre remains exclusively white. Their reaction was different. Inchley continues, 'Black audience members, according to Edwardes, "lapped up the West Indian dialect that was hard for me to follow". Suddenly Edwardes was in the minority, struggling not only with an alien dialect, but with culturally alternative norms of response and behaviour.'[10] Edwardes's struggle serves to highlight the linguistic and cultural dexterity that Briton's black communities work with on a daily basis. It is not surprising then that black British playwrights and actors will now choose to avoid a 'tendency to dilute' a culturally specific dialogue so that 'everyone understands'.[11] Would this clarity in later black artists have come about had Talawa not produced its Caribbean work when it did?

Talawa's performance history demonstrates that the company made a concerted effort to move away from the stereotypical work of the black theatre movement of the late 1970s and early 1980s. In so doing, the company created a canon of work within the contemporary Caribbean genre by producing thirteen contemporary Caribbean plays between 1986 and 2001, all of which were steeped in Caribbean performance and Caribbean language forms.

In Gates's *The Signifying Monkey*, Gates expresses that black artists in the West learn by what they are exposed to. The result is that they produce black work from a Western tradition that is differentiated by their 'Black

---

[7] Inchley, *Voice and New Writing*, 98.
[8] Ibid., 171 note 78.
[9] Ibid., The reference given is Charles Spencer, 'Review of Elimina's Kitchen', *Daily Telegraph*, 31 May 2003, in *Theatre Record*, 23 (2003),701–6 (703).
[10] Inchley, *Voice and New Writing*, 100. The reference given is Jane Edwardes, 'Review of Elmina's Kitchen', *Time Out*, 25 June 2003, in *Theatre Record*, 23 (2003), 701–6 (704).
[11] Ibid., 98. The reference given is Roy Williams in Natasha Tripney, 'Roy Williams', *The Stage*, 10 April 2014, 21.

English vernacular tradition'.[12] Whilst Brewster's Caribbean productions are undeniably Western in their format, she ensures the characters' black vernacular is key to their oral language of performance. Similarly, she makes the African traditions these characters come from evident in the non-spoken performance vocabulary of her work. This is demonstrated in her productions of *The Black Jacobins*, *The Dragon Can't Dance*, *The Lion* and *Beef, No Chicken*.

The Black Jacobins

The motivation to revolt

Talawa's 1986 revival of C. L. R. James's *The Black Jacobins* took place at the Riverside Studios Hammersmith between 21 February and 15 March 1986. Talawa's performance was fifty years after the first London performance in 1936.[13] This earlier production was seen with scepticism:

> the play is altogether too propagandist. Propaganda – in this case the cause of the negro races – is all very well in its proper place, but it is not permissible in a play which purports to be substantially true to history. The coloured races have certainly been persecuted by the whites, but the author's bias in their favour would appear to deny the whites a shred of nobility of character or honesty of purpose. In his play the blacks are white and the whites are black.[14]

Conversely, the response to Talawa's performance revealed that pockets of the mainstream press now saw a place for black theatre on the British stage: 'But how marvellous to see a large scale project presented by the newly formed Talawa company, but full of familiar faces tackling such important and pertinent historical issues.'[15]

---

[12]Henry Louis Gates Jr., *The Signifying Monkey: A Theory of Latin American Literary Criticism* (New York: Oxford University Press, 1988), xxii–xxiii.
[13]In 1936 Paul Robeson played James's Toussaint in *Toussaint L'Ouverture* (later re-titled *The Black Jacobins*), at the Westminster Theatre, London, 15 and 16 March.
[14]Anon, 'Toussaint L'Ouverture' (review of the performance of *Touissant L'Ouverture* of 15 March 1936), *Stage*, 19 March 1936, 9.
[15]Michael Coveney, 'The Black Jacobins/Riverside Studios', *Financial Times*, 27 February 1986, 27.

James's motivation for writing the play, which documents the successful 1791 slave revolt in San Domingue that led to the establishment of an independent black republic, stemmed from his feeling that 'there weren't any plays that said black people had created any distinct events of the time.'[16] Similarly, Brewster was motivated to direct the play due to her dissatisfaction with what she perceived to be the unacceptable lot of black theatre in Britain. She explains, 'I'm not very impressed with the black theatre over here. There's too much grovelling, too much emphasis on how marvellous it is that blacks are actually at last being allowed to do their own thing in a white man's country, too many introspective plays about racism: too many blacks laughing at the comic stereotypes of themselves.'[17]

This new production allowed Talawa to demonstrate James's concern to a new generation of black people in Britain whilst simultaneously giving contemporary black performers in Britain access to the fringes of British theatre. Additionally, the production would challenge uninformed perceptions of black theatre, provide a fresh start of what could be made accessible to black theatre practitioners in Britain, and mark the beginning of Talawa Theatre Company's performance career.

Oral language of performance: We speak black

C. L. R. James's text is generally written in 'standard English'. The occasions where the text indicates a specific language style are rare and generally point to class, cultural and political differences between characters. The language of Talawa's video performance demonstrates a clear shift away from the text in its move away from 'standard English' speech. Throughout Talawa's performance the hierarchy of languages in San Domingue is highlighted, showing French at the top, the language of the rich white land-owning class, and Creole and pidgins beneath, the language of the black land-workers. The darker the speaker the lower the status and the more African-sounding the language.[18]

---

[16]Daryll Cumber Dance, *Conversations with Contemporary West Indian Writers* (Leeds: Peepal Tree Books, 1992), 18.
[17]Tom Vaughan, 'Haiti – The Roots of Rebellion', *Morning Star*, 17 February 1986, 4.
[18]This notion was explored in Aphra Benn's *Oroonoko: Or, the Royal Slave. A True Story* (London: Will Canning, 1688).

Talawa Theatre Company

Whilst the use of pidgins may be seen as debilitating in British society, as they are associated with the presumed stupidity of the speaker,[19] the language of Talawa's production was aimed at black people who speak and understand it. Those outside of this group, facing the intelligibility questions discussed above, may question the relevance of the work to them. Their singular experience simply mirrors the general one of black people at mainstream British theatre performances. It is usually not for them.

All of Talawa's black characters in the performance use a non-'standard English' voice. The black cast made up of a range of native West Indians and black British performers offers a range of authentic Caribbean and black British voices. Due to the trademark African-Caribbean linguistic mix, the performance reinforces a sense of black national linguistic identity for black British theatregoers. Simultaneously, this language use promotes black culture in a theatrical setting that had been stifled by English imperialism.

Brewster's linguistic choice illustrated the potential range of the black British voice, both on and off stage. This heightening of black cultural identity through voice and language sees Brewster labelled as political. Whilst being black and speaking in the mainstream is often a political act, this outer politicization is a necessary labelling by the mainstream to signal danger from those who are unwilling to fit into the boxes set out for them. Where historical and current societal attempts to ensure black lives remain at the lowest echelons of every society are unsuccessful, a label must be given. Brewster's presentation of this language was a freedom of black expression. Sartre explains, 'What then did you expect when you unbound the gag that had muted those black mouths? That they would chant your praises? Did you think that when those heads that our fathers had forcibly bowed down to the ground were raised again, you would find adoration in their eyes?'[20] Given her chance, Brewster's adoration was reserved for black language and black cultural history. The central characters of Toussaint L'Ouverture, Maire-Jeanne, Dessalines and Moïse demonstrate the outcome of this directional decision.

As Toussaint L'Ouverture, Norman Beaton provides a consistent example of linguistic accommodation. He adapts L'Ouverture's language to sound

---

[19] Viv Edwards, *Language in a Black Community* (Clevedon: Multilingual Matters Ltd, 1986), 24.
[20] Jean Paul Sartre, *Orphée Noir* (Paris: Presses Universitaires de France, 1948), ix. The English translation is taken from Frantz Fanon, *Black Skin, White Masks* (London: Pluto Press, 1986), 29.

more like his French masters when he is speaking to them. This linguistic flexibility is used strategically to point out how L'Ouverture uses language to achieve his political ambitions. Additionally, Beaton's L'Ouverture uses local speech to highlight his conviction that whilst he wants San Domingue to remain a French colony, he and his fellow islanders are determined to maintain their own local identity through their use of local language. The message mirrors Talawa's emergence as a black British theatre company that chose to display its cultural roots by performing culturally specific themes in non-'standard English'.

Beaton's L'Ouverture has a specific Guyanese accent. This voice is definable as the 'standard' educated West Indian voice of the kind Cassidy attributes to the educated English-speaking man anywhere, with his regional differences.[21] Beaton's L'Ouverture presents the voice of the well-to-do black man whose colonial politics are revealed in his voice. His voice is similar to that of those Europeans who have traditionally been classed as his oppressors. Although he does not want to be ruled by them, neither does he want to have complete control of his country: 'France will be elder brother, guide and mentor.'[22] His inner desire to remain linked to them is demonstrated in his choice to use speech that approximates that of the colonial rulers. For Talawa's black audience, generally unused to seeing Caribbean language forms used with consistency and in leadership roles on the British stage, this creates a momentary sense of esteem for an aspect of their home language, even if used to emulate Europe.

Mona Hammond's Marie-Jeanne is orally characterized by her use of verbal repertoire. This is a feature of black British speech, described by those who use it as 'flexing'. In black British society 'flexing' refers to the mixing of 'standard English' speech in combination with African-Caribbean language forms, from one sentence to the next. The script does not indicate that the character is linguistically dextrous, as all of her text is in 'standard English'. Talawa's performance highlights then the subtlety and range of language used by some black Britons. The character's verbal repertoire reflects the question of language choice linked to identity as experienced by black Britons, who change their speech according to how they wish to be perceived in a given environment. Edwards's discussion of the motivation

---

[21] Frederic G. Cassidy, *Jamaica Talk: Three Hundred Years of the English Language in Jamaica* (London: Macmillan, 1961), 26.
[22] Rehearsal script, 389.

of language choice of black Britons points to speakers choosing between 'standard English' and code switching within their patois usage.[23]

Decades on from Talawa's debut show, black Britons use verbal repertoire more openly as a fact of life. When featured in performance, even today, this quickly becomes an important part of academic discussion. Inchley comments on Kwame Kwei-Armah's *Fix Up* (2004) and how voice is used to show allegiance with racial identity.[24] Similarly, in her discussion of Kwei-Armah's *Statement of Regret* (2007), Inchley points out how the black characters make linguistic choices to hide their background, on their road to success. This is seen in Kwei-Armah's black policy think tank founder Toks, who uses his 'authentic West Indian accent when he wants', but 'his straight English accent defies his working class roots'.[25] Inchley further highlights the effects of verbal repertoire usage: 'These are some of the most insidious manifestations of code switching as success leads not to defiance of the gangster, but to secretiveness, shame and snobbishness about cultural, racial and class origin.'[26]

This was played out nineteen years earlier by Hammond's linguistic portrayal of Marie-Jeanne, which allowed Talawa to highlight bilingual–cultural aspects of black British existence. Throughout the performance Hammond's Marie-Jeanne mainly uses 'standard English' speech. She reverts to her native Caribbean and in this case Jamaican language when she is either angry, or in a comedy situation. Notably, she opts for 'standard English' when she wants to be taken seriously. This indicates the low status of native speech on the island and by extension of Caribbean speech in Britain.

Hammond's portrayal of Marie-Jeanne's sexual relationship with General Hédouville of the French army highlights how their intimacy exposes her use of verbal repertoire. Her accent is Jamaican when she accuses him of wishing she were a white woman. This language choice points to her blackness and moves away from the whiteness she perceives Hédouville wishes on her. She cannot be what she thinks he wants, but she can use her language to show him who she is.

Hammond shows Marie-Jeanne not only moving physically and sexually through the full range of society, but also linguistically as she

---

[23]Edwards, *Language in a Black Community*, 116–17.
[24]Inchley, *Voice and New Writing*, 85.
[25]Ibid., 87.
[26]Ibid.

communicates comfortably with blacks and whites alike. Her speech mirrors the verbal repertoire of members of the black British audience and wider community as she uses her artistic license to adapt her character's linguistic codes strategically according to her desired outcome with each interlocutor.[27] Hammond's mixed 'standard English' and Jamaican speech, coupled with Beaton's Guyanese accent, highlight the generic nature of Caribbean language use by Talawa in this production. Brewster explains, 'The company chooses to use the natural voices of its Caribbean actors when the aim is to represent the Caribbean generally. In order to make the voices comprehensible to most English speaking listeners, Caribbeanisms which would identify a speaker specifically to an island are avoided.'[28]

In BBC1's television adaptation of Andrea Levy's novel *The Long Song* (2010), a similar approach was taken.[29] Although set in Jamaica and depicting the slave rebellion of Christmas 1831, the Caribbean accent is generalized for British television. Do the accents need to be specific when the story is excellent, needs to be told and reminds us that this is just one of many untold stories?

The production received praise, with little comment on the accents.[30] Where the accents were pointed out, this was to state how inaccurate they were. This was immediately followed by a debate on whether the accents mattered, given the enormity of the subject matter.[31] Simply put, native language matters when placing characters accurately. The fact that Brewster's actors were native speakers avoided post-production discussion of accuracy of voice.

By remaining culturally specific, Brewster's choice of flexible uniformity would automatically include both British and native Caribbean forms. Brewster's aim was to allow black performers to begin defining themselves

---

[27]Gilbert and Tompkins, *Post-Colonial Drama*, 177.
[28]Yvonne Brewster, Personal Interview by David Johnson, London, 30 March 1999.
[29]*The Long Song* (2018), [TV programme] BBC1, 18 December 2018.
[30]https://www.radiotimes.com/news/tv/2018-12-20/bbc1-slavery-drama-the-long-song-review/, https://www.theguardian.com/tv-and-radio/2018/dec/18/the-long-song-review-a-sharp-painful-look-at-the-last-days-of-slavery/ (both accessed 6 April 2019).
[31]Read more: https://metro.co.uk/2018/12/18/long-song-viewers-enraged-harrowing-slavery-drama-lenny-henry-wows-performance-8263087/ (accessed 6 April 2019).

linguistically, rather than 'to find a space within something else, thus giving them less exposure and less historical reference'.[32] Whilst the Caribbean performers use their native voice to display their linguistic accommodation and verbal repertoire, the black British performers display what R. B. Le Page refers to as linguistic behaviour. This is seen in Trevor Laird's and Brian Bovell's respective performances of Dessalines and Moïse. Both performers worked to Brewster's specific oral remit: 'I needed the actors to use their voices to show that they were rebellious but to speak in a way that the black audience could identify with.'[33]

Laird's Dessalines, sometimes aided by the suggestion of a pidginized language form, through incomplete sentences and a lack of clear sentence structure in the text adopts a British-African voice. This speech choice reveals the identity of the underdog in a society where he would be more acceptable if his speech were closer to the 'standard' form. This strategic voice is a form of linguistic rebellion, described by Hodge and Kress as an antilanguage. In this context the voice mirrors one of the uses of a black British voice as a way of distancing oneself from mainstream British society by using speech divergence. Such speech behaviour may be seen as the speakers' attempt to regain power in a society where they otherwise feel powerless.

As Laird's Dessalines develops professionally, his attempts to hide his 'savage' past are shown in his quest to develop his language and education, and become more European. His language is different from, though politically reflective of, that of the black British community. Native black British speakers, though they can sound like their white counterparts, can also choose to sound differently in what may be interpreted as a desire to assert their cultural identity. This is now also seen with white British teens that choose to identify with their black peers.

Laird's Dessalines, despite his concerted efforts, is unable to sound like the French when he decides that this is what he wants to do. This can be understood by the fact that he was neither born, nor ever lived, in France. Laird's portrayal of Dessalines stresses that his character's desire to accommodate linguistically is a constant effort. The more prosperous he becomes, the less African he aims to sound. When faced with the French, English and American army men Laird's Dessalines is almost robotic in his

---

[32]Brewster Interview, 16 January 1997.
[33]Brewster Interview, 30 March 1999.

attempts to control both his speech and accent. When he is later accused of whipping slaves on his plantation his controlled voice represents his attempts to learn the power-based behaviour he experienced at the hands of the French.

Starting with his oral language, Laird shows throughout his performance how Dessalines has systematically tried to eradicate the most obvious elements associated with his blackness, all in the hope that this will make him more acceptable to those he aspires to be like. This is epitomized at the end of the production by his stilted dance, symbolic of the manner and language of his colonizers. Talawa's audience laughs at the difficulty with which he dances. In attempting to disguise his blackness, he becomes ridiculous because he has an unworthy, and in his case unachievable, aim.

James has written the character to appear to ultimately despise his physical blackness. Whilst he cannot change his skin colour, he works to erase all other aspects of his blackness and sees having a wife who is close to the white phenotype as desirable.[34] Similarly, to escape poverty and be deemed more acceptable in a white dominated society, a mixed race bloodline is deemed preferable to being pure black. This is voiced in Levy's *The Long Song*, when Tamara Lawrance's Ms July tells Jack Lowden's Robert Goodwin, with embarrassed pride, 'I am a mulatto, not a negro.'[35] Laird's Dessalines cannot claim this and makes every outward effort to disguise the purity of his blackness.

In contrast to Laird's Dessalines, who moves from antilanguage in rebellion to attempted linguistic accommodation in 'prosperity', Bovell plays Moïse using language that fits both antilanguage and overt language forms throughout the performance. As any linguistic accommodation is temporary, Bovell demonstrates that his character never truly rejects antilanguage forms of speech. Bovell Africanizes Moïse's speech, adding a hint of a French accent to an African, though audibly London-based, voice. Bovell's choice of language represents the ex-slaves of San Domingue as the voice of the oppressed. It maintains the character's cultural roots in Africa alongside the European influence of France.

For the British audience the London voice helps define the actor as black British. His chosen voice carries with it the dual culture of the character and

---

[34] Carl Stone, *Class Race and Political Behaviour in Urban Jamaica* (Kingston: Institute of Social and Economic Research, 1973), 120.
[35] *The Long Song*, [TV programme] BBC1, 19 December 2018.

part of the native culture of the actor's reality. The exposure of this language in an environment where exposure has remained limited is threefold: it liberates it, reveals the rebellious nature compromising language is associated with, and alters 'the overwhelming power of English'.[36] Inchley clarifies why black performers are on occasion allowed this space: 'In theatre, where there is generally empathetic regime, voices that are censured elsewhere are often given temporary licence.'[37]

In Levy's *The Long Song*, this temporary licence is granted for the television production. The whites speak 'standard English' and the blacks speak a form of Jamaican English as the two groups communicate directly. Both sets of speakers are bilingual but only speak the language of the cultural group they belong to. Lawrance's Ms July unnecessarily translates between the black workers and her white slaver lover, Lowden's Robert Goodwin. She stops when he tells her he knows what they are saying.[38] This moment recognizes their black English as a language. Bovell's Moïse, in refusing to attempt any form of 'standard English' speech, validates his choices in a wider island community that would prefer that neither he nor his language existed.

With the French, English and American army men, Bovell's Moïse slightly accommodates his antilanguage speech. Thus where his character's natural regional speech will not be advantageous he accommodates it. This is an attempt to ensure that he gets his message across to those who do not share his politics. Equally, this keeps his antilanguage speech sacred as it remains kept from those who look down on it. Consistent with Bovell's portrayal of his language, Moïse's behaviour as written by James is equally rebellious, resulting in his murder early on in the play. For the colonials he has little in common with, he is a threat that must be removed. At this point, a similar message is being relayed to the black British audience that they should integrate into European society at the expense of losing their own culture and language, in order to survive.

Through the range of black language forms demonstrated in *The Black Jacobins*, Talawa invited British theatre to open its doors to the voices of a community of British people whose voices were seldom heard on the British stage. This section of the British Empire was working creatively on

---

[36]Gilbert and Tompkins, *Post-Colonial Drama*, 177.
[37]Inchley, *Voice and New Writing*, 41.
[38]*The Long Song*, [TV programme] BBC1, 19 December 2018.

a linguistic level and becoming part of an institution that had generally remained out of its grasp for centuries. This time, however, it was working from home.[39]

Non-spoken performance vocabulary: Colonialism and Voodoo

The non-spoken performance vocabulary of African-Caribbean theatre in Britain may be characterized by the inclusion of both music and movement: 'Everyone expects black performances to have singing and dancing.'[40] Brewster was concerned her work should not be regarded as generally multicultural: 'Multiculturalism is an excuse for ad hocism, I think cultural concerns have to be specific.'[41] In *The Black Jacobins*, Talawa uses its non-spoken performance language to explore the culturally specific themes of colonialism and Voodoo.

The theme of colonialism is expressed throughout with music. The suffering and ultimate rebellion caused by colonialism is signalled, as written by James, by the black population through the recurrence of the song 'La Marseillaise'. Originally a French revolutionary song, it has also been the French national anthem for most of the period since the revolution of 1789. Its adoption by the slaves in St Domingue makes their claim that 'liberty' cannot be limited to freeing whites from class oppression, but must also include freeing blacks from oppression based on race.

Although the script states where the song should be sung, 'To arms Citizens' are the only words given. Brewster chooses to use the French translation, 'Aux armes citoyens'. The song is used as a bonding device within the ex-slave community. This offers an aspect of black history from a black perspective which 'allows black, and in particular, mixed race people, who often find themselves not wanted by either side, the chance to resource themselves with heritage facts'.[42]

'La Marseillaise' moves from being a song of rebellion whilst the blacks are slaves, to a song of freedom once they have been set free. In both cases the song points to the oppression caused by colonialism. Brewster filters

---

[39]Dahl, 'Postcolonial British Theatre: Black Voices at the Center', 39.
[40]Brewster Interview, 30 March 1999.
[41]Brewster Interview, 16 January 1997.
[42]Brewster Interview, 2 October 1998.

it through the production at critical points prior to any action where the characters are being incited to take up their weapons and fight.

Prolonged use of the song throughout the production is innovative and appropriate. When Bovell's Moïse announces the arrival of Monsieur Bullet at the beginning of the production, it is to the undercurrent of the song. Whilst things appear to be well, the song sung low symbolizes that something is brewing in the fields. Shortly after, it is announced that all blacks are free. By this time the rendition of 'La Marseillaise' is loud and wild, indicating that the slaves can no longer be controlled by their former masters.

Talawa reintroduces the song at the end of the first act when Beaton's L'Ouverture sends his constitution to Keith Hazemore's Napoleon. Throughout the scene, the song is whistled in the background. This points to the brewing anger felt by the black population and the unrest that may be caused if Hazemore's Napoleon does not agree to the constitution. The additional introduction of continuous whistling in the distance creates the menacing effect of warriors on the fringes of a battlefield waiting for orders to attack. Brewster has extended the significance of 'La Marseillaise' from a rebellion song to the war anthem of the blacks.

'La Marseillaise' becomes the war anthem of the past once Beaton's L'Ouverture is perceived to be too weak and a rival, more militant and less compromising faction emerges around him. The new rebels adopt the song of the man of the people, David Haynes's Samedi Smith. Each time the song of rebellion goes against the politics of the black leader, those who are caught singing it are condemned to death. Brewster's cast sing Samedi Smith's song off stage in French, whilst Laird's Dessalines translates it to Bob Philips's Christophe and by extension the audience. This bilingual performance of the song presents two sides of black rebellion to the black British audience. There is the rebellion of those who want complete control of their existence, in contrast to those who wish to remain linked to their colonial history. Through her production Brewster allows both the characters and the audience to use theatre 'to re-examine and re-imagine' their history.[43]

The European side of colonialism is expressed through regular interjections of classical music. From the outset, Jean Hart's Madame Bullet's signature is Mozart, sung in Italian. The language of opera further

---

[43] A. Ruth Thompsett, 'Re-imagining History: An Introduction to the Black Theatre Conference Papers', *Black Theatre in Britain*, 1 (1996), 6. Tompsett quotes Hazel Carey.

distances the white plantation owners from their black slaves. Brewster, however, gives the snippets of opera an African dimension. When Hart's Madame Bullet discusses and sings opera with Hammond's Marie-Jeanne, at the beginning of the production, we are aware of the beat of African drumming in the background. The beat acts as a reminder to the general unrest and gives the feeling of intrusion from the blacks that live on the other side of the luxury of the plantation walls.

After her initial appearance, Hart's Madame Bullet is scarcely seen and when she is, there is no theme tune. Her signature has been passed onto her servant Hammond's Marie-Jeanne for the rest of the production. This signals that she is of both African and European descent. Whilst she prepares for the arrival of Ian Collie's General Hédouville the theme has been adapted. Now, accompanied by her servant Jenny Jules's Celestine, to whom we imagine she has taught the song, Hammond's Marie-Jeanne sings with a pronounced Caribbean intonation and performs a calypso dance. The sense is that further African influences are later incorporated into the theme when performed between Hammond's Marie-Jeanne and Jules's Celestine, due to the latter's influences. Whilst the music highlights the difference between Hammond's Marie-Jeanne's mulatto cultural heritage and Jules's Celestine's African roots, both are drawn in musical contrast to their colonial rulers. What once musically represented white colonialism is incorporated into black existence. The through line from Hart's white Madame Bullet, to Hammond's mulatto Marie-Jeanne, to Jules's black Celestine demonstrates a Eurocentric path by which blacks Africanize white culture.

Hammond's Marie-Jeanne's calypso-style version of her Mozart theme is used when she writes to inform Beaton's L'Ouverture that Collier's General Hédouville is his enemy. This cultural performance adaptation is akin to what Schechner refers to as 'culture of choice'.[44] Brewster has taken the colonials' Mozart and dressed it for a contemporary black British audience, enabling them to grasp the subtleties of cultural differences within the black community as written in James's play. The audience can see then that the work has been created for them, both by James and Brewster.

As seen in the earlier discussion of ritual, the knowledge of the existence of Obeah and other forms of witchcraft permeate black British existence.

---

[44]Richard Schechner, 'Interculturalism and the Culture of Choice', in *The Intercultural Performance Reader*, ed. Patrice Pavis (London and New York: Routledge, 1996), 41–50.

Staging the concept and ritual of Voodoo in *The Black Jacobins* allowed Talawa to present an aspect of black culture relevant to the black British community, as performed from a black perspective. Olanyian explains, 'Blacks across the three continents studied are questing for cultural identity not because they are black but because they are black and dominated.'[45] Talawa's exposure of blackness partly challenges this domination within the performance arena.

The performance of the ritual, which features the dance of Laird's Dessalines and Jules's Celestine moving into a state of possession, is introduced musically by 'La Marseillaise'. Talawa's inclusion of the ritual in the form of a loosely choreographed performance is in line with the company's commitment to use cultural rituals and African performance forms in its work.[46] The performance of the ritual possession unexplained but performed as a natural aspect of the characters' lives gives it credence. Those who are possessed appear drunk.[47] This cultural styling contributes to Brewster's aim towards the development of a distinctive black British performance voice.[48]

The voice Brewster was explicitly developing with this production also adheres to the five performance goals Teer set for her National Black Theatre (NBT): 1. Raise the level of consciousness; 2. Be political; 3. Educate; 4. Clarify issues; 5. Entertain.[49] Brewster's less specifically verbalized approach was doing precisely this. Her work also paralleled the first and third of six additional explicit goals Teer developed with her company. The first was to perpetuate a black art standard, which Teer describes as 'A way of working blackly – so that an artist can work naturally from his own spiritual energies, by using the language, environment, and all elements which distinguished black people from other nationalities'.[50] The third was to re-educate audiences by presenting aspects of life that were relevant to its Harlem

---

[45]Tejumola Olaniyan, *Scars of Conquest, Masks of Resistance: The Invention of Cultural Identities in African, African-American, and Caribbean Drama* (New York and Oxford: Oxford University Press 1995), 140.
[46]Yvonne Brewster, Personal Interview by David Johnson, London, 13 June 1996.
[47]Laennec Hurbon, *Voodoo Truth and Fantasy* (London: Thames and Hudson, 1995), 110.
[48]Brewster Interview, 30 March 1999.
[49]Thomas, 'Barbara Ann Teer: From Holistic Training to Liberating Rituals', 359. The reference given is Harris, 'The National Black Theatre', 283-4.
[50]Ibid., 350. The six goals listed are taken from a pamphlet entitled 'NBT Is a Celebration of Life and a Rebirth of Power' (New York, 1973), 6.

The Island Plays

community and that gave the audience 'new information about themselves, so that they leave uplifted, reaffirmed and enlightened'.[51] As there was little black history in British education at the time of the performance, Brewster's choice and direction afforded her black audience an opportunity to glean heritage facts. Here the facts were specific to Haiti, but given that black experience is widely mirrored internationally, all black facts are relevant where few are generally offered.

Through *The Black Jacobins*, Voodoo rituals are presented to the audience along with the range of black reactions to it. Voodoo was a way of life for the poor and a threat to the wealthy that were often embarrassed by it.[52] Laird's Dessalines, who is featured dancing in the possession ritual, has become anti-Voodoo by the end of the play. This is in line with his desire to promote European values over indigenous culture. The presentation of the ritual, coupled with the question of why some blacks may want to reject their cultural heritage, tacitly asks the black British audience what is the cost of total assimilation?

The black community of the production is resourceful in its suffering. Religious bonds are created through need. Whilst European thought believed that mixing Africans from different areas would limit the possibilities of communication, a whole new form of religious communication developed in Voodoo. Such was the power of Voodoo that Jean Price-Mars in his discussion of the politicization of Voodoo claims that were it not for 'Voodooist participation in the revolutionary movement, Haiti would not have become an independent nation in 1804'.[53]

Talawa's production provided the message that, through theatre, black British audiences can develop a deeper understanding of aspects of their lives and complex communities. Also that black lives are worthy of performance on the British stage, by actual black people, who are able to fully represent them, and accurately tell the intricacies of their multilayered stories. The positive response to Talawa's first production was seen in the 82 per cent black audience and the final weeks being sold out.[54] There was

---

[51] Thomas, 'Barbara Ann Teer: From Holistic Training to Liberating Rituals', 351. The reference given for this is Harris, 'The National Black Theatre', 285.
[52] Michel S. Laguerre, *Voodoo and Politics in Haiti* (London: Macmillan Press Ltd, 1989), 19–20.
[53] Ibid., 101.
[54] Saunders, *British Theatre Companies*, 90. The reference is Letter from Nick Owen to Jodi Myers, 'National Tour of The Black Jacobins by Talawa Theatre Co', 25 June 1986, ACGB 92/1/1.

clearly an audience for the work. An audience whose attendance Cumper describes as a 'political act'.[55]

The positive reviews pointed to the fact that there was also space for African-Caribbean theatre on the British stage. Gordon praises Norman Beaton's portrayal of L'Ouverture, describing it as 'a dignified performance of moral weight'.[56] Coveney goes further, stating that the production is the sort of show 'that lends dignity and credibility to the British black theatre movement'.[57]

Brewster sensed black theatre history in the making at the time of the performance. The Haitian attaché to Europe had loaned Brewster an etching of Toussaint L'Ouverture which she featured in her poster. Brewster ensured there was a subliminal message that she would not reveal, in *The Black Jacobins* and all her later Talawa show posters. She explains, 'That is my little trick, the only thing that is going to outlast us is if the thing is defensible.'[58] The attaché attended the opening night: 'He patted me on my knee; I'm not a #metoo. None of that!' He patted when there was something he liked, but had to leave in the interval. Brewster continues, 'You know what had happened [why he left]? The second Haitian Revolution took place on the night of our first performance of the first Haitian Revolution.'[59]

The Black Jacobins set Talawa on a unique creative path that would become characterized by the company's intention to make whatever work it did its own.[60] There was instant credibility because of the quality of the work and because, in spite of the significant funding made available, there was a profit in excess of £20,000.[61] Four nights of preparing the application and setting up Talawa as a company had paid off. The success was tinged with the usual racism as shown in the distrust of the costume hire company, Angels. When Talawa's stage manager went to pay, Angels realized the costumes were hired by a black company: 'D'you know what they said? Bring back payment in cash. They wouldn't rent it to us. We had to go back with a cart load of cash to pay.'[62]

---

[55] Allfree, 'The Big Interview: Talawa Theatre Company, from Feisty to Philosophical', 54–3.
[56] Giles Gordon, 'Haiti's First Revolutionaries', *Observer*, 2 March 1986, 23.
[57] Coveney, 'The Black Jacobins/Riverside Studios', 27.
[58] Brewster Interview, 31 October 2014.
[59] Brewster Interview, 26 November 2018.
[60] Brewster Interview, 30 March 1999.
[61] Brewster Interview, 31 October 2014.
[62] Ibid.

What had started as a one-off commission led to Talawa becoming an established black theatre company. *The Black Jacobins* came to mark the beginning of both Talawa's performance life and the birth of a new black British theatrical voice that changed the face and raised the profile of black theatre in Britain. Nine years after the production Dahl's general comment on black British theatre describes the commitment and energy of black theatre practitioners. Her statement is as relevant to Talawa's debut as it is to the practitioners, many of whom worked with Talawa along their journeys throughout the end of the 1990s and into the new millennium: 'Certainly a new generation of black British Theatre workers are already on the field of play. Their tactical command of theatre's disciplines, and their diverse strategies are, I believe, producing visions of culture and of the new Britain that – like their histories – will not be contained, repressed or denied.'[63]

The Dragon Can't Dance

A chosen ethnicity

Talawa's *The Dragon Can't Dance*, co-produced with the Theatre Royal Stratford East, was performed between 29 June and 4 August 1990. This was Talawa's fourth Caribbean play. Writer Earl Lovelace produced the script from his original 1979 novel of the same name. The play was first performed during Trinidad's Carnival in Port of Spain in 1986. The new play form faithfully presented the novel's central theme of the power of Carnival over the lives of the island's underprivileged, in particular that of the protagonist Aldrick.

When Talawa emerged with its version four years later, Lovelace was concerned that as the work is culturally specific, the British production might only enjoy limited audiences. He did not want his work to be seen as just another black play: 'Literature is literature anywhere. It is universal. It doesn't come with a tribal scar.'[64] Brewster, in agreement with Lovelace, declared her opposition to specific ethnic labelling of the work: 'It is a very handy label to come up [with], black theatre. What that means is that black people presenting their arts, their culture, their life, can be ghettoized. When in fact stories like this are for everyone and speak to everyone.'[65]

---

[63]Dahl, 'Postcolonial British Theatre: Black Voices at the Center', 53.
[64]Biyi Bandele-Thomas, 'Conversation with Earl Lovelace', *Voice*, 5–11 July 1990, 21.
[65]Liz Gilbey, 'Dancing the Dragon', *What's on in London*, 27 June 1990, 39.

Performing this play gave Talawa the opportunity to widen both press and public perception of Trinidad and Carnival. Would Talawa expose Carnival 'as a great resource from which an indigenous drama can be fashioned', as Hill put it, or would it be more fitting of Walcott's description, 'as meaningless as the art of the actor confined to mimicry'?[66] By directing a Trinidadian play, Brewster's culture of choice was, as with *The Black Jacobins*, outside of her native Jamaican roots. As Schechner explains, this notion was not new in itself: 'There is probably more conscious and freely chosen ethnicity around now than there has been in the past. And it is possible to have ethnicity without racism. That's the Utopian dream anyway to have difference which is chosen and which is culture-specific, without it necessarily being hierarchical and authoritarian.'[67] By choosing to work with an ethnicity close to her own, Brewster was more likely to achieve success in the accuracy of its performance.

Oral language of performance: It ain't reach yet

Both Lovelace's novel and his script are in 'standard English' flavoured with Trinidadianisms. We see 'it have' for 'there are' and 'it ain't reach yet' for 'it hasn't come yet' and 'coulda' for 'could have', along with wider Trinidadian terminology. Lovelace's chosen language style acts both as a means of bringing alive the community in question and asserts his refusal 'to submit to the dominance of the imposed standard language and to subscribe to the "reality" it sustains'.[68]

The language demonstrated in Talawa's performance is generally overt language behaviour. This, along with the company's attempts to bring Caribbean English speech to Britain in an established forum, went against the early theories of language-conscious anticolonialists who believed that exposure to 'proper' English after colonialism would eradicate Creole speech patterns.[69] These thinkers did not envisage that once free, colonized people would seek to revive their cultural identity through language. As aspects of cultures and languages are passed down from one generation to

---

[66]Olaniyan, 'Agones: The Constitution of a Practice', 77. The reference for Walcott's comment is Walcott, 'What the Twilight Says,' 37, 34–5.
[67]Schechner, 'Interculturalism and the Culture of Choice', 50.
[68]Gilbert and Tompkins, *Post-Colonial Drama*, 169.
[69]Hubert Devonish, *Language and Liberation: Creole Language Politics in the Caribbean* (London: Karia Press, 1986), 88.

the next by merely living in a community, with no conscious effort made to pass on, the eradication of 'improper' English would take generations, or a concerted effort to stamp it out.

The fact that approximately half of Brewster's cast were native Trinidadians helped with overall accent authenticity. This also allowed linguistic access to native Trinidadian speech for the non-Trinidadian performers. Absolute accuracy of accent was not, however, Lovelace's and perhaps by extension Brewster's primary concern. Lovelace explains:

> The actors in this production of Dragon will not have Trinidadian or Tobagonian origins. They should not let this trouble them too much. Calvary Hill, in the time in which work is set, would have been one of the areas in Port of Spain to which immigrants from the nearby islands in the Eastern Caribbean would have settled as they came to seek opportunities in the bigger, more prosperous Trinidad, and it would not have been surprising to find a variety of islands' dialects sprinkling The Hill, making it, what I would like to signify, a Caribbean yard.[70]

This approach suits the varied black British performer and theatre audience. It reflects both the mixed language of their community and that of their parents. For Brewster, the language formed part of a more important whole: 'We are not just putting on Trinidadian accents and swanning around. This is a serious play.'[71]

In line with elements of Bell's theory of language style as audience design, language use in *The Dragon Can't Dance* was influenced by the expected black audience. The presentation of the diverse languages of Calvary Hill helped authenticate the voices of Talawa's black British audience whose speech shows the hallmarks of its particular multicultural existence. The general stage Trinindadian voice used in the production allowed the patronage of the widest possible English-speaking audience whilst remaining culturally specific.

As in *The Black Jacobins*, the performers' use of verbal repertoire is a feature of the production. Here the verbal repertoire features predominantly

---

[70]Lovelace makes the statement in Talawa's publicity programme of the performance. See Talawa's production archives, *The Dragon Can't Dance*, publicity file.
[71]Gilbey, 'Dancing the Dragon', 39.

amongst the black British actors. Geff Francis in his portrayal of Fisheye provides a clear example of this. Francis, commonly recognized for his role as Michael, the Bank Manager, in Channel 4's 1990s sitcom *Desmond's*, here demonstrates an aspect of his Caribbean linguistic range. His accurate movement from a working class Trinidadian voice to an upper working class London accent attests to his black British bilingual cultural reality, and that of Talawa's black British audience.

His handling of both voices with ease points to the possibility of a completely bilingual–cultural existence. His language use in *The Dragon* is notably working class Caribbean speech that is seen in greater contrast to the middle class speech he uses in *Desmond's*. His use of verbal repertoire crosses class and culture. If Francis, as a black Briton, is able to absorb the central language forms of his mixed cultural existence, then it is likely that other black Britons do the same. His onstage performance may encourage the off stage usage of the Caribbean aspect of the black British audience's verbal repertoire. Along with the range of oral behaviours in the performance are non-spoken performance vocabularies that root the performance in aspects of its cultural heritage.

Non-spoken performance vocabulary: 'All A We Is One' – music, calypso and Carnival

Talawa's performance informs its audience of how calypso is an integral part of the Trinidadian institution of Carnival. It also provides a forum for stereotypical images around Carnival to be challenged whilst entertaining the audience. The range of calypso styles and music used in the production make the work innovative. This is partly achieved through the original calypsos and music written specifically for the production. The audience is ushered into the auditorium to the sound of live steel pans to prepare them for a British-Caribbean theatrical experience. The sound of the steel pans highlights the genre's 'links with the "percussive cultures" of Africa'[72] This is followed by nine calypso-style songs and various musical interludes that recur throughout the performance.

Talawa uses its opening number 'All A We Is One' (song one) to set the lively Carnival tone of the piece. The song also demonstrates the power

---

[72]Gilbert and Tompkins, *Post-Colonial Drama*, 85.

that calypso has in bringing the racially and economically divided areas of Trinidadian society briefly together, as everyone has a part to play in Carnival. This simultaneously points to the stark reality of a generally socially divided Trinidad and by extension the rest of the Caribbean. This division and coming together mocked in the satirical title of the song may be recognized by the British audience, whose own annual Notting Hill Carnival enjoys the mixing of both British and international races, along with all classes of people, for two days each year.[73] After that, black people are a lot less popular.

'Tro Me Out A She Yard' and 'Sylvia Ain't Have No Man' (songs two and three) show calypso being used to express a range of everyday situations and emotions. From feelings of unrequited love, as expressed by Oscar James's Philo in 'Tro Me Out A She Yard', to the importance of getting the right costume for Carnival, in James's Philo's 'Sylvia Ain't Have No Man'. The production shows calypso as a Trinidadian life force. Edwards explains, 'Calypso was the music in which we criticized the government, gossiped about our neighbors, commented on world affairs, and gave advice on everything from how to cook pig knuckles and rice to how to marry.'[74]

Calypso, then, is the heartbeat behind every event in every life, every day. Although we understand that Laura Beckford's Sylvia has no costume and that James's Philo has been rejected, the pleasant sound of each calypso brings hope to their situations. This is seen in the more popular calypso sound used for 'Dance Dragon' (song four) as sung by Susan Aderin's Yvonne. The lively pace of Talawa's composition detracts from her message that society's down trodden should rebel. The same song reappears as song nine to end the show with a calypso pulse.

Talawa uses varying styles of calypso to enhance the message within a song. This is well expressed in 'Come Out In The Road Warrior' (song five) which acts as a musical indicator to the rebellious badjohns. The calypso sound, though recognizable, is accompanied by a clear African drum bass. The heavy drumming represents both Africa and the rebellious streak of Francis's Fisheye and Cyril Nri's Aldrick. It indicates their feeling for their African roots and their move away from what they perceive to be the Europeanization of Carnival and calypso. Nri's Aldrick is given a second musical interpretation with 'Man Alone' (song six). Talawa uses the

---

[73]Darnell Cadette, 'Carnival's Bumpy', *Voice*, 24 August 1990, 31.
[74]Edwards, 'Caribbean Narrative: Carnival Characters - In Life and in the Mind', 110.

song as the character's anthem. Like songs two and three above, it does not strictly fit the popular calypso genre. It is slow with steel pans and a guitar accompaniment and is used to express the non-rebellious, solitary and despairing side of his character.

James's Philo's 'Hooligans in Port of Spain' (song seven) is used as the character's song of attack. This musical attack is responded to by both Francis's Fisheye and Nri's Aldrick who intercut the song with their own message of James's Philo being a sell-out. In an appropriate semi-reprise, Nri's Aldrick sings 'Man Alone' to the same beat as 'Hooligans in Port of Spain'. This is immediately followed by the angry 'Come Out In The Road Warrior'. The combination of the three songs, each with its own mood carried by a calypso beat, again stresses the flexibility of the calypso genre. This range of music highlights the versatility of the steel pan which is generally regarded with low musical status in British music.

At the beginning of the second act Talawa uses more general calypso music to create the atmosphere of the Carnival. The steel pans create the feeling of excitement and fill the theatrical space with the movement and celebration of Carnival, as if to prove Stone's comment that 'No novel, however, can convey the pulsating force of Carnival with the immediacy of theatre'.[75] In the second half of Act Two the music depicts the everyday life of those on Calvary Hill, and what has happened to them since Nri's Aldrick and Francis's Fisheye have been in prison. A slow calypso highlights the tranquil atmosphere of the Hill five years on. As the pans play we watch the inhabitants of the Hill go about their new daily routines. Both the oral and musical performance of the production bring out Lovelace's original musical style. Stone explains, 'The music of *The Dragon* – calypso, rapso, road march, parang – is fully integrated with the drama, making Lovelace's adapted novel, rather than *Moon*, or any other precursors from the Calabash Folk Theatre, the first authentic yard musical'.[76]

Talawa presents the penultimate song 'We Believe In Miracles' (song eight) in a cappella. This is doubly effective as it momentarily breaks away from the expected musical style. The song taking the form of a gospel church song is accompanied by hand claps and later drumming. The rendition is used to explain why the police did not stop the rebellious rampage and what happened in court before Nri's Aldrick and Francis's Fisheye were sent

---

[75]Stone, *Theatre: Studies in West Indian Literature*, 86.
[76]Ibid., 85.

to jail. This musical style impresses upon the audience the notion that the essential spirit of Carnival and the music of multiple steel pans is long gone. Now they have only their voices.

The musical direction moves effectively away from calypso when Dhirendra's Pariag tells King's Dolly that he wishes they could have all got on better with each other. The move is to Indian music. This highlights their cultural identity that has been musically ignored throughout the performance, mirroring the way the couple are treated generally by their neighbours. The music is briefly used to point to their most intimate thoughts and feelings that separate them from their Creole neighbours. Earlier when the couple describe how they were ignored at Christmas the music accompanying the scene remains appropriately calypso. The music reminds us that they are celebrating Christmas because they are with Christian Creole people and they want to be accepted.

Additionally Talawa uses music instead of straightforward dialogue. This is seen in Chan's Cleothilda. Her distress at Dhirendra's Pariag acquiring a bike is shown in the regimented marching reggae chant, 'Something new happening in town, the crazy Indian coming down.'[77] Strategically the heavy beat is drawn in contrast to the calypso she has sung and danced to earlier. Her anger expressed through an African beat is a theatrical device to point to the character taking sides in the community. She wishes to disassociate from the Indian. Her chant demonstrates that at this point she wants to be regarded as more similar to the non-racially mixed black people in her community.

Similarly, music is later used to enhance the tension that Chan's Cleothilda wishes to cause once she has lost her Carnival spirit. Her solitary complaint about dog mess in the streets is accompanied by the stark rattling of spoons on bottles and bongo drumming. The hollowness of the spoons on the bottles echoes the emptiness she feels for those around her and the vacuum that she perceives to exist in the community once Carnival is over. This is in contrast to her earlier rendition of the Christian hymns 'Rock of Ages' and 'Forty Nights'. Brewster employed the hymns to occupy the emptiness within the character prior to the Carnival celebrations. In the aftermath of Carnival and before she can return to her hymn singing, there is a silent void. With no music to fill it, her life is miserable.

---

[77]Rehearsal script, 22a.

Whilst the production demonstrates the intricate level to which music is used to pre-empt, highlight and heighten the tone and action of each scene, equal attention is given to displaying the importance of the history and institution of Carnival. Although Carnival is now a black-controlled event, this was not always the case. Prior to the abolition of slavery in Trinidad in 1834, the 'upper class community' consisted of the white landowners that mimicked the songs and dances of their slaves during Carnival. Many came from the French settler elite.[78] Olaniyan explains, 'Introduced by the whites, the Trinidad carnival was for long kept up and sanitized against the participation of other racial groups. A strictly hierarchical society, the recognized distinctions were, in order of importance, "Whites, Free Persons of Colour, Indians and Slaves".'[79] The period directly after emancipation saw the participation of former slaves and the poor. This caused whites to pull out of Carnival, now regarding it as a 'disorderly amusement for the lower classes'.[80] Once there was no white involvement there was also little money to spend on Carnival celebrations.

For the black populace who spent much of the year looking forward to Carnival, post-emancipation lack of funds did not act as a barrier but rather pushed their resourcefulness to the limit. The best example of this was seen in the 1940s with the invention of the steel pan, made from oil drums discarded on the island by American military bases.[81] Grant points to the ingenious nature of this development: 'The very poorest people invented a musical instrument . . . which is beautifully tuned, looks beautiful, you can play all types of music [on it, and] it's being played all over the world.'[82] The instrument carried with it part of the history of the underprivileged who were forced to work within the little that they had. Its creation can be likened to the new rituals developed in slavery. Similarly, Elaine Savory refers to this innovation as a strategy for survival, borne out of repression and the need to reconnect with past ancestry destroyed by centuries of colonialism.[83]

---

[78]Gilbert and Tompkins, *Post-Colonial Drama*, 79.
[79]Olaniyan, 'Agones: The Constitution of a Practice', 68. The reference is to Errol Hill, *Trinidad Carnival* (Austin: University of Texas Press, 1972), 10.
[80]Olaniyan, *Scars of Conquest*, 15.
[81]Winston Normans, 'Celebration in Diversity', *Carnival 89*, August 1989, 8.
[82]Grant, *Blackgrounds* Interview, May 1997.
[83]Elaine Savory, 'Stategies for Survival: Anti-imperialist Theatrical Forms in the Anglophone Caribbean', in *Imperialism and Theatre: Essays on World Theatre, Drama and Performance*, ed. J. Ellen Gainor (London and New York: Routledge, 1995), 245.

The Island Plays

As Carnival had taken on a new significance with mostly black participants, the emergence of the steel pans and the bands playing them became an important aspect of life in Trinidad. For some, Carnival may have become the only important event in their lives: an event which Hill describes as providing 'a striking record of mass participation in what was undoubtedly the greatest annual theatrical spectacle of all time'.[84] Brewster's production examines the notion of Carnival being the most important event in a character's life. This is done through the portrayal of Francis's Fisheye and an exploration of his physical violence in relation to the Carnival theme. The performance also comments on Nri's Aldrick and his internal intellectualization of life inspired by his preparations for Carnival.

Becoming part of a steel band legitimizes Francis's character's existence both in his own eyes and those of his new community. Francis's performance demonstrates how Carnival is used to allow a man weakened by society, as his professional and financial status is low, to show his physical strength and hold on to part of what he perceives to be his manhood. Belonging to the band and playing the badjohn means he can be part of an underprivileged whole, look out from the gutter, yet empower himself by physically intimidating those in his community who are willing to conform. By making his presence felt and metaphorically shouting loud, he is able to add meaning to his existence and attest to Wiley's notion that 'Most black people can't afford to be quiet'.[85] Francis's performance suggests emotional and psychological death would be the result of his character remaining silent.

The suffering he reveals behind his macho stance parallels that of black Britons and their weak outsider position in British society. Many of those who migrated from the Caribbean to Britain between 1948 and the 1960s were forced into positions of weakness by the strong arm of British society, which caused them to feel frustrated.[86] In the cases of the many men who found they were unable to support their families, having anticipated that they would be able to before their arrival in Britain, their frustration sometimes led to relationship breakdown.[87] Those black Britons later born

---

[84]Edwards, 'Caribbean Narrative: Carnival Characters - In Life and in the Mind', 110. The reference is to Hill, *Trinidad Carnival*.
[85]Ralph Wiley, *Why Black People Tend to Shout: Cold Facts and Wry Views from a Black Man's World* (New York: Penguin 1992), 2.
[86]Selvon, *The Lonely Londoners*, 73.
[87]Dodgson, *Motherland: West Indian Women to Britain in the 1950's*, 43.

here were equally frustrated, when they discovered their situation mirrored that of their parents, as British society actively denied them the opportunity to progress.

This weak outsider position became an indisputable national reality in Britain in 2018. This was when the political impropriety referred to as the Windrush scandal came to light. It saw the wrongful detention, denial of legal rights, deportation and denial of re-entry to Britain of many British-Caribbean subjects. This was a result of the government's 'hostile environment' policy. The policy consisted of measures aimed at making staying in Britain as difficult as possible for those without leave to remain. It was hoped that making it hard to stay, for those who were now no longer wanted, would encourage them to leave. The policy was first announced in 2012 under the Conservative–Liberal Democrat coalition. This illustrates the kind of continued effort since slavery and Caribbean colonization designed to ensure black people cannot control their environment and remain displaced. Francis' Fisheye's plight is eminently familiar to that of his black British audience.

Francis portrays Fisheye as a man who is only able to feel content when he can control his environment. He can only achieve this through unpredictable violence. Whilst his violent character is written in the script, Francis uses his physical size to dominate those around him, serving to highlight the reality of his character's weak position in society. In the decades since the performance, the feeling of weakness amongst young black men in certain sections of British society has partly resulted in their involvement in the current so-called 'knife crime epidemic' of 2019. In the same timeframe and as a response to the same feeling, many more black men have chosen to excel in education and all areas of professional working life, whilst maintaining both their masculinity and their blackness.

Francis shows Fisheye needs to assert himself to those he can, as he is unable to access the authorities that have caused his situation. The anger he demonstrates at James's Philo's success leads him to slap Philo's lady friend. His violence is aimed at humiliating Philo by taking away some of the added manhood he has achieved by winning the calypso crown. The manhood that Philo has gained by compromising his approach to his area of Carnival is mirrored by the loss of manhood that Fisheye experiences through his unwillingness to do the same. Francis's character is further weakened and his entire existence threatened by the intervention of the sponsors offering to fund the band and excluding him for fighting. Gilbey explains the change sponsorship brought:

It was only in 1950s when this sponsorship and the destabilization of Carnival began: a steel band might do something really important like all wear clean T-shirts. Now they were taking to a uniform provided by a sponsoring company and conforming. Carnival became glamourized and pretty. For a whole year a community would sustain their dragon man: he was their community arts worker, if you like, a microcosm of society and culture. Sponsorship undermined this.[88]

Through Francis's Fisheye and the effects of steel band sponsorship on him, we are made aware of both the new politics of Carnival that emerged due to the availability of financial backing and how poor black Trinidadians lost control over their Carnival. Britain's Notting Hill Carnival experienced a similar fate in 1998, when sponsorship fell through and Carnival organizers contemplated the possibility of cancelling the event. Richard Branson's Virgin Atlantic stepped in with the funds. Cadette comments, 'Quite a timely move on Mr Branson's part as there are a series of scheduled Virgin Atlantic flights to the Caribbean this year! Well, business is business.'[89]

For Francis's Fisheye, being in the band made him somebody, and throwing him out to suit the sponsors makes him nobody once more.[90] Talawa's audience witness the effects of both Fisheye's unstructured rebellion and his ultimate decision to toe society's line. Both in rebellion and once he has compromised, his situation remains the same. He is poor, powerless and black. In contrast, Talawa's presentation of Carnival through Nri's Aldrick shows how this character represents the articulate voice of the people. Savory explains, 'In Caribbean plays, the least articulate folk are likely to be the most elite and often white, whereas the most verbally dextrous are most likely those who came from the poorest and most African-centred masses.'[91]

Nri's Aldrick, then, introduces Talawa's audience to the internal and psychological effects of Carnival on those for whom it forms an integral part of their existence. For him, this is a yearlong process that begins the

---

[88]Gilbey, 'Dancing The Dragon', 39.
[89]Cadette, 'Carnival's Bumpy', 31.
[90]Stone, *Theatre: Studies in West Indian Literature*, 86.
[91]Savory, 'Strategies for Survival: Anti-imperialist Theatrical Forms in the Anglophone Caribbean', 252.

moment the last Carnival is over. At this point he turns his attention to himself and looks at his innermost emotions, demonstrating the Carnival tradition of 'self-reflective criticism'.[92] The making of his next dragon costume encourages this contemplation. As he sews, his conviction is that he cannot settle with anyone until things are put right on the island. This political commitment is didactic and a new experience for many black Britons who have not had to start battles against racial discrimination and poverty from scratch. They have always had some form of foundation set for them by their politically active ancestors.[93]

The superficial aspects of Carnival are challenged as Nri's Aldrick continues to make his costume, and Talawa's audience come to appreciate the sincerity of his claim: 'This is my whole life here.'[94] Whilst conducting her research for the show, Brewster stayed with Lovelace in Trinidad. She soon realized, 'Carnival is religion in Trinidad. Not in a religious sense but in that it gives people something to believe in.'[95] Lovelace took her to meet the man playing the dragon. She watched him finish his costume, use it, destroy it and start again for the following year.[96] Carnival was indeed his entire existence.

Nri's Aldrick's chosen masquerade, repeated each year, is symbolically that of the dragon.[97] Both this costume and those like Nri's Aldrick, who are concerned about the political rebellion that Carnival has represented, are becoming extinct. The constant dragon masquerade symbolizes Nri's Aldrick's rebellion and his fight against what he sees going on around him. Each day is based on adding to his new dragon costume. With each addition he cements the minor aspects of his life from the previous year to create the greater picture of his current existence. As with James's Philo's calypsos and Francis's Fisheye's fighting in the band, Nri's Aldrick's dragon is both his life and manhood.

Once incarcerated, Nri's character realizes the full extent of the hopelessness of his people's situation. It is this understanding and

---

[92] Gilbert and Tompkins, *Post-Colonial Drama*, 95.
[93] Paul Gilroy, *Small Acts: Thoughts on the Politics of Black Cultures* (London and New York: Serpent's Tail, 1993), 230.
[94] Rehearsal script, 12a.
[95] Brewster Interview, 26 November 2018.
[96] Ibid.
[97] Stone, *Theatre: Studies in West Indian Literature*, 85. Although the dragon is one of the oldest masquerades, it is being driven to extinction.

acceptance of it that distinguishes him from his neighbours who remain satisfied with what Carnival offers them. Once he recognizes that he has moved on spiritually, psychologically and emotionally, he can no longer dance the dance of the dragon, as he now views this type of rebellion as both misunderstood and fruitless. Lovelace asks: 'why the dragon couldn't dance, why he couldn't perform, you know, you couldn't carry on that one-dimensional almost rebellion all the time. And I suppose a question that man has to face, I mean even beyond Carnival is, "Can one continue to rebel all the time in a certain dimension?"'[98] Lovelace's comment is pertinent to Britain's Notting Hill Carnival today. Whilst some support sponsorship others feel that it takes the spirit of Carnival away, leaving the original spirit of Carnival in a state of permanent disrepair.[99] As of 2019, Notting Hill Carnival is known to be Europe's biggest street party. The notion of party far outweighs any spirit of political rebellion and is a far cry from Grant's determination that Carnival is something within the human psyche.[100]

Brewster's decision to do this show and make the cultural statements she does encourages greater understanding of the Caribbean Carnival process. An additional reason for her forging ahead within this genre was to provide the opportunity for black Britons to get a grounding in a part of who they are. As Brewster explains, the cost of an ungrounded generation of black Britons is high: 'The black people that are born in England, they're split. It's not bipartisan, it's more schizoid. They don't know which way to go sometimes.'[101] Brewster's work offered them undiluted access to a part of their heritage that could challenge an inner feeling of otherness. At home in Britain they are perpetually asked where they really come from, whilst in the Caribbean they are considered British. Brewster's conclusion is that it is for black British artists to answer their questions of who they are and where they belong in their work.[102]

---

[98]Dance, *Conversations with Contemporary West Indian Writers*, 156. Taken from interview with Earl Lovelace.
[99]Nigel Carter, 'Multi-cultural or Multi-commercial?', *Caribbean Times incorporating African Times*, 15 September 1992, 30.
[100]Grant, *Blackgrounds* Interview, May 1997.
[101]Brewster Interview, 26 November 2018.
[102]Ibid.

Talawa Theatre Company

The Lion

The Lion by Guyana's Michael Abbensetts was Talawa's seventh Caribbean play and fourteenth production in total. The production marked two important firsts for the company: it was Talawa's first commissioned play in its West End home, performed at the Cochrane between 30 September and 23 October 1993 and directed by Horace Ové; it was also the company's first internationally touring production, directed by Brewster.[103] The production offers Talawa's black audience food for thought as it presents a range of black identities and the clashes between them.

Oral language of performance: Speaky spokey

Damourette and Pichon's idea that 'every dialect is a way of thinking' is demonstrated in this section as we see how three English language forms mark fundamental differences in people who have both a history and culture in common.[104] The forms are middle class Caribbean speech, black British speech, and working class Caribbean speech performed by a British actor.

The script of *The Lion* is written in 'standard English', peppered with Caribbeanisms. One of the language forms featured in the performance is presented in the publicity programme with a quote from the production: 'Yuh seat of government is dis sofabed.'[105] This could lead programme readers to imagine that the Caribbean language of the performance would be that of the monolingual patois speaker. Whilst this speech is used in the performance, it takes second place to the varying forms of British and Caribbean black middle class speech performed.

Talawa's production presents the Caribbean black upper middle class voice as presented by the protagonists Stefan Kalipha's Ramsey James and Madge Sinclair's Isabella.[106] This black middle class speech in both the Caribbean and Britain, and the presentation of the lives of its speakers on stage, demonstrates both David Mamet's belief that 'As the society changes

---

[103] In November 1993 the British cast did a ten-day run of the show at the Ward Theatre, Kingston, Jamaica.
[104] Fanon, *Black Skin, White Masks*, 25.
[105] Rehearsal script, 34, 'This sofabed is your position in government'.
[106] The language that they use is essentially 'standard English' with a Caribbean accent and some regional differences.

the theatre changes', and Talawa's tenacity in showing rarely performed black lives.[107] Talawa points its audience to the fact that post-emancipation black culture has developed its own middle class both in Britain and the Caribbean. Due to its colonial history, the black Caribbean class system is akin to that of Britain, where social hierarchy is demonstrated by language use and accent.

Where previously in colonial history black skin served as a barrier to upward mobility, Talawa's performance of *The Lion* shows how whilst lighter skin colour is advantageous, black skin need not be the hindrance it once was provided that the black speaker's language demonstrates an 'acceptable' level of education. This is seen in Sinclair's Isabella. In the treatment for the stage play, Abbensetts describes Isabella's language: 'She has two ways of speaking: she can sound very English, and then suddenly break into a bit of a Caribbean dialect.'[108]

Embarrassment about Caribbean black working class language and manners in Britain is presented by Selvon in *The Lonely Londoners*. Selvon's section on the character Harris describes how he is black and imitates all that he regards as British and, more specifically, English. He wears a bowler hat and carries an umbrella with a briefcase and *The Times* under his arm.[109] He has used language to climb socially and is put on edge by his fellow countrymen whom he feels do not speak or act in an appropriately English manner around his white friends.

The need that some African-Caribbean people newly arrived in Britain throughout the 1950s had to demonstrate the ability to use 'standard English' was unnecessary with ensuing generations. This is seen in all of the aforementioned black British theatre companies that emerged throughout the late 1970s and 1980s who used African-Caribbean speech forms as their major mode of performance expression. This is also seen in the wealth of African and Caribbean English language productions that Talawa has produced since its inception and reflects changes in British society as a whole.

The linguistic prejudices once levelled at blacks by whites in the Caribbean have become the preserve of the middle class black Caribbean community. In imitating their ex-colonial masters, they mock black

---

[107]David Mamet, *Writing in Restaurants* (New York: Viking, Penguin Inc., 1986), 19.
[108]The treatment for the stage play is found in Talawa's production archives files for *The Lion*, general file.
[109]Selvon, *The Lonely Londoners*, 110–22.

working class uneducated speech. They see this speech as inferior to their own linguistically recognized West Indian Standard speech (WIS). This is seen in *The Lion* when Isabella corrects Hendrick's language:

HENDRICKS: Come 'n get it!
ISABELLA: Hendricks, you're in Britain now. Here they say 'coffee is served'.[110]

Her correction serves to enlighten him and point to her elevated status. In his discussion of the case of Jamaica, David De Camp gives a clear indication of the social status of Sinclair's character's type of speech in relation to other 'standard English' forms. Those who head the continuum are Jamaicans who speak the most highly respected varieties of Jamaican English. They recognize that this is not the same as 'standard English'. Expatriates who speak public school 'standard English' do not even enter on the continuum as all expatriate speech is outside it.[111]

Kalipha's Ramsey also uses educated middle class speech. His stated claim for this is based on his British education. This highlights the important fact to the British audience that not all those who came from the West Indies arrived in Tilbury Dock on the *Empire Windrush* in 1948.[112] The adoption of middle class speech adapted by blacks to suit their Caribbean environment was a marker of upward mobility in both the pre- and post-independence Caribbean. This speech became the norm for the islands' rich and powerful.[113] Those in power like Kalipha's Ramsey are fully aware of the cultural consequences surrounding their linguistic choices. Opting to imitate the language and manners of the old colonial rulers would serve to keep society as divided as it had been under colonial rule. Similarly, those who know how to use this language stay on top.

It is through Colette Brown's Sonia and Danny Kwasi Sapani's Gideon that Talawa's audience experiences the theatrical voice of the black British

---

[110]Rehearsal script, 3.
[111]David De Camp, 'Social and Geographical Factors in Jamaican Dialects', in *Creole Language Studies II*, ed. R. B. Le Page (London and New York: Macmillan, 1961), 83.
[112]Yvonne Brewster, Personal Interview by David Johnson, London, 16 March 1999: 'People here like to think that all black people came here on the *Windrush* to look for work.'
[113]Errol Miller, 'Educational Development in Independent Jamaica', in *Jamaica in Independence: Essays on the Early Years*, ed. Rex Nettleford (London and Kingston: Heinemann Caribbean, 1989), 207.

middle class. This voice is identical to that of their white counterparts and here it is drawn in linguistic contrast to the other characters that represent opposite ends of the Caribbean class system. This use of general middle class British speech is beneficial to Talawa's wider representation of itself, as it both expands and demonstrates the verbal repertoire of the company, whilst unveiling a second level of overt language behaviour. This overt language behaviour, like Caribbean middle class speech, is uncommon to the contemporary black British stage. Black British middle class speech remains generally unexplored in black British theatre for two main reasons: firstly, its similarity to 'standard English', and secondly, it shows blacks with a black identity that is not steeped in poverty and struggle. Such poverty is often mistakenly taken to be representative of black culture.[114]

Both Sapani's Gideon and Brown's Sonia are born into middle class families due to their fathers' political professions, though neither was raised with them. As for their mothers, little is known. Additionally, both characters are middle class by their own profession as both are teachers. Intentionally, there is nothing in either performance that reflects their full cultural heritage. For Brown's Sonia this is easily explained. She was raised by an English mother and did not have any long-term direct contact with the Caribbean. For Sapani's Gideon the case is quite different. His mother raised him as a single parent and is from St Judes. If he has been at all influenced by his mother's speech, his Caribbean linguistic knowledge could feasibly be wider than is demonstrated by his language use in the play. Like Sinclair's Isabella, Sapani's Gideon could realistically use some form of the Caribbean expression he has heard all his life from his mother. Equally, given the passionate nature of his situation and the fact that he is surrounded by Caribbean people from St Jude's, it is conceivable he would use the occasional Caribbean word and reflect his bicultural life.

The fact that he does not do this is a strategic marker in Talawa's aim to highlight his entire 'Britishness' and the difference that he sees between himself and the Caribbean characters. This exemplifies the chosen linguistic and cultural differences between Caribbean nationals living in Britain and their black British counterparts who move away from orally expressing a Caribbean identity. When Sapani's Gideon tells Kalipha's Ramsey that he is proud of being a black Briton, his linguistic tone reflects this. He uses the

---

[114]Rex Nettleford, 'Cultural Action in Independence', in *Jamaica in Independence: Essays on the Early Years*, ed. Rex Nettleford (London and Kingston: Heinemann Caribbean, 1989), 326.

language of where he feels he belongs as he provides food for thought for Talawa's black British audience.

The language of Sapani's Gideon and Brown's Sonia may have no place on any black language continuum as it is indistinguishable from that of their white counterparts. There are, however, many black British professionals who use this speech. Despite this, when this voice is presented in the black British performance arena, it is often used to highlight the speaker's entire loss of cultural identity, instead of as a partial expression of mixed cultural roots and life experience.

This notion of black middle class speech portraying the user as having a cultural identity problem was illustrated in the 1970s ITV comedy series *Rising Damp*. The series ran from September 1974 to May 1978 and starred Trinidadian-born Don Warrington. He played Philip, the African Prince student doctor, who shared a flat with his white friend, affectionately referred to as 'the layabout', played by Richard Beckonsale. Warrington's character became widely known as 'the posh black man', indicating a perceived incompatibility of his speech with his skin colour. Four decades on, is the presence of black newsreaders on every mainstream British television channel enough evidence that black skins and 'posh' speech are compatible?

In Talawa's production of *The Lion*, it is the working class Caribbean speech of David Webber's Hendricks that is seen as the more commonly expected way of speaking for blacks. Talawa illustrates the verbal repertoire of the black community with this choice of voice. The linguistic dexterity is heightened as Webber is British and is using this Caribbean voice in performance. This third linguistic form, as is seen through Talawa's work, has been shown where the text requires the depiction of a black working class environment. For Talawa, the voice has tended towards Jamaican working class speech. In this production, this speech choice is partly due to the writer's Jamaican nationality. In the case of non-Jamaican writers, this working class speech style is used to illustrate a Jamaican situation using Jamaican speech, as is demonstrated by Walcott.[115]

Webber's Hendricks has spent much of his life on the Caribbean Island of St Jude's. His voice should reflect his linguistic history. As the island is fictitious, there is no model for the actor to follow. He must draw his

---

[115] This speech is used in the following Talawa Caribbean productions to depict the black working class: *An Echo in the Bone* (Dennis Scott), *O Babylon* (Derek Walcott), *Smile Orange* (Trevor Rhone), *Maskarade* (Sylvia Wynter).

own conclusions based on his experience of Caribbean speech and adapt it for performance on the British stage.[116] The result is a recognizable stage version of working class monolingual Jamaican patois speech. His chosen voice is defined enough for it to be culturally and socially identifiable, whilst demonstrating a clarity that makes it comprehensible to non-patois speakers. Webber's chosen voice is effective because it demonstrates the essential class difference needed between the characters.

His language is akin to what De Camp refers to as Quashie Talk. This is the lowest form of language on the Jamaican continuum and is generally used by comedians.[117] This is fitting for Webber's character who by the nature of his uneducated speech is given comic status. Through the varying speech styles offered in the production, Talawa gives its black British audience a picture of Caribbean language hierarchy which relates directly to them. Many will be as familiar with the working class speech of Webber's Hendricks as the middle class speech of the other characters.

The production equally offers clues as to how Webber's Hendricks's monolingual patois speech, coupled with his personal taste and manners, places him at the bottom end of St Jude's hierarchical society. From this, Talawa's audience can judge for itself whether black Britons like Webber's Hendricks are similarly pigeonholed in British society. Drawn as the polar opposite to his employer, his musical taste leans towards ragga and reggae, as opposed to Kalipha's Ramsey's love of opera. Throughout the production he is the only character who regularly uses expletives, despite their absence in the script. The suggestion is that he is incapable of demonstrating the same kind of linguistic 'sophistication' as his employer, and that his language then legitimizes his expected poor treatment by those in a higher social group.

In 1953 a form of Creole was described as 'Inferiority made half articulate.'[118] From Webber's portrayal of Hendricks and his treatment in *The Lion*, this opinion remains widespread both in the Caribbean and in Britain. Much of Talawa's black British audience would have grown up hearing this type of monolingual patois speech at home. They would also have attended

---

[116]Brewster Interview, 16 March 1999: 'David was familiar with the voice because of his Jamaican background.'
[117]De Camp, 'Social and Geographical Factors in Jamaican Dialects', 83.
[118]J. Edward Chamberlin, *Come Back to Me My Language: Poetry and the West Indies* (Chicago: University of Illinois Press, 1993), 82.

Talawa Theatre Company

British schools with their 'historical exclusion of "plantation English"'.[119] Talawa's performance shows its commitment to, along with the necessity of, placing such speech forms centre stage. As Nettlefold puts it, 'The use of Standard English for official and formal discourse is not incompatible, after all, with the common usage of a tongue created by the Jamaican people over 300 years for their own use and to describe their own reality.'[120]

The simultaneous introduction of upper middle class Caribbean language, black British middle class professional language and working class Caribbean speech to the black British stage is threefold. Audiences are invited to acknowledge the three forms and the class based language and culture systems within Caribbean society. These divisions are overlooked in Britain in preference of placing all black people into a singular and identical black group. Secondly, the three forms are shown to work together, as they do in real life. Finally, there is a clear hierarchy that once again places the voice of the monolingual patois speaker beneath all other sections of society.

Notions of black identity: Black . . . ish Brit . . . ish

Talawa's production of *The Lion* raises questions around notions of black British identity, differences between black Britons and West Indians on issues of masculinity, and how the Caribbean working class character Hendricks, as portrayed by Webber, adapts to life in Britain.

Confusion around black British identity stems from the range of views that exist on what it is. Enoch Powell believed that West Indians born in England were not Englishmen, whilst Mary Karen Dahl points to black British as meaning 'anyone in Britain who is not white'.[121] Caribbean definitions that exclude black Britons complicate the question further. Nettleford describes Dawes's definition of a Jamaican as 'anyone white, black or mixed who grew up in Jamaica and traces Jamaican ancestry back to the period of the institution of slavery in Jamaica'.[122]

---

[119]Inchley, *Voice and New Writing*, 81. Additionally, Inchley points to the education reports throughout the 1970s, 1980s and 1990s which stigmatized black speech (166 note 4).
[120]Nettleford, 'Cultural Action in Independence', 292.
[121]Dahl, 'Postcolonial British Theatre: Black Voices at the Center', 41.
[122]Rex Nettleford, *Caribbean Cultural Identity: The Case of Jamaica, an Essay in Cultural Dynamics* (Jamaica: Institute of Jamaica, 1978), 4. Nettleford quotes Neville Dawes in his address to the Lions Club Montego Bay, 2 May 1974.

Sapani's Gideon uses the term black British to describe himself. His cultural roots are however entirely Caribbean. Brown's Sonia is half white and perceived, due to inheriting her father's skin colour, to be black in British society. Her father's British nationality is irrelevant to how she is classified in Britain. Whilst Brown's portrayal of Sonia reveals an acceptance of the definition wider society has given her, for Talawa's black audience her Britishness comes mostly from her white cultural roots.

Neither Sapani's Gideon nor Brown's Sonia view their Caribbean roots as helping to attribute underdog status to them in British society. Like many black Britons, they have not lived the Caribbean side of their heritage. Their quest for their Caribbean heritage is shown in their love–hate relationship with the Caribbean based on their relationships with specific Caribbean individuals.

Through Sapani's Gideon, Talawa's audience is made aware that his rejection of the Caribbean is based on the political career of the president for life and the fact that the president killed his father. When he tells Kalipha's Ramsey, 'It's no wonder some of us don't really want to be West Indian anymore', his statement is layered.[123] As far as the character is concerned, he personally does not want to be like Kalipha's Ramsey because of his political hypocrisy and tyrannical rule. For the audience, his reaction highlights the fact that some black Britons reject their Caribbean roots. This exposure invites the crucial questions as to why this happens.

Talawa's performance illustrates that black British cultural heritage, as with all bicultural people, is flexible.[124] Those living biculturally select what they consider to be the most appropriate cultural forms for their existence. They are faced with a challenge, however, when they need to catch up on the heritage facts of the less dominant culture but find that those depended upon to fill in the cultural gaps are unprepared to help them.

This is highlighted through Brown's Sonia. Once she has her father with her she needs to question him about her Caribbean relatives. This black Briton has a need for her self-discovery through her cultural line.

---

[123]Rehearsal script, 32.
[124]Julie Stone Peters, 'Intercultural Performance, Theatre Anthropology, and the Imperialist Critique, Identities, Inheritances, and the Neo-Orthodoxies', in *Imperialism and Theatre: Essays on World Theatre, Drama and Performance*, ed. J. Ellen Gainor (London: Routledge, 1995), 199–213.

There are two main reasons why Kalipha's Ramsey does not recognize or understand his daughter's need to equip herself with this information. Firstly, he can only think about himself, and secondly he would rather forget the experiences he had with his family because they were bad for him.

For the black Britons represented by Brown's Sonia, this message is mixed. She is meant to recognize her cultural heritage is important, yet accept exclusion from it. Talawa's production presents then the opportunity for its black British audience to confront questions of belonging to the cultures they are sandwiched between. Who are they? Where and how do they fit? This inadvertently echoes the teachings of Teer, her five performance goals and her third company goal to re-educate, as discussed earlier.

Kalipha's Ramsey plays on the black Briton's perceived lack of identity when he asks Sapani's Gideon, 'To me you're a black Briton, but to the British who the blasted hell are you?'[125] He sees Sapani's Gideon as black British due to his black skin and his legal British status, and because he seeks to reject any likeness between them. He will not accept Sapani's Gideon as Caribbean as this would connect them. His rhetorical question suggests that black Britons have no real identity and their bicultural existence reduces them to being incomplete, as they face rejection from all sides. Whilst the characters debate black British identity, the audience is left legitimately questioning whether the dreamt up category of 'black British' is nothing more than a white construct, on a par with Powell's unattainable 'Englishness' above, designed to ensure forever inequality between whites and blacks in Britain both on and off stage.

It is on issues of perceived masculinity that a further cultural distance is shown between the black British and Caribbean characters in Talawa's production. Throughout, the masculinity of the Caribbean upper middle class and working class man is drawn in contrast to the masculinity of the black British man. The differences are stark and often adhere to fixed stereotypes. The conflict and contradictions form part of the continued identity question for black Britons that ultimately have to negotiate where they best fit.

Kalipha's Ramsey is unable to see Sapani's Gideon as a real man because of his profession. He regards his teaching of cookery and his

---

[125]Rehearsal script, 33.

The Island Plays

linguistic aptitude as having diminished his masculinity. His comments are understood within the context of his situation as an exile abroad that has been stripped of his power and hence robbed of an aspect of his manhood. His insults to Sapani's Gideon stem from his frustration and recognition of the fact that the black Briton is in many ways in a stronger and therefore more masculine position. This is because Sapani's Gideon is on his home soil, is still master of what he does, has control over Brown's Sonia, and despite Kalipha's Ramsey's physical attack on him is the younger and physically stronger man of the two.

Along with the perceived power that is attached to the Caribbean notion of profession is the connection of sexual prowess to masculinity. Webber's Hendricks, as the basest of the three men, openly discusses his sexual exploits. As he has no other accepted power he measures the mark of his masculinity by his escapades. Both Webber's Hendricks and Kalipha's Ramsey are described by Brown's Sonia as dinosaurs in regard to their 'outdated Caribbean' attitude to women. Once again, Sapani's Gideon is shown in contrast to the Caribbean men.

Talawa's presentation of a 'standard' modern black British middle class man, in Sapani's Gideon, is rare for the time. This is by virtue of the fact that his background, educational attainment and middle class lifestyle are not common to the majority of black British, or white British, men. He is part of a small minority within a minority. Talawa's black male audience has the opportunity to decide if it has anything in common with him, as each finds his place on the vast masculinity continuum between Webber's Hendricks, Sapani's Gideon and Kalipha's Ramsey.

Whilst Webber's Hendricks's motivations surrounding his masculinity are sexual and Kalipha's Ramsey's are political, initially those of Sapani's Gideon are couched in his need for revenge. He has become romantically involved with Brown's Sonia in order to get to her father. As his central focus is with Kalipha's Ramsey and his present sex life is a by-product of his decision to deal with him, sex in itself is not a central focus for him. It is used strategically as a weapon. Whilst the Caribbean male characters advertise their sex lives, he keeps his private life low key. This is in part because he is playing a game, but simultaneously contrasts his black British attitudes with those of the other men.

Through David Webber's Hendricks, we see that it is the Caribbean characters as well as the black British characters that are affected by questions surrounding their black identity. Webber's Hendricks's behaviour and ability to adapt from a colony to the motherland is reminiscent of

Gilroy's claim that modernism began with slavery, as it was African slaves who first had to cope with and find their way around the problems of modern society.[126]

As Webber's Hendricks makes a conscious effort to adapt to and make the most of his new environment, he takes up both betting and wine drinking: 'I'm in Englan' now. I'm not so crass an' crude anymore. I'm changin'.'[127] He associates his new activities with having a certain amount of 'class'. He is acquiring a 'Britishness' that takes away some of his Caribbean 'roughness'. The boasts of his chosen changes are tongue in cheek in the knowledge that he gambled and drank what was available to him in the Caribbean. His momentary contentment suggests that positive change is readily available to Caribbean men of all classes in modern Britain. Talawa presents us then with the gulf between the colonial postwar promises of a wonderful life in the motherland and the stark reality of British-Caribbean subjects once in Britain. This reality continues to be passed from one black British generation to the next.

For Talawa's audience Webber's Hendricks represents the kinds of experiences they are more familiar with of the first generation working class Caribbean man making his way in Britain. He is the character with the least in terms of material resources or connections but makes the most of the situation that he finds himself in. He is able to adapt to British life without compromising his Caribbean identity. He is also living from day to day.

Brewster directed the production for the tour to The Ward Theatre in Kingston, Jamaica between 3 and 13 November 1993. Sponsored by the British Council, Brewster was told to make the piece more Jamaican. In Britain it had passed as Caribbean enough. Brewster had three days to change the political ethos to fit Jamaica.[128] The performance became so Jamaican that when Webber faced post-show queues of fans wanting his autograph, they insisted he was putting on his native Mancunian accent and pretending to be British when he spoke to them.[129]

---

[126]Paul Gilroy, *The Black Atlantic: Modernity and the Double Consciousness* (London and New York: Verso, 1993).
[127]Rehearsal script, 26.
[128]Brewster Interview, 26 November 2018.
[129]Ibid.

The Island Plays

This speaks to Webber's authenticity as Hendricks. This black Briton was playing the kind of first generation Caribbean man he knows. A part of himself. Edwards explains, 'We must train our artists to be true to themselves and their culture, I believe, because it has been rigorously trained out of them.'[130] Webber was able to do this through his experience at Talawa and using the only vehicle he has for acting: himself.[131] Talawa's performance of *The Lion* and the issues it raised surrounding black language and identity in Britain support Stone Peters's theory of one of theatre's uses: 'Theatre has a special place in history because it offers an aestheticized brand of performance, of the ways things happen on the political stage or the stage of war, in the courts and on the streets.'[132] Here the 'aestheticized brand of performance' shone an intricate light on black life and illustrated that Talawa's work is not 'white theatre in black face' but rather a performance genre that speaks directly to its target and wider British audience.[133]

Beef, No Chicken

Beef, No Chicken was Talawa's twenty-second production and tenth Caribbean work. The company performed the play at the Tricycle Theatre Kilburn from 18 December 1996 to 1 February 1997. Prior to the opening of the play Brewster had anticipated that performing the play at the Tricycle meant audience numbers could be higher than for shows performed in less popular venues. This in turn could give greater exposure to both Talawa and Derek Walcott, one of the Caribbean's leading literary figures.[134] Culturally, the show takes its audience to a small Trinidadian town, Couva. It highlights local power and resistance to change when a local restaurant owner, Otto Hogan, refuses bribes that lead to the delay of a new motorway in Couva town centre.

---

[130]Gus Edwards, 'Part IV Performance, Introduction', in *Black Theatre: Ritual Performance in The African Diaspora*, ed. Paul Carter Harrison, Victor Leo Walker II and Gus Edwards (Philadelphia: Temple University, 2002), 313.
[131]Ibid, interview with Douglas Ward.
[132]Stone Peters, 'Intercultural Performance, Theatre Anthropology, and the Imperialist Critique, Identities, Inheritances, and the Neo-Orthodoxies', 200.
[133]Edwards, 'Part IV Performance, Introduction', 313. The reference is to Louis Mason, '"The Electronic Nig Meets the Gold Dust Twins," Interview with Ed Bullins and Robert Macbeth', *Black Theatre* (May–September 1969).
[134]Yvonne Brewster, Personal Interview by David Johnson, London, 20 November 1996.

Talawa Theatre Company

Work on the play started in June 1996 when the company's production of *Medea in the Mirror* was running at the new Shaw Theatre in Brixton. Brewster chose this play at this juncture as she felt obliged to remind British theatregoers of the fact that talented Caribbean playwrights exist and because the company had dedicated the earlier part of the year to new and unknown writing.[135]

Brewster: Directing language

As a performance researcher, I followed the four-week rehearsal period and documented the journey Brewster arranged for her cast during rehearsals for *Beef, No Chicken*. This had a central focus on developing linguistic accuracy. Brewster's linguistic approach is symbolized by her text-based methods. Like the majority of the Caribbean texts, the language of *Beef, No Chicken* is generally 'standard English' with Caribbeanisms, in this case from Trinidad. Brewster was raised with the idea that Jamaicans should speak as clearly, with their own accent, as possible, as did the two Jamaicans, Dwight Whylie and Dick Pixley, whom she heralds as speaking perfect English on the BBC's overseas radio service in the 1950s. She describes the aim of her language work with Talawa as a need to get all of the voices of the text in harmony like a symphony: 'You're not going to listen to a whole symphony with bassoons.'[136]

Many of the performers had been directed by Brewster in a previous Talawa production. She explains, 'All of these established faces were new black actors at one point and some of them not too long ago. I like to give work to people that I know will work well together, but at the same time take a risk on a new face in almost every production.'[137] The majority of the cast members were either native Caribbean or black British performers. Each associated their character's language with similar voices from the Caribbean island of their childhood, or that of their parents. These were from Grenada, Jamaica, St Vincent and Trinidad. The one performer of Ghanaian descent, Freddie Annobil-Dodoo, also linked his characters' voices with those of the Caribbean.

Brewster built the confidence of those black Britons attempting a Caribbean voice on stage for the first time. These performers were guided

---

[135]Ibid.
[136]Interview with Yvonne Brewster by David Johnson, Talawa offices London, 9 March 1997.
[137]Ibid.

in reasserting a part of their cultural heritage that is rarely given a public forum. In order to produce such a voice, some speakers had to surmount psychological obstacles developed by being told not to speak like their parents during their childhood.[138] They were reacquiring a lost or unexplored part of their voice and culture through Brewster's rehearsal process.

Brewster initially allowed each cast member to develop a wide range of possible voices for their character. Where cast members needed to produce multiple voices, as in the case of Sandra Bee and Annobil-Dodoo, they worked through Brewster's process for each character until each had its own distinct voice. Brewster coaxed the performers into working with a voice that resembled the stereotype of the character. This exaggerated form was used to examine the mouth movements needed to create the voice. It could then be watered down to make the character a person rather than a caricature.

It is Brewster's belief that if performers feel they have real input into their character's development, they will be comfortable with their work and natural speech will follow. Additionally, she was aware that performers learn voices through varied techniques and so did not expect the entire cast to perfect their accents at the beginning of the rehearsal period. Instead, she saw each stage in the rehearsal process as offering a further opportunity to get to grips with the required voice.[139]

The performers' initially hesitant reading of the text highlighted the skill required in working simultaneously with 'standard English' and Caribbeanisms. Brewster explained difficulties as they occurred, thus demonstrating her critical role in training a new generation of black British performers capable of working within this genre. In addition to her own language work, Brewster knew that for this particular production she would need the practical help of native Trinidadians. This help came firstly in the form of choreographer Greta Mendez.

On 19 November 1996 Mendez ran a workshop aimed at helping the cast develop its characters' voices. Mendez's philosophy for developing specific speech for performance was that if the character becomes a living being for the performer through an understanding of the character's movement, and if the performer is able to give the character a life outside of the text, a natural voice for the character should follow.

---

[138]Sam Adams, Personal Interview by David Johnson, London, 26 November 1996.
[139]Brewster Interview, 20 November 1996.

Mendez gave the performers the initial task of improvising waking up and taking a walk in their local area. The work highlighted that those who already had the correct oral voice for their character were able to easily develop movement and a life outside of the text. Those learning the voice for the first time produced movement that highlighted the difference between their character's current voice and that which was required. This was exemplified in Annobil-Dodoo playing the limer. There was a direct correlation between the actor's rigidity of movement and the lack of confidence and accuracy he expressed orally. Annobil-Dodoo's disadvantage was that he was the least experienced cast member in the voice he was required to produce. Brewster had pointed out, 'Some do it immediately because they can, others just pick it up when they hear it around them. Most really get going when they get to grips with the script; Freddie will do it with the voice coach.'[140]

Mendez's next step was to allow the characters to improvise in varying situations that they could conceivably find themselves in outside the text. Much of the rehearsal centred around a game of dominoes being played by all of the male characters whilst the female characters flitted in and out. The end result was once again that those who had already grasped their voice ran with it. Mendez had anticipated that not all of the performers would produce the voice that they required through the above two exercises and prepared a third route. She supplied a range of audio cassettes with Trinidadian music and lectures so that performers would be able to simply listen and copy.

27 November 1996 was a linguistic turning point in the rehearsal process. It was the first day of two voice coaching workshops run by Claudette Williams. The detailed and practical voice work session dealt intensely with the shape of the mouth and the positioning of the tongue. Williams offered straightforward point of reference practical advice by suggesting that the performers aim to keep their tongues forward and lips tight, as if smiling. Becoming more confident the performer would be later able to produce the same sounds with less stress on tightening lips and positioning of the tongue, thus finding their own Trinidadian voice. Additionally, performers were given voice exercises that focused on producing a powerful sound. This was achieved by restricting the performers' speech by covering their mouths.

---

[140] Ibid.

The Island Plays

When released, the performer instinctively acted as if still constricted. This made their speech much stronger. The final practical advice they were given was to practice their lines using the above methods.

The following day, those cast members who had already demonstrated an ability to use the Trinidadian voice continued to do so. Those who had previously had more difficulty were now using Brewster's, Mendez's and Williams's techniques and were approximating a Trinidadian voice. Annobil-Dodoo, in accordance with Brewster's earlier prediction, was now producing an accurate Trinidadian sound. The positive results brought a higher degree of linguistic accuracy to the cast generally and enabled the physical dimensions of each character to come through. The combined methods proved that the performers were able to get the correct sound with the right training.

The main character, Otto Hogan, was played by Trinidadian Shango Baku. Linguistically Baku was able to produce the appropriate voice with ease, as well as provide continued coaching to other performers. Jim Findlay, playing Mongroo and Deacon, is also Trinidadian, and again was able to provide ongoing voice coaching to cast members. Ram John Holder, playing Franco, used his native Guyanese accent. The black British performers – Geff Francis, Sam Adams, Annobil-Dodoo and Sandra Bee – had the biggest task in developing the correct Trinidadian voice.

Francis had previously performed a convincing Trinidadian voice in Talawa's *The Dragon Can't Dance*. He was equally successful with the same voice used for the Mayor in *Beef, No Chicken*. Francis's Grenadian family background helps explain his facility with the Trinidadian accent, although this skill is not to be taken for granted as not all black British-born performers are able to reproduce the voice of their parents. Francis benefited from the voice work done during rehearsals where he was able to perfect his Trinidadian sound. In his role as Cedric Hart he uses an authentic American accent. No training was provided for this voice as many American influences are part of British contemporary culture, allowing performers great access to this speech style. Similarly successful in playing a role requiring Trinidadian and American accents was Sam Adams.

This black British performer was familiar with the Caribbean sounds of the eastern Caribbean, being of Vincentian parentage. Producing an approximation of the voice was a revelation to her that she had maintained part of her linguistic heritage without realizing it. Adams, playing Drusilla, as with many black British performers working with Talawa for the first time, had only previously worked in 'standard English'. This new linguistic dimension and personal discovery of an enhanced cultural identity for performance expanded her possible range of work.

The success of her Caribbean voice in *Beef, No Chicken* also bonded her with her black community on a linguistic level she had until then never experienced: 'This performance gave my friends and family an opportunity to see me in a new light.'[141] Whilst this may be said of any performer in any production, the 'new light' referred to here was one that was more fully culturally and linguistically representative of her. On and off stage, Adams was now able to use her re-awakened Caribbean voice and more developed cultural identity.

In the same role, Adams was easily able to produce an American accent. Like Francis, Adams produced two contrasting voices for the performance and like Francis she was starting from a lifetime's aural experience of an eastern Caribbean voice. The experience of the show allowed her to practice both voices and hone these specific elements of her craft, as well as serve as testimony to Brewster's ability to set young black talent on the road of self-discovery and professional theatrical work.

Annobil-Dodoo, playing the parts of the limer and the second bandit, worked in three main voices. These were the Trinidadian lower register as the limer, a New York street style speech in a rap as the limer, and monolingual Jamaican patois as the bandit. In presenting three types of black language it was in his rendition of the New York rap voice that Dodoo achieved most accuracy. His performance, along with that of Adams and Francis, sheds light on the ease with which many black British performers reproduce an American accent in performance.

Is it due to the American accent having higher status than any Caribbean form that makes it easier for black British actors to reproduce? As there is no stigma attached performers can feel free to imitate and get it wrong until they get it right. With Adams and Francis their Caribbean voice is produced from a sense of cultural and linguistic pride that increased their desire for accuracy.[142] For Annobil-Dodoo this is not the case. His Caribbean point of reference is limited in comparison to the other performers.

---

[141] Sam Adams, Personal Interview by David Johnson, London, 12 June 1997.
[142] Sam Adams and Geff Francis, Personal Interview by David Johnson, London, 26 November 1996.

With the two Caribbean language forms Annobil-Dodoo achieved an equal degree of accuracy. Although voice coaching was received for the Trinidadian form only, the performer presents a recognizable Jamaican voice. The question of language and its importance to identity is raised once again. The young black man identifies strongly with black British youth culture and language, 'which is more Jamaican in style than any other Caribbean language form'.[143] He is already then partly versed in a watered down version of the voice needed for the bandit in this performance, and his everyday linguistic experiences reflect the developing heavily Jamaican voice of the black British community.[144]

Sandra Bee, performing three voices, demonstrates how black British performers may use all of their experiences to develop a range of voices for performance. For the character of Sumintra the voice is a lower middle class Trinidadian Indian speech style. This speech has clear Indian inflections within its Caribbean voice. For Mitzi the voice is an educated middle class general Caribbean voice with Trinidadian overtones. Finally, for the part of the bandit the voice is the monolingual Jamaican patois male voice as used by Annobil-Dodoo. Brewster comments on Bee's efforts, 'Sandra Bee does three accents: Indian Trini, upper Trini and lower Jamaican, and she does them all brilliantly.'[145]

Bee's monolingual Jamaican patois form may wrongly be taken for granted because her background is Jamaican. Appearing in the BBC black sitcom *Brothers and Sisters* at the time, Bee was already working actively using a form of the Jamaican voice. A pride in her origins enabled her to break down any barriers regarding negative feeling about her Caribbean language status. As Bee uses 'standard English' and patois in her daily speech, adopting a further language form would prove easier for her than a monolingual speaker of any language, as she is familiar with the concept of language change.[146] The fact that she needed to use other forms of Caribbean language, which she did not regard as having lower status, enabled her to concentrate entirely on the language and her task of getting it right.[147]

---

[143]Freddie Annobil-Dodoo, Personal Interview by David Johnson, London, 26 November 1996.
[144]Ibid.
[145]Brewster Interview, 20 November 1996.
[146]Sandra Bee, Personal Interview by David Johnson, London, 28 November 1996.
[147]Ibid.

Talawa Theatre Company

In playing the part of the Indian Sumintra there is no attempt to make Bee look more Asian. This reveals the depth to which she is able to produce the correct sound for her character. The fact that the performer is clearly of African-Caribbean origin does not upset the audience's understanding of the Asian extraction of the character she is playing. Her identity is clear both by her Indian accent and her sari. Additional stereotypical Asian symbols would have made the actress seem like she was presenting a caricature and would have allowed her to rely almost entirely on her physical appearance. The way she is presented allows for a subtlety that encourages Bee to reveal her character's identity from the inside, through voice, and from the outside, through movement.

When the press commend Talawa's performances, it is often the performers who achieve the highest degree of linguistic accuracy who are noted when the critics have enjoyed a production overall. The following review extracts of *Beef, No Chicken* show how some journalists approach the aspects of Caribbean performance work by expressing a range of language-linked views. Kate Bassett explains:

> I'm looking, I'm listening, but frankly I'm having difficulty following. This is, of course, partly because I am a honky and cannot keep up with the patter. However, you do tune in after a while and the language in which the locals squabble and get saucy is a delightful combination of lyricism and comic inventiveness, lilting but delivered at a fair lick.[148]

Bassett happily refers to herself as a 'honky'. This distances her from blacks in Britain and the performance. It is unlikely that black reviewers failing to understand a white show would explain that it is because they are 'sambos'. The reason Bassett does not understand the 'patter' is not to do with her being white, but because she has little experience of the Caribbean language used in the production. Conversely, white people who have lived alongside their black neighbours are more likely to follow the 'patter'.

This is the all too familiar cry of at least one reviewer of any black British and Caribbean language-based play: 'I just couldn't understand it.' Why not? Black people in Britain have to negotiate every second of every day in a varyingly welcoming environment and learn whatever speech style is going. White people are just not used to having to make this kind of effort.

---

[148] Kate Bassett, 'A Complicated Menu with Plenty of Spice', *Daily Telegraph*, 15 January 1997, 15.

The Island Plays

Either it's the white way in the 'white space', or it's the white way in the 'white-space'. Anything outside of that runs the risk of being written about with patronizing 'appreciation' and incredulity.

A second review by journalist Francis James commits to highlighting individual efforts that I believe stand out because of their linguistic accuracy. James writes:

> Everyone's work is of the highest calibre. But having said that, two people are worthy of special mention – Shango Baku who plays the put upon central character Otto, and Geff Francis, who is outstanding in his two roles as a smooth as silk TV anchor man, and the rotund mayor longing for corruption, rape and other heinous crimes to bring his small town into the twenty first century.[149]

Finally, John Thaxter's review of the production in *The Stage*, again without mentioning language work, hails the performances of those who are linguistically adept in their roles. Thaxter notes:

> Quite outstanding is roly-poly, lightsome Sandra Bee, with delicious cameos and as an operatic short-order cook in an Indian sari, a mafia-style gangster in Ray-Bans and the council's pinkly fashionable secretary reading back her shorthand notes in mincing ladylike tones. Equally remarkable is Geff Francis doubling as a suave, redheaded television newscaster and as the pot-bellied mayor.[150]

Talawa's work in this genre at the time demonstrated that the language of black British theatre was both diverse and developing. This is unsurprising when black Britons are viewed through the historical context of having an ever-changing identity imposed upon them by the dominant white culture, where they have had to be linguistically dextrous in order to survive. Brewster's productions illustrate her tenacity in bringing this dexterity to the British stage. This type of unapologetic, concerted effort must be continued by today's British theatre practitioners, both black and white, for a nuanced range of black British voices to become commonplace on the British theatre menu.

---

[149] Francis James, 'A Tour de Farce by Top Class Group', *Kilburn Times*, 9 January 1997, 17.
[150] John Thaxter, 'A Meaty and Happy Revival', *Stage,* 9 January 1997, 12.

CHAPTER 5
THE BLACK SOUTH

Refusing exclusion from the American genre

It is the American plays that make up the smallest proportion of the company's work during the Brewster era. There were three productions: Ntozke Shange's *The Love Space Demands*, Dr Endesha Ida Mae Holland's *From the Mississippi Delta* and Pearl Cleage's *Flyin' West*. These productions were all written by black American women. They focus on black female characters specifically, whilst exploring the plight of black people generally. Each play requires the black British actors to use an American accent, as Talawa's productions illustrate how aspects of black American and black British life are connected.

Whilst the plays have obvious links, Brewster wanted to ensure that those she contracted to direct, as well as those that came after her, sought to push the company forward. She explains, 'Whoever takes over from me should expand and not marginalize the company. As a black company, if we produce too much of the same thing, we have had it, it becomes too difficult to be seen for anything else.'[1] Igweonu highlights Brewster's view: 'it is worth noting that while these American plays address issues from a female perspective, Brewster did not necessarily see their production by Talawa as being defined by feminism.'[2] Lizbeth Goodman goes further and explains that the promotion of a feminist agenda was not Brewster's main aim in doing the work.[3] Brewster's strategic goal for working in this genre was rather to broaden Talawa's performance repertoire.

Brewster's work expanded the two groups of American theatre that have been a common staple on the British stage throughout the twentieth and

---

[1] Yvonne Brewster, Personal Interview by David Johnson, London, 14 March 2000.
[2] Igweonu, 'Talawa', 252.
[3] Lizbeth Goodman, *Contemporary Feminist Theatres: To Each Her Own* (London: Routledge, 1993), 150.

the first two decades of the twenty-first centuries. The first group is made up of contemporary American classics produced by internationally renowned American writers in the last seventy years. These include Tennessee Williams (1911–83), Arthur Miller (1915–2005), Edward Albee (1928–2016) and David Mamet (b. 1947). Their work remains a regular feature of the British stage. This is seen in the West End of London, across the regions on the fringe circuit, as well as in amateur theatre. Although their writing is varied, covers universal themes and takes place where black people are prominent, black lives do not feature in these plays.

Williams's play *The Glass Menagerie* (1945) was first performed at London's Haymarket Theatre on 28 July 1948. His later plays *A Street Car Named Desire* (1947) and *Cat on a Hot Tin Roof* (1955), the latter winning the Pulitzer Prize in the same year, have also been continually performed in London since their creation. His 1961 play *Night of the Iguana* was performed in London at the Noel Coward Theatre throughout summer 2019. Williams's work depicts white American southern life.

Having an equally successful career at the same time was fellow American Arthur Miller. The Miller plays that boast an extensive life on the British stage include *All My Sons* (1947), *Death of a Salesman* (1949), also the 1949 Pulitzer Prize winner, *The Crucible* (1953) and *A View From The Bridge* (1955). *All My Sons* was performed at London's Old Vic theatre as recently as June 2019. Miller's work presents moral issues for his characters to work through. The issues often highlight a past wrongdoing which the characters are forced to deal with in the course of the play.

The third of the American writers is Edward Albee, perhaps best known for his plays *Who's Afraid of Virginia Woolf?* (1962) and *A Delicate Balance* (1964). In 1967 *A Delicate Balance* won the Pulitzer Prize. A production of *Who's Afraid of Virginia Woolf?* was staged in London in May 2017 at the Harold Pinter theatre. Albee's *The Goat, Or Who Is Sylvia?* was also a feature of the London stage in 2017 at the Theatre Royal, Haymarket. Albee's work explores and attacks the 'contentment' of middle class suburban America, corruption and life in theatre.

In 1976 Mamet produced three Off-Off Broadway plays: *Duck Variations, Sexual Perversity in Chicago* and *American Buffalo*. This was followed by *The Woods* (1977), *Edmund* (1982) and *Glengarry Glen Ross* (1984), also the 1984 Pulitzer Prize winner. Mamet is a prolific writer and his work is routinely performed on the British stage. A production of *Glengarry Glen Ross* was performed at London's Playhouse Theatre from 2017 to 2018.

Mamet's work is appreciated for his specific language use and his characters' mixture of nerve and obsession.

American playwrights have found a second niche on the British stage in musical theatre. This theatrical form has had an active life on the London stage throughout the last century.[4] This is seen in *A Trip to Coontown* (1898), *Clorindy, the Origin of the Cakewalk* (1898), *In Dahomey* (1903), *Show Boat* (1927) and *Porgy and Bess* (1935). This musical genre often depicted black life through a mammy-style minstrel lens that concentrated on white inventions of black stereotypes. Despite depicting blacks as servile non-thinkers the work was hugely popular with British audiences.[5]

In 1975 British musical theatre saw an important addition in this domain with the two African productions *Ipi Tombi* and *Kwa Zulu*.[6] Although this work came from Africa and did not depict any aspect of black British life, by the nature of its existence it created a non-American black presence in mainstream British theatre.

In the last forty-five years popular American television shows and films have experienced a successful transformation to the format of musical theatre. These have attracted large audiences with production runs lasting several years. Representing this phenomenon are the following American musicals which were being performed in London during 2000: *Annie* (1970), *The Wiz* (1975), *Grease* (1978), *The Little Shop of Horrors* (1982), *Beauty and The Beast* (1993), *Fame* (1994), *Bugsy Malone* (1997), *The Lion King* (1997), *Saturday Night Fever* (1998) and *Titanic* (1997).

None of this work deals with any aspect of black life with the exception perhaps of *The Wiz*, a contemporary performance of the *Wizard of Oz* (1903) featuring an all-black cast. This century, musicals have featured specific black artists or white artists who worked predominantly with black artists. These include *Thriller* (2007) about Michael Jackson, *Motown* (2013) about Berry Gordy and his Motown acts, *Dream Girls* about Diana Ross and the Supremes (1981 and 2018), *Beautiful* (2015) about Carole King and featuring the black artists she worked with, and *Tina* (2018) about Tina Turner. They all show how entertaining black people are in that singing and

---

[4]Stanley Green, *Encyclopaedia of the Musical* (London: Cassell and Company Limited, 1976).
[5]Brian Rust, *London Musical Shows on Record 1897-1976* (Middlesex: General Gramophone Publications Ltd, 1977), 43.
[6]Ibid., 145 and 159 respectively: *Ipi Tombi*, Her Majesty's Theatre, 19 November 1975, *Kwa Zulu*, New London Theatre, 24 July 1975, transferred to Piccadilly Theatre, 23 September 1975.

dancing sort of way. Brewster's work offered British audiences something new. Working in this genre allowed her to tap into the longer-established history of black writing in America and add to the creation of a wide body of black theatrical performance in Britain.

The Love Space Demands

Between 1 and 31 October 1992 Talawa presented its tenth show and first American work with a production of Ntozake Shange's *The Love Space Demands* at the Cochrane Theatre, London. The piece, which discusses the writer's black American female perspective on sex, love and relationships, was part of the launch of the C. L. R. James Institute. It was also performed to commemorate James's ninetieth birthday. It was fitting that Shange's work was used for the occasion as James held her in high regard: 'I have read no finer modern poet.'[7] Brewster also intended her production to 'exhibit and celebrate the wealth of creative talent now at ease with itself, after decades of frustration through having no sense of belonging'.[8]

Piecing it together: The structure of the work

The structure of Talawa's performance was set by the text. *The Love Space Demands*, called a 'choreopoem', is a series of poems loosely linked by their theme and style to create a sequence of short performance pieces. Each piece flows into the next to form a single longer performance. Shange constructed this format as she felt it best suited her purpose of creating poetry that was specifically written for performance.[9] Shange describes *The Love Space Demands* as 'A collage of experience, the poems and monologues are real questions I have asked and the sharp edges of the answers'.[10]

Like Teer's earlier decision to evolve a black art standard, Shange wanted to create her own work that expressed what she wanted to say, how she

---

[7] Talawa's production archives for *The Love Space Demand*s, publicity file and production flyer.
[8] Ibid.
[9] Carole Woddis, 'Enuf Said', *What's On in London*, 30 September–7 October 1992, 13.
[10] Shange describes her work in the production flyer.

wanted to say it. Brewster directed the poem in the order set by Shange in its three equal sections as outlined below:

Section One:

Devotion to one lover or another.

Serial Monogamy.

Intermittent Celibacy.

Section Two:

A third generation geechee myth for yr birthday.

Male English as a second language.

If I go all the way without you where would I go?

Section Three:

Loosening strings or give me an 'A'.

Open up/this is the police.

Crack Annie.[11]

This uniformity of structure gave the piece a balance that was drawn in stark contrast to the stream of consciousness effect delivered by Jean Binta Breeze in the leading role. When Brewster asked Shange for the rights to the play, she also explained that she wanted Breeze to do it. She was warned against casting Breeze due to her schizophrenia and for being unreliable. Brewster knew she would have to accept Breeze's rituals, as she had done years before, 'of praying to Gods and sprinkling white rum' in her dressing room before each performance.[12] Brewster remained undeterred in her decision to cast Breeze for two reasons: 'She's a wonderful example of someone who can overcome things like that in life' and 'Once she came on stage, you just believed her'.[13] Shange's structure enabled Brewster to divide each piece with a musical interlude. This allowed the company to run the entire production with no interval. This directional strategy maintained the experimental nature, intensity and roller-coaster feel of the piece.

---

[11] Each title is written as it appears in the production programme for the show. Shange, however, does not use any capital letters for her titles in the script.
[12] Brewster Interview, 26 November 2018.
[13] Brewster Interview, 31 October 2014.

Talawa Theatre Company

Oral language of performance: Speaking from her heart

Although Shange does not give a specific direction as to how the text should be spoken, the text itself indicates how the play should sound. The attempt to clarify the sound of the work is achieved by Shange's writing semi-phonetically. Words that would normally end in 'ing' are shown as ending with 'in', as in askin', stoppin', demandin'. Shange frequently uses her own spelling of the following words: 'About' is written as 'abt' or 'bout', 'because' as 'cuz', 'could' as 'cd', 'full of' as 'fulla', 'mother fuckers' as 'muthafuckahs', 'wouldn't' as 'wdn't', and 'your' as 'yr'.

Additionally, the writer chooses not to use any capital letters. Her work benefits from three kinds of punctuation only: question marks, speech marks and a sign written as / which indicates a comma. The majority of the language of the script remains, however, in 'standard American English'. Shange's written speech clearly influenced the work of later writers. Amongst these are Ketih Antar Mason who punctuates similarly and penned his own choreopoem, *For Black Boys Who Have Considered Homicide When The Streets Were Too Much* (1982). His title is reminiscent of Shange's earlier work *For Colored Girls Who Considered Suicide When The Rainbow Is Enuf* (1975). Shange's abbreviated language is also a forerunner to internationally used text speech.

Shange's choice of written language becomes an antilanguage form as it rejects 'standard American English' and cultural norms. She does not want her characters to aspire to the ways of affluent American life that they are excluded from. This linguistic specificity meant the success of the production hinged on Breeze's ability to find an appropriate range of language and voices for her characters that would work with Talawa's audience. Brewster explains, 'The language was determined by Breeze. I didn't have to do any work. Jean and the cast worked through the octaves of the piece by discussion. My job was to give it an even keel.'[14]

Breeze had no difficulty producing two American accents. Her accuracy is attributed to the fact that she lived and worked in America for many years. For the first poem, 'devotion to one lover or another', Breeze's character's accent is that of the deep American south. For the second piece, 'serial monogamy', the accent of the upper middle class nondescript strata of American executive society is used. Breeze's use

---

[14]Yvonne Brewster, Personal Interview by David Johnson, London, 6 January 1997.

of multiple accents highlights Talawa's presentation of verbal repertoire as well as the ease with which Talawa's performers often work with an American accent.

In the piece 'open up/this is the police', Breeze speaks Spanish with conviction and accuracy of accent. This use of Spanish further diversifies Talawa's linguistic dexterity whilst highlighting Breeze's remarkable talent. Unlike the majority of Talawa's work, with *The Love Space Demands* the voices of the performance have a dual status when compared to the company's general language use at that time. On one level, the status of American English and Spanish is higher than the Caribbean language forms used in Talawa's Caribbean plays. On another level, their status is lessened because they are black American English and working class Spanish speech forms.

Some of the Spanish provided by Shange's text was omitted in favour of introducing a Caribbean blackness to the language through Breeze's use of her native Jamaican monolingual patois. Here Breeze's fourth speech style is demonstrated intermittently with the same ease with which she performed the entire poem. This was a strategic artistic decision that would aim Breeze's character's language use at Talawa's black British audience.

The violent language of the work is seen in the use of words that have become a normal part of working class black American life. Whilst words such as 'niggah', as seen in 'a third generation geechee myth for yr birthday' and 'muthafucka' in 'intermittent celibacy' are part of everyday speech in some American communities, they have a greater impact on black British audiences. This language is encountered less on the British stage than in British society generally and illustrates Brewster's preparedness to break new linguistic boundaries for Talawa and black British theatre generally. This is further demonstrated by the sexual language of *The Love Space Demands*.

Breeze interprets the sexuality of the poems to deliver a range of sexual voices. There is the sensual sexual voice she offers in her performance of 'devotion to one lover or another' where talk is of flowers, their petals and erotic baths. Breeze introduces the sexual voice of flirtation with 'serial monogamy', as she imagines her various lovers. She then produces a sexual voice laced in animal passion in 'intermittent celibacy', to demonstrate the losing of one's virginity. This voice is continued in 'mesl (male english as a second language): in defence of bilingualism'.

In 'mesl', Breeze's character observes a group of men watching baseball. She believes they reach a collective state of orgasm due to their excitement of the game and the language they hear when listening to it. Breeze finds a passionately sexual voice that demonstrates how her character achieves sexual fulfilment, when she creates her own game out of being neglected by a man addicted to sport. She makes herself the centre of the game enjoying all the sexual pleasure she reads into it, and ends the piece with a heavy orgasmic sigh. Breeze's character's pleasure and indeed her presence go entirely unnoticed by her partner who is part of the male group watching the game.

It is Breeze's performance in 'crack annie' that is the most sexually violent. The references to 'new pussy' and the use of sexual language to describe the horror of child abuse introduce an uncommon voice to Talawa's audience. Black British theatre-going audiences of shows such as the Oliver Samuels monolingual patois-speaking popular variety were familiar with slapstick sexual language in performance. The sexual language and voices Breeze finds for her characters in *The Love Space Demands* are however not gratuitous. Since Breeze's performance in 1992, the open debate on sex, sexual language, sexual acts, gender issues and child abuse has been commonplace in all the mainstream media. Perhaps it was work like Talawa's, in unashamedly telling horrific personal stories, that also inadvertently opened up the debate in the ensuing decades.

Non-spoken performance vocabulary: The psyche and dancing the dialogue

In Talawa's earlier productions music was generally used in the following three ways: incidental music, music as a direct part of the background action where accompanying a dance, or music as a central aspect of a performance where the protagonist or cast sing as part of the action.

In *The Love Space Demands* the company uses music in a less obvious and more intense way. It is used throughout the performance to symbolize the psyche of Breeze's characters, or other characters around them. Breeze's characters' internal and outer battles are developed through their relationships with the men they confront and whose answers they coax through the three male musicians playing the double bass, the drums and the flute. The responses that Breeze's characters imagine the musicians give them are not specific, but their musical tone and Breeze's characters' further responses give the audience a clear indication of the progression of each debate.

Brewster uses the musical instruments for more than the music they provide, as they act momentarily as symbols of the men Breeze's characters feel they have been let down by. This is seen in 'loosening strings or give me an "A"' where Breeze's character describes a sexual experience through her interaction with both the double bass player and the dancer. Breeze's character is free to move around her sexual partner in the piece, the double bass. The double bass player does not have the same freedom of movement. He responds to her through his music whilst the male dancer represents him physically in the background. The instruments and their music then become part of the dance and movement.

Brewster further uses dance and movement to explore and express the emotions of Breeze's characters. The two dancers Prince Morgan and Andrea Whiting, as choreographed by Greta Mendez, appear throughout the piece and give a physical dimension to the characters' monologues. At times the choreography simply serves to communicate the literal story being told.

In the solo pieces this is seen in 'devotion to one lover or another' where the dance reflects the bathing ritual that Breeze's character discusses. In 'intermittent celibacy' the female dancer presents Breeze's character's desire for sex. Her solo reflects the isolation that Breeze's character feels in not being able to find a sex partner. In 'a third generation geechee myth for yr birthday', the female dancer's solo interprets Breeze's character's childbirth theme. The same technique is used effectively for both dancers in 'serial monogamy' where they act the flirtation scene described by Breeze's character, and in 'if i go all the way without you where would i go?' where togetherness and sexual energy are interpreted.

The choreography is also used to predict the spoken words. The effect is one of surprise and echo. The surprise element is in the fact that what is said does not immediately match the change in mood as performed by the dancers. Usually Breeze's character is passive whilst the dance has progressed into a more lively stage of the argument. The echo is experienced when Breeze's character, in telling her tale, describes the action that the audience has already seen interpreted through dance.

This is seen in 'mesl (male english as a second language): in defense of bilingualism' where Breeze's character's description of her game follows the movement of the dancers. Through the dancers, the audience is made aware that her game is an amalgamation of the games that keep her partner away from her. The dancers reveal how the new game revolves around Breeze's character's sexual fantasies and ultimate orgasm, before we hear her version of it.

Brewster employs the same technique to disturbing effect in 'crack annie'. Whilst Breeze's character expresses confusion and tries to explain her reason for allowing the events that happened, the dancers perform the child rape scene before Breeze's character can describe it. Breeze's character's speech is a form of filling in the gaps as we learn that the victim is her daughter, used for sex by Breeze's character's drug-pusher.

The use of music, dance and movement mirror each other throughout the performance. The seriousness of the issues then is increased by being interpreted in multiple art forms. Whilst the audience was presented with many modern sexual and violent questions, was Talawa's show also predicting what society was going to become in later decades, or simply holding up a mirror to what it already was, at a time when victim's voices did not matter? Kate Bassett describes the work:

> Jean 'Binta' Breeze oozes ease and energy, embracing poetry, dance and music with brilliant laid back panache. Her monologue is a string of Ntozake Shange's poems on sex and affection: a radical and outspoken work ('niggers' and 'new pussy') ranging from the comic sketches on 'serial monogamy' to a painful poem on child sexual abuse.[15]

When Talawa performed *The Love Space Demands*, the company was six years old. Perhaps the choice to do the work at that point reflected an innocent desire to shock and rebel, or possibly it was a case of the black American theatrical sister showing her reality to her British sibling, or maybe neither. What the work clearly showed, however, is that life is often uncompromisingly harsh if you are American, poor, female and black. It also illustrated that under Brewster, Talawa was not going to be a staunch black theatre company performing for a black middle class audience that did not want to be offended. Brewster had taken a risk with this creative departure and the mainstream reviews proved that her decision was appreciated.

---

[15]Kate Bassett, 'The Love Space Demands', *City Limits*, 15–22 October 1992. No page number available.

All of the mainstream press found something positive to say about Talawa's production. Michael Billington comments, 'I'm not sure how to describe Ntozake Shange's *The Love Space Demands*, presented by Talawa, but it's certainly impressive.'[16] Bassett is equally enthusiastic: 'the choreography rises to excellence (capes fluttering like falling petals and a sexual deflowering powerfully symbolised by a foot forced through a skirt) ... It's an interesting artistic format rarely seen in the UK, and Talawa are well worth a look.'[17] Nick Curtis states, 'it's a remarkable, lyrical experience of live poetry.'[18] Additionally, Jean Breeze's performance is heralded as a success in every review. Her performance is described as 'mesmerising',[19] and Gould suggests 'Jean "Binta" Breeze must surely be one of the more fascinating people to have graced the stage at Talawa's Cochrane Theatre'.[20] Brewster's gamble on Breeze had paid off.

The critical response illustrated that in spite of the character's very specific gender, race and life situation, the work had a much wider appeal. Director and screenwriter Gina Prince Bythewood comments on her film *The Secret Life of Bees* (2008), starring Queen Latifa, Alicia Keys, Jennifer Hudson and Sophie Okonedo: 'Why are we narrowing the audience because up on screen there's black women? ... the moment you put black characters in a film it becomes not universal and that's just not true.'[21] Brewster had proven that in theatre, where the work works, the appeal will be wide and at least appreciated, even if not fully understood. For Brewster, Shange's response to the production also gave her confidence that the show had been a success. The writer arrived at the theatre on the opening night in a limousine, pink dress and shiny shoes. After the show, she agreed that Talawa's production brought out elements of the play that she had not previously seen.[22]

Brewster's production received the kind of general audience reaction that Teer wanted to experience for herself in theatre. Teer was explicit in her desire to 'attend a theatre where she could see plays that validated her

---

[16] Michael Billington, 'The Love Space Demands', *Guardian*, 7 October 1992, 36.
[17] Bassett, 'The Love Space Demands'.
[18] Nick Curtis, 'The Love Space Demands', *Independent*, 7 October 1992, 23.
[19] Anon, 'The Love Space Demands', *Mail on Sunday*, 11 October 1992, 40.
[20] Helen Gould, 'Life's a Breeze for Binta', *Stage*, 1 October 1992, 6.
[21] *Black Hollywood, They've Got to Have Us: Black Is the New Hollywood* (2018), [TV programme] BBC1, 27 October.
[22] Brewster Interview, 26 November 2018.

Talawa Theatre Company

as a black woman and left her feeling exhilarated'.[23] Talawa's production of *The Love Space Demands* illustrated that whilst some could come out validated, everyone could feel exhilarated by the quality of the work. As well as the success of the performance, the rebellious nature of the work set a precedent for the company's American plays. This is demonstrated in Talawa's next American production, *From the Mississippi Delta*.

From the Mississippi Delta

Between 1 April and 1 May 1993 Talawa presented its thirteenth production in total and second American work, with its run of Dr Endesha Ida Mae Holland's *From the Mississippi Delta* at the Cochrane Theatre, London and the Contact Theatre, Manchester, directed by Annie Castledine. The play tells the true story of how Holland was raped as a child, turned to stealing and prostitution to earn a living, and then became a civil rights activist. In the process, she turned her life around, earned a doctorate and become a celebrated writer. The play depicts the struggles of black lives in American society from the 1940s, where they had and were expected to be nothing. Holland was the exception to that rule.

Oral language of performance: Delta voices

The language of the script of *From the Mississippi Delta*, like that of *The Love Space Demands*, reflects the writer's attempt to present a form of American speech that suggests how her script should be spoken. It is the voice of the black American south. The script is generally written in 'standard American English' with American phraseology and some southern American spellings. The pronunciation of the black south is highlighted by the repeated use of phonetic spellings in the text. Commonly used are 'Dat' for 'That', 'Dis' for 'This', 'Wit' for 'With', 'Den' for 'Then', 'bout' for 'about', 'Chilluns' for 'Children', 'Aint' for 'Aunt', 'Nawth' for 'North', 'Useta' for 'Used to', 'Wimmens' for 'Women', 'Moe' for 'More', 'Gie' for 'Give' and 'Kin' for 'Can'.

No attempt was made to change any aspect of the language and Castledine employed dialect coach Charmion Hoare to give ten workshops to her cast. To help her audience with the language, Castledine took the step of

---

[23]Thomas, 'Barbara Ann Teer: From Holistic Training to Liberating Rituals', 347.

providing a glossary in the production programme. This step had not been taken with Talawa's earlier African, American or Caribbean productions.

It was because of the language of her script that Holland encountered problems in putting on the production in America. Simi Horwitz points out that Dr Holland's work 'Did not fare well with several well-known black actresses',[24] and quotes Holland: 'They refused to even consider the play because of the black dialect, they did not want to be identified with it.'[25] They feared career stigmatization. That was then.

In America where the pinnacle of acting success may be measured by a performer's celebrity in Hollywood's film industry, there was a notable lack of black performers at the time of Castledine's Talawa production. This changed considerably between 2016 and 2019. The suggestion that black American performers aiming to get to Hollywood are held back by the black roles they play, and by extension the black language that they use, was less obvious in this three year time frame than when Holland was turned down by black American actresses.

Those that have bucked the trend include Mahershala Ali, who made history when he became, after Denzel Washington, only the second black actor to win more than one Oscar. Ali won the Oscar for best supporting actor for his portrayal of Juan, a Cuban drug dealer in *Moonlight* (2016). As Juan, Ali used black American speech. Similarly using black American speech was black Briton Naomie Harris, playing a drug addict, also in *Moonlight* (2016). She was nominated for the Golden Globe, Bafta and Oscar for best supporting actress for her efforts.

Both winners of the Oscar in the supporting actor category in 2019 were black Americans. Regina King won best supporting actress for her portrayal of working class black American Sharon Rivers in *If Beale Street Could Talk* (2018). Ali won best supporting actor for his portrayal of Don Shirley in *Green Book* (2018). Ali's Shirley acts in a way that Americans arguably perceive to be white: he plays the piano, he does not eat fried chicken and he speaks 'standard American English'. A previous portrayal as a drug dealer had not been used against him, or was that because he won an Oscar for it?

Whilst black American speech is less of a career hindrance than it was in 1993, the work of Hollywood's most celebrated contemporary black

---

[24]Simi Horwitz, 'From Prostitute to Playwright: The Life and Times of Dr. Endesha Ida Mae Holland', *Theatre Week*, 16–22 March 1992, 24–8.
[25]Ibid.

performers illustrates that where black performers are used in Hollywood films, it is rarely because they are simply the best performers for the parts. The fact that they are black is often relevant to the roles. This fact may still encourage black performers who wish to work in the mainstream to steer away from work that uses 'black accents' or 'black characterization'.

In Britain a parallel can be drawn with the potential theatrical marginalization of black British performers. Once seen in black work using a 'black voice', black actors in Britain run the risk of being viewed as black actors only suitable for such roles, rather than as an actor who appeared in a particular production. There is perhaps less stigma, however, where they use a black American voice as its sound is not representative of any area of British society. There is currently a growing list of black Britons who have reached star status both in Britain and America by playing the widest possible range of characters. These include John Boyega, Idris Elba, David Harewood, Naomie Harris, Marianne Jean Baptiste, Daniel Kaluuya, Thandie Newton, Sophie Okonedo, David Oyelowo and Antonia Thomas. Through their work, performing the appropriate speech of a character is proving not to be the career barrier it once was.

A cappella actresses: The performances

The power of Talawa's performance of *From the Mississippi Delta* comes from the a cappella voices of the three performers, who swop roles throughout the piece to recount the life experiences of Dr Endesha Ida Mae Holland.

Pauline Black

Black, most famous for being the lead singer in her chart topping British group Selecter (1979–81), here generally plays Aint Baby, Dr Endesha Ida Mae's mother. Black's performance was outstanding specifically for its linguistic accuracy. Her oral precision is perhaps explained by her general unassuming attitude to developing a character. In relation to creating Caribbean roles, Black points out: 'Because I don't have that tradition of the Caribbean, have not grown up in a West Indian family, when I do a West Indian play I have to approach that play afresh as I would if I were trying to be a Russian in a Chekhov play.'[26]

---

[26]Rees, *Fringe First*, 143.

The Black South

Black's accurate use of American language once again serves to highlight the verbal repertoire of Talawa's black British performers in this area. As Black's natural speaking voice is recognizable for its 'standard English' and her singing voice for its unique quality, her American accent in this production appears all the more impressive, as it has no link with the voices that she is known for.

Black's unquestionable talent gives rise to questions as to why she is not a major theatrical player in mainstream British theatre. Along with the myth of there not being enough black parts when she emerged, was Black too light-skinned for white directors who wanted what they saw as a 'real' black actress in their shows? Perhaps in the past her colour precluded her from leading lady roles on the British stage, as it may now for older female characters, or maybe once younger actresses of a similar hue became prominent – Sophie Okinedo, Tandie Newton and Naomie Harris – unimaginative producers could not fit them all in.

Black's refusal to become marginalized by limiting herself to black culturally specific work, along with the fact that she is not prepared to accept every part that she is offered, may also have contributed, along with her successful singing career, to her being seen less in mainstream acting roles than her talent deserves. As for her decision to star in *From the Mississippi Delta*, she explains, 'I like the piece because it gives a very positive image of black people. As long as there are plays around like this I will want to do more.'[27]

Joy Richardson

After Black's introduction to the protagonist Talawa's audience is further introduced to her as an eleven-year-old through the performance of Joy Richardson. Richardson's overall performance wavers due to her struggle to find the correct voice. This causes a movement from the theatrical reality created by the performers who get the voice right, to the more familiar sound of Richardson's South London accent. She is given due credit for her performance: 'Joy Richardson was able to turn a nasty cough into a character, but didn't quite capture the Southern dialect.'[28]

This was an exceptional learning experience for Richardson, sandwiched between two of Britain's leading black female theatre performers of the

---

[27] Michael Owen, 'America, Japan - and Kilburn', *Evening Standard*, 2 April 1993, 26.
[28] Winsome Hines, 'From the Mississippi Delta', *Voice*, 20 April 1993, 27.

day. It was the kind of opportunity that all performers need to further develop. As this chance was rarely available to black performers at the time, Richardson's lucky break also carried with it the burden of accurate black representation. A white actress at this juncture in her career could reasonably use this type of early professional work to focus on honing her craft. Richardson and other black performers, both then and currently, never have this 'luxury' due to the irregularity with which black performers are seen on the British stage in leading roles.

Despite the growing numbers of successful black British actors in the past two decades, many still suffer the same burden of representation as Richardson did in 1993. Of the three actresses in the production, only Richardson had benefited from British drama school training. The fact that she had most difficulty producing the Southern American accent, despite her three-year course, points to the role that Talawa plays in developing black British performers. The company offers them a professional platform to work in and create a range of black characters.

Josette Bushell-Mingo

We first meet Bushell-Mingo when she explains how Aint Baby became the second lady doctor. With each role she adopts and through the range of voices she uses for her varied characters, her American accent is consistently credible. Like Black, Bushell-Mingo was able to reveal her verbal repertoire by giving each character its own easily identifiable sound. Whilst Brewster had begged Castledine to direct the show, Castledine agreed that she would only do it if she could get Bushell-Mingo.[29]

Bushell-Mingo performs almost every character that features in Aint Baby's life, as well as Aint Baby herself. She plays a variety of male characters throughout the performance, including the drunk mourner at Aint Baby's funeral. From the unexaggerated deep voice she uses and the doddering hooked stance she adopts, the audience is immediately able to define the obvious outer characteristics of this man. Her performance of his incomprehensible speech and total drunkenness, which causes him to fall into Aint Baby's grave, steal the attention from anything else that is happening on stage.

---

[29] Brewster Interview, 26 November 2018.

Bushell-Mingo, like Black, demonstrates a unique ability to capture her audience. Despite the fact that many of the male characters she plays are negative because of their involvement with drugs and crime, the accuracy of her oral and physical performance generally focuses the audience on the immediate message that Holland is giving through her character, rather than stoking anger at seeing black men portrayed in a negative way. Often her portrayal uses their tragedy to provide comedy. The tragedy that Bushell-Mingo's drunken old man has turned to blurring his reality with alcohol, although understood, is lessened by her comic presentation of him. Whilst highlighting his tragedy, Bushell-Mingo's comic approach endears him to Talawa's audience. The fact that she is a woman removes the audience from some of the tragedy of the male characters she presents. As a black woman she is not offended by them, but is rather part of them with all their faults and idiosyncrasies. Bushell-Mingo's skill as a performer is as equal an aspect of Talawa's audience's appreciation as is the despair of the situation that she has performed.

Critical reception

Talawa's production under Castledine's direction received nominations for the *Manchester Evening News* award for best production, along with nominations for best actress for both Pauline Black and Josette Bushell-Mingo. Bushell-Mingo won the award. Additionally, every review of the production was positive thus marking the piece as one of Talawa's major successes. Carole Woodis comments:

> This, I would venture to say is the play which and the production that should at last put Yvonne Brewster's Cochrane theatre on the map . . . This is not just a play for these performers it is also about their lives and when they inhabit Ida Mae's world as they do here, they are transformed by it. So too, are we. An event not to be missed – and this time I really mean it.[30]

Woddis's comment suggests that the mainstream had been waiting for Talawa to prove it deserved its West End home. It also illustrates what the mainstream thought black theatre should be at that time. At this juncture,

---

[30] Carole Woddis, 'Joyful Blues: From the Mississippi Delta, Cochrane', *What's On in London*, 14–21 April 1993, 47.

her positive review was more valuable than she may have intended, due to the insecurity that Talawa was facing with questions over the renewal of its lease, and continued residency at the Cochrane.

Louise Stafford Charles contributes to the enthusiastic write-ups with: 'This is a production which can only go to strengthen the already excellent and deserved reputation which Talawa holds.'[31] Deborah McLauchlan adds, 'I will say that if you never go to the theatre, see this anyway; if you can't afford it, save up; and if you haven't got the time, cancel something else.'[32] McLauchlan's comment is backed in almost identical sentiment by Joy Morgan: 'Even if you are not a regular theatre-goer, you must make an exception for this latest Talawa Theatre production.'[33] Morgan continues with her support for the production: 'The three actresses give a passionate performance of each phase of Holland's life and throw themselves into their roles with jubilation and complete dedication. Their individual strengths and talents work in perfect balance and the production flows with a natural ease.'[34]

Across a full range of critics the three black British female performers were given solid recognition for the artistic quality of their work. Helen Adkins sums up the achievement: 'Just when there seems to be too much to be told in too little time, when the sheer number of characters runs the risk of incoherence the thread is always picked up by the extraordinary performances of Pauline Black, Josette Bushell Mingo and Joy Richardson.'[35] Overall, this sent a positive message to black theatre practitioners that wider British theatre accepts some kinds of black British theatre in its mainstream.

Three black British women had very successfully performed the life of a black American woman. American director and actor Kasi Lemmons believes that playing American blacks is less challenging for the British to do, without having experienced American slavery, than for the black Americans to play themselves, having survived it. She explains, 'It is somehow easier both for the performer and for the audience, taking out that specific genetic component.'[36] Is that genetic component in black Britons really so different?

---

[31]Louise Stafford Charles, 'Through Life's Compelling Journey', *Stage*, 6 May 1993, 11.
[32]Deborah McLauchlan, 'From the Mississippi Delta', *City Life Manchester*, 12 May 1993, 37.
[33]Joy Morgan, 'From the Mississippi Delta', *Weekly Journal*, 15 April 1993, 11.
[34]Ibid.
[35]Helen Adkins, 'Sweet Humour Out of Bitter Horrors', *Tribune*, 16 April 1993, 9.
[36]*Black Hollywood*, BBC1, 27 October 2018.

The two American productions Talawa had performed up until this point received the best reception from the critics. The issues and language of Talawa's other styles of work, whilst serving an important purpose, were not as appealing to theatre critics as to Talawa's audience. Were the favourable reviews a result of the critics having a better understanding of the genre, as American culture has a firm place in British theatre and on British television? Or was it because the critics found there was less of a language barrier than with the Caribbean plays? Could the critics simply have felt able to write freely because the work was American and did not exclusively belong to Talawa culturally? Whatever the answer, at least part of it lies in the fact that they enjoyed the show on every artistic level.

Talawa's production of Holland's earthy tale was not selected for shock value. This is in contrast to the way Holland introduced herself to new students at the start of each academic semester: 'I'm from Greenwood Mississippi. I'm an ex-whore and an ex-thief. My mama ran the whorehouse. My brothers were two town drunks.'[37] Brewster's reasons for having the production staged by Talawa were much more simple: 'This is a good play and will entertain our audience whilst giving some insight into an interesting black American life; people's lives can be interesting.'[38]

Along with the interesting life that the show presented, the overt discussion of sex and violence and the plight of blacks attempting to take a fighting stance against white American society gave Talawa, at least momentarily, a more feisty and politically militant identity than some of its previous Caribbean productions may have done. This may well have been a by-product of wider mainstream understanding and engagement with the piece. Although the production reflected the black situation in America, the response to the show suggests that Brewster was correct to believe that black British theatre was an appropriate forum for this straightforward language and the political issues the play presented.

Talawa's success with this production demonstrates the company's continued determination to take risks and move black theatre into the mainstream and forefront of theatre in Britain. In Horwitz's article cited above, Holland states, 'When I was growing up I never even knew a black

---

[37] Horwitz, 'From Prostitute to Playwright', 28.
[38] Yvonne Brewster, Personal Interview by David Johnson, London, 26 April 1996.

person had ever written a book.'[39] At the time of the performance, for many black Britons, Talawa was the first they would see of established black British theatre. Talawa then made a significant impact in the slow erosion of the possibility of British blacks being able to ever remember a time when quality black theatre did not exist in Britain.

Flyin' West

Talawa's third American play and twenty-third production in total was the company's performance of Pearle Cleage's *Flyin' West*. The play ran from 5 to 28 June 1997 at London's Drill Hall. Prior to the abolition of slavery in America in 1865, Kansas had officially become a free state in 1861. This was a safer place for black people to be and begin a new life. *Flyin' West*, set in the all black town of Nicodemus Kansas in the autumn of 1898, tells a story of black pioneer life on the western frontier. A light is shone on the tough existence of black women and the advantage of being mixed race. Brewster saw directing the production as a 'reclamation exercise'.[40] Stories of cowboys and Indians had routinely omitted the black cowboys of Kansas.

When Brewster met Cleage in North Carolina, whilst she was on a biannual lecturing tour speaking on the matriarch in Caribbean theatre, she was surprised by Cleage's appearance: she looked 'almost white'.[41] After Cleage confirmed the correct pronunciation of her name and further discussion followed, Brewster was struck again: 'She is the blackest person I've ever met. In America, one drop [of black blood] and that's enough.'[42] Whilst they talked about *Flyin' West*, Brewster confirmed she knew that there were many black cowboys in 1898 Kansas.[43] This heritage fact would be new to much of her audience. Brewster would pass on many more such facts through her production of the play written by the blackest white-looking person she had ever encountered.

---

[39] Horwitz, 'From Prostitute to Playwright', 27.
[40] Brewster Interview, 26 November 2018.
[41] Brewster Interview, 31 October 2014.
[42] Brewster Interview, 26 November 2018.
[43] Ibid.

The Black South

We need heritage facts: Research package and the company's response to it

Having followed Brewster's creative process with her cast, as performance researcher for *Beef, No Chicken* (1997), it was clear how her explanations of the background to the text and of the text itself enhanced both the rehearsal process, as well as the work the cast subsequently produced. With this in mind, I suggested the *Flyin' West* cast should be given a research package along with their script prior to rehearsals. Brewster kindly left this in my hands.

The pre-production research process began with a meeting between Brewster and myself on 1 March 1997. The aim was to discuss the themes in the play and Brewster's vision of how they would impact Talawa's audience. Brewster's main concern was that her audience should see the strength of the four black female protagonists. She explains, 'When black people here complain about how hard life is they don't know what they're talking about. These women had to do everything men did and still find time to raise their families.'[44] Her intention then was to use theatre didactically and politically, and encourage black women in Britain to see themselves as able to better any situation that they find themselves in. This notion echoed Brewster's entire working life.

The focus on black female characters would highlight the plight and resourcefulness of these individuals. Their resilience would be held up as examples to Talawa's audience. Whilst the play and Talawa's performance of it show black men and women pitted against each other, both highlight the disastrous circumstances of the black men in these women's lives. Only two black men feature in the play. They are seen fleetingly and are drawn in sharp contrast to each other. Wil, played by David Webber, is passive and shy, whilst the other is the wife-beater Frank, played by Ben Thomas. Their existence serves to reveal how these black women deal with their black men.

In addition to exposing the plight of black pioneer frontier women, Cleage's play raised many areas of black interest. The research package would:

- provide structured and comprehensive, general, historical and cultural information on the background of *Flyin' West*

---

[44] Yvonne Brewster, Personal Interview by David Johnson, London, 1 March 1997.

- ensure the black history presented in the play was highlighted with the aim of actively building heritage facts
- point those who wanted it in the direction of how to find out more[45]

Brewster wanted her cast and audience to learn the heritage facts in the play and hoped that they would be motivated by them. She asked everyone involved with the production to comment on the impact working on the production had on them. This information was then used in the publicity programme. Brewster took this step as she understood the weight and importance of the heritage facts the play revealed: 'it has allowed us to explore creatively so many aspects of under-recorded Black history, attitudes and taboos as they existed in the nineteenth century. It also highlighted the relevance of these issues here in multicultural Britain a hundred years later.'[46]

---

[45]The research package contains explanations of:

The American Civil War

Focus is on the key role slavery played during the war and highlights the differing opinions of the northern and southern American colonies, formed in 1783, on this issue.

The American Constitution

Changes to the American constitution after the Civil War that helped the advancement of blacks are outlined.

The Farmers' Alliance

White farmers formed the Alliance in 1877 to work together and protect themselves on their land. This later included black farmers and a Coloured Farmers' Alliance in the south.

Black Life in the West

This highlights the crucial and unacknowledged role that blacks played in America's development.

The Homesteaders

The two main factors that encouraged black people to go west are presented:

1. The Homestead Act of 1860. This offered 320 acres of land to American citizens prepared to settle in the west.
2. White supremacy in the south which led to the Exodus of 1879 and saw twenty to forty thousand blacks migrate to Kansas in the hope of owning their own homes and land.

Black Laws

This explains how the laws worked against black people.

The Black Cowboys and Leading Frontier Personalities

The Black Infantry and Cavalry

Black Women on the Last Frontier

[46]Yvonne Brewster, production programme of *Flyin' West*, 7.

Both Anni Domingo, playing Miss Leah, and Angie Le Mar, playing Fannie, experienced a reawakening in this production. Domingo expresses her gratitude for the process: '*Flyin' West* has certainly been an informative and joyous journey into the world of sisterhood. It has helped me remember and celebrate the strength, tenacity and love of Black women through the ages.'[47] Le Mar states, 'When you know what has happened you realize that Black women and their experiences should be applauded and cherished. I question when will the backbone to the Black race ever rest! Only in peace. Coloured to black – still no changes.'[48] What Brewster created here was more than theatre. It was a coming together of a past black experience with that of the contemporary black and other audience. Le Mars's final comment points to at least one question the production brings to the audience's mind: 'That was 1898: where are we now?' [49]

David Webber's contribution, focusing on love, illustrates how infrequently positive black love is portrayed on the British stage:

> *Flyin' West* offers a powerful message of hope for Africans everywhere. The sight of two strong and successful Black people, so clearly in love is almost revolutionary in today's theatre. I am delighted and absolutely thrilled to be part of it. Pearl Cleage clearly loves our people and manages to show how awesome we can be and that the tremendous bonds of sisterhood complement and enhance the Black man. Let us celebrate. One love.[50]

Webber's comment brings us back to the similarities between what Brewster offered her actors instinctively and that which Teer intentionally aimed to extract from hers. The results are similar. Teer's seven-hour *Master of Liberation Workshop* aimed for her actors to own who they are and to have a more satisfying life by 'removing the notion that black people are oppressed.'[51] Similarly, in her *Pyramid Processes*, stages one and two, Teer further helped her actors in their liberation process. Stage one aimed 'to enable participants to present themselves fearlessly to the world and to enjoy

---

[47] Anni Domingo, production programme of *Flyin' West*, 7.
[48] AngieLe Mar, production programme of *Flyin' West*, 8.
[49] Ibid.
[50] David Webber, production programme of *Flyin' West*, 8.
[51] Thomas, 'Barbara Ann Teer: From Holistic Training to Liberating Rituals', 354. The reference is to 'NBT Opens New Season', *New York Amsterdam News*, 12 November 1977: D14.

that presentation of who they were'. Additionally she wanted each actor to 'express himself in a whole new way so that he can perform effortlessly and without fear'.[52] Webber was able to extract good things about being a black man from his process and experience. This, along with his notion that the strength of the female relationships in the play is also beneficial to black men, should be taken within the context of the character he plays.

Through Webber's performance Talawa's audience sees how Wil is brought into the sisters' fold, once they perceive him to be entirely harmless and on their side. He is welcomed as part of the family. On the other hand, the sisters deal with the perceived threatening behaviour of the other black man, Thomas's Frank, by killing him. They had to kill Frank. He was an outsider due to both his aggressive behaviour and his mixed race heritage. We see then that these women are only hostile to men who endanger them.

Through the family and sisterhood that Brewster offers her audience via Cleage's characters, she points to one of the most important aspects of black life anywhere in the world: black family structure. The production offers its audience an image of a sense of belonging to a community within an otherwise at best disinterested and at worst unfathomably hostile wider environment. This is epitomized in the women's welcoming of Webber's Wil.

Comments on the impact of the show were also welcomed from Talawa's administrative team. These were similarly printed in the production programme and reflect the significant impression the play had across the company. Alf Desire explains:

> As much as Medieval jousting, Gothic Architecture and the six wives of Henry VIII interested me as a child, it was never going to answer a number of nagging questions. Questions like, 'Why am I the only black face in this classroom?', 'Why do schools only teach the slavery aspect of Black history?' and 'Why do they keep putting me in the football team?' I learned as I went along. A strong sense of origin and purpose helped. The understanding process would have been aided if the other children in that classroom could have taken home something positive about my heritage. *Flyin' West* redresses this and will light the touch-paper to the further learning of our roots and culture.[53]

---

[52]Ibid.
[53]Alf Desire, marketing officer for Talawa, production programme of *Flyin' West*, 8.

Desire's notion that this kind of information would have been beneficial to his white classmates points to the importance of sharing cultural information, if people living in a culturally diverse society are to understand each other. The fact that Desire was able to voice his opinion in this forum created the possibility for other young black people in Talawa's audience to see that their experiences were sadly commonplace. Perhaps there was some comfort to be found in that. Less comforting is the fact that these experiences remain widespread for black Britons.

For Sonji Clayton, '*Flyin' West* is about knowledge, "overstanding", fear and finally gaining the truth, a test of strength that four strong black women pass with Flyin' colours.'[54] Once again, what Brewster had achieved through the production across the board with her staff was akin to what Teer did in the second stage of her *Pyramid Process* which she called the *Ritualization of Communication*. This aimed to do away with notions of self-consciousness and lack. Teer's exercises involved 'decrudding' to eradicate 'feelings of worthlessness and contempt' and promote the 'love affair with self'.[55] Was this not what Desire and Clayton had experienced?

As a black British woman Clayton was able, as Brewster had intended, to draw inspiration from the lives of the characters and benefit from the heritage facts in the play. Clayton demonstrated a yearning for information relevant to her from the outset of Talawa's work on *Flyin' West*. When the research package was presented to Brewster's team, Clayton requested a personal copy, commenting, 'I want to be able to study this and have something that I can refer back to, and show my friends.'[56] Had Clayton's British education provided information that empowered her, the research package would have been less important. Brewster's work was partially helping to fill another British educational gap. Her approach also demonstrates how effectively heritage facts can be disseminated through the theatre forum off stage, as she dedicated three pages of the production programme to details taken from the research package. Offering this printed information to Talawa's audience meant that it was accessible long after the performance event.

Brewster was certain that the cast's majority view of the research package was that it benefited the development of their practical performance.

---

[54]Sonji Clayton, secretary/administrative support for Talawa, production programme of *Flyin' West*, 8.
[55]Thomas, 'Barbara Ann Teer: From Holistic Training to Liberating Rituals', 355.
[56]Sonji Clayton, Personal Interview by David Johnson, London, 12 April 1997.

Ben Thomas, of mixed race, playing Frank, described in the text as a light-skinned black man, also of mixed race, saw the research package as 'serious information that helped me to know more about myself and my character. We really need to know this stuff'.[57] Thomas had experienced emotionally comparable situations to his character, induced by both black and white sections of British society.

Thomas explains he was never conscious of any hostility from the white community he lived in, but was aware of its perception of his difference. He felt like them, but saw he did not look like them. In relation to the black community, Thomas did not notice any bad feeling towards him there either, and although as a child he did not live amongst a black community, he knew that he belonged, at least in part, to it. He could see that his appearance was similar, but sensed he was regarded as other. Thomas experienced this notion of difference cast on him further from the black community once he was living in London, where he felt he was seen as living separate to them.[58]

Thomas maintains that the play and the research package helped him to understand some of the kind of black history that encouraged a divide between black and mixed race people. He had not wanted or needed to choose to be on one side or the other, though his formative family life experiences saw him living happily within a white community. Through working on *Flyin' West* and studying the research package he saw how this era of black history had forced people of mixed race to identify either with the black struggle or to aim to pass for white and enjoy some of the many privileges of that community. The black perception, as explored in *Flyin' West*, that being of mixed race was seen as advantageous partly explained to Thomas some of the difference that he felt the black community saw in him. Oscar Watson expands on Thomas's notion: 'I think there is still a school of thought that sees lighter-skinned black people as more acceptable and that doesn't get addressed very much.'[59] Watson's comment is still relevant in 2019 where the specific circumstances of light-skinned people are rarely, if ever, explored in performance.

---

[57] Ben Thomas, Personal Interviews by David Johnson, London, 8 December 1998, and London, 5 July 2019.
[58] Ibid.
[59] Anon, 'Flyin' West', *Attitude*, June 1997, 38. The writer quotes Oscar Watson who was Talawa's administrator at the time of the production.

Thomas felt that the wider knowledge he gained on the American Civil War also helped to fully contextualize Cleage's work and this aspect of black history: 'I now knew how black people got to this part of America. None of the films that I ever saw about Cowboys and Indians ever included any black people.'[60] He also used his new knowledge of the pioneer black women on the western frontier to understand their plight and delve into the psyche of the light-skinned black man he played. He explains, 'The research package made it easier for me to understand the motivations of the women around Frank. Whilst he waited for his inheritance from his white father, these women were trying to get on with life. You can see why they acted the way they did when he tried to take their land away from them.'[61]

Thomas being of mixed race and playing a bad character of mixed race potentially presented the issue of the role continuing, or developing a negative stereotype. This was of no concern to Thomas: 'It is rare to see the bad guy being portrayed as such because he is of mixed race.'[62] The reality is that Thomas's colour does not allow him the same kind of freedom as his white counterparts. They can indulge in the performance of negative heritage facts because there is a wealth and range of work for them. They have the good fortune of playing any role, without their work appearing to be a reflection of all white men.

Through the production, Thomas learnt about the laws of the time that actively discriminated against blacks. This made him question what these laws would mean to his mixed race character and by extension himself. Thomas's interest was enhanced by the fact the production did not deal purely with black and white but significantly with people of mixed race. It was about him.

As more and more black Britons become more culturally mixed, but remain defined wholly as part of the black British community, heritage facts should not be presented to them as a by-product of other cultural facts. This could be to the exclusion of half of who they are. For black performers in Britain, unless they are performing in a black production, it is unlikely they will receive positive heritage facts as a normal part of their stage work. This

---

[60] Thomas Interview, 8 December 1998; Thomas Interview, 5 July 2019.
[61] Ibid.
[62] Ibid.

is in stark contrast to white performers who are likely to receive heritage facts from most productions they are involved in.

This points to the necessity of creating more black and colour-blind work. This would ease the burden on contemporary black theatre practitioners who may feel a need to give only positive information about the black characters or communities they portray. This type of professional approach to their work is a reaction to the generally negative mainstream theatrical offerings on black life. Such a reaction highlights the importance of Brewster's work and the black theatre practitioners that continue to create performances with all aspects of black life at their core. Author Toni Morrison does this.

In a 2017 interview, Jana Wendt explains to Morrison that she has marginalized whites. Wendt wants to know why Morrison has no interest in white people and if she will ever substantially incorporate white lives into her books. Morrison explains, 'You can't understand how powerfully racist that question is, can you? You could never ask a white author, "When are you going to write about black people?" Even the inquiry comes from a position of being in the centre, being used to being in the centre.'[63] Morrison continues to compare her situation as an African American writer to a Russian writing in Russian for Russians who is also read by others: 'It's a benefit or a plus, but he's not obliged to consider writing about French people or Americans or anybody.'[64]

Similarly, black British theatre practitioners must feel incentivized to create the work that is of them. Brewster facilitated this type of movement with her work generally and with this production of *Flyin' West* specifically. With enough black work out there, the type of interview Morrison endured will hopefully become extinct. It is not enough to marvel at Morrison's great answer. She, Brewster and many other black people across the planet can field this line of racist questioning with ease. This is because they have been doing it all their lives. Real change will come on the British stage, when, like Brewster, black British artists uncompromisingly tell their stories in their authentic British voices ad infinitum, and when the white mainstream resists defining itself in its production of the same work.

---

[63]Toni Morrison, interview by Jana Wendt 2017, Youtube, http://youtu.be/DQ0mMjll22l, accessed 16 April 2019.
[64]Ibid.

Critical reception

The critics' response can be grouped into three types: those that avoid mention of the production in their writing, those that dislike it and those that celebrate it. Of those that avoid discussing the actual production, this seems to be because their intention is to highlight another area of the work. This is demonstrated by Winsome Hines in *The Voice*.

Hines's first article is entirely dedicated to one of the lead performers, Syan Blake, who plays Minnie.[65] This is because Blake, at the time, was one of Britain's up and coming leading black performers due to her role as Frankie Pierre in the BBC's *Eastenders* (1996–7). The article focuses more on Blake's ability to cope with her new role in the public eye than her role as a battered wife in *Flyin' West*. When Hines comments on the play in a later article, it is only to provide a brief description of the action.[66] The tragic and unpredictable irony was of life imitating art when, after depicting Minnie's suffering domestic violence, Blake was murdered, along with her two sons, by her partner in 2015.

A similar focus is evident in the write-up of the production in *The Stage*.[67] The writer's entire attention is placed on a black British celebrity rather than any aspect of the production itself. On this occasion the artist is stand-up comedian Angie Le Mar. A third of the reviews on the production dedicated their whole piece to the above two performers with only the merest mention of the production. These reviews did no harm to the company by giving positive publicity to the performers concerned.

Whilst it is reasonable not to like the work, some of the negative reviews made little attempt to explain themselves. Douglas McPherson states, 'Unfortunately, the play is as slow as an arthritic snail in an advanced state of depression. The pace may evoke for you the laid-back atmosphere of a sun-baked cotton field ... or it may just send you to sleep. Given the important matters at the heart of the work, that is a very great shame.'[68] Similarly, James Christopher took an inexplicable personal swipe at Brewster, in addition to showing a lack of understanding of the importance of this work to her audience:

> Yvonne Brewster has misspent most of her directing career trying to turn messages about black empowerment into frontline theatre.

---

[65] Winsome Hines, 'Once Burnt Syan's Shy', *Voice*, 2 June 1997, 23.
[66] Winsome Hines, '*Flyin' West*' *Voice*, 16 June 1997, 52.
[67] Anon, 'Jokes Are on Hold for Now', *Stage*, 19 June 1997, 10.
[68] Douglas McPherson, 'Flyin' West', *What's On in London*, 18–25 June 1997, 58.

She must imagine that her stilted productions have been dropping rednecks on their knees for 20 odd years. Let's get real. This is the Drill Hall, the cultural epicentre of the politically correct. To all but the converted Pearl Cleage's 'Flyin' West' is not news it is worthy rubbish.[69]

The fact that this view is in direct contrast to the black performers highlights the need to arm black performers and their audiences with more 'worthy rubbish'. Christopher is clear that black advancement, or shows depicting historical events that do so, should not make mainstream theatrical productions. Once again, whites know what is best for black theatre.

The critic has the power to comment in an influential public forum on work that is representative of a non-mainstream aspect of British culture. This work should be understood by the critic for its relevance to the section of the population that it primarily aims to serve. Here, Christopher is keen to consign decades of work to the dustbin. This kind of unqualified criticism can help ensure companies like Talawa never progress. Is that the plan? Christopher's comments also reveal a personal irritation towards Brewster, her production of *Flyin' West* and the company's work generally. Can a critic working from this starting point make a fair judgement? Whilst the attack on Brewster's production is unjustified , it provides a perspective when she says, 'I have taken a lot, because people can be very unkind.'[70] For an artist in the public eye, unfair criticism is part of the territory; it is debatable, however, whether this hurling of personal abuse is acceptable. It does, nonetheless, serve to illustrate the need for this genre of theatre in contemporary multicultural Britain.

Dominic Cavendish's starting point is equally questionable when he comments, 'What should offer a powerful conflict between people who have been driven to extremes, becomes a simplistic stand-off between a demonic wife-beater and women who seem to spend more time celebrating their strength than minding the crops.'[71] Cavendish has not recognized the value that an oppressed people put on celebrating the strengths and achievements of those that have gone before them and who have helped them to get to

---

[69]James Christopher, 'Cry Freedom, Loudly', *The Times*, 13 June 1997, 36.
[70]Brewster Interview, 31 October 2014.
[71]Dominic Cavendish, 'Flyin' West', *Time Out*, 18–25 June 1997, 139.

where they are today. At this point in Talawa's development, this kind of representation was, and still is, an important aspect of the company's work. It offers the black British audience specific cultural information which Cavendish may feel is largely irrelevant to him.

Conversely and unsurprisingly, the black press is supportive of the production: 'What holds the action together, apart from the quality of the writing, is Brewster's excellent stage direction . . . Talawa theatre has been going for ten years and on the strength of this production, it should keep going, pioneering Black European theatre for many more.'[72]

The difference in perception between the black critic and the white mainstream critics about the same piece of work is striking. This is perhaps due to differing expectations partly formed by each critic's past experience of British theatre generally. For the black critic the appreciation of Brewster's work may be due to the fact that Brewster is bothering to do the work at all. She is therefore catering to a group that the critic belongs to that is likely to be otherwise unrepresented. The fact that Brewster's quality and style of work are also praised here suggests this critic has a clear understanding both of what it is Brewster is trying to achieve, as well as the degree to which she has been successful in her aim. Brewster had pleased her primary target audience.

For others to reach and have a similar impact in the mainstream, the mainstream needs to expand its expectations of British theatre to genuinely include more culturally diverse work, as produced by the recognized experts in each area. Part of the issue of Talawa's work not always receiving positive recognition from the mainstream at the time may have stemmed from, and remain in part due to, the nature of the work being both black and British.

If the work were one or the other, theatrical styles and themes rooted in the theatrical histories of Africa, Britain or the Caribbean could be expected. The black British genre is a comparatively new and developing phenomenon that is welcomed by black Britons as they experience a greater sense of belonging and ownership of all aspects of British society. Their white counterparts, however, before they can fully appreciate it, may need more time to come to terms with the existence of the genre and the fact that Britain is no longer completely white.

Not all mainstream British theatre critics have the same opinion, level of interest or understanding of black British theatre. John Thaxter comments,

---

[72]Uju Aslka, 'Flyin' West to Freedom', *Journal*, 18–24 June 1997. No page number available.

'The result is a witty, hugely enjoyable melodrama.'[73] It is the anonymous comment in the *Big Issue*, however, that seems to have fully grasped at least one of the messages to be taken from Talawa's performance: 'The Talawa Theatre Company addresses the difficult questions of cultural identity and of the women's struggle to survive in a harsh and unforgiving frontier land. It certainly puts paid to the Spice Girls' claims to have invented girl power.'[74]

My eyewitness account

On 28 June 1997, the Drill Hall was filled to 80 per cent capacity and the ticket-paying audience was 100 per cent black. The white audience members were Drill Hall staff. The set held the physical hallmarks of a Talawa show. This is in part due to the fact that designer Ellen Cairns had at that time created over 70 per cent of the sets for Talawa, including *Flyin' West*. On each occasion she developed an ambience of the main themes of the play through her minimalist designs.

The sparse two-tiered set for this production left ample space for Talawa's performance. Brewster had warned Cleage, 'It's gonna be your play, but I don't know if I can ask my actors to sit around a table for one and a half hours.'[75] There was no table in the end. Instead the cast used a cloth that became whatever they needed it to be. Everything was reduced to the bare minimum: 'Instead of an apple pie we had an apple.'[76]

For any audience member who followed Talawa's work at the time, the fact that many of the actors' faces were recognizable from previous Talawa shows was immediately evident. As the majority of Talawa's work had been within the Caribbean genre, those who had performed in these shows had demonstrated their ability to work with a Caribbean voice. In *Flyin' West* all of the performers with previous experience of Talawa now demonstrated that they were also able to give a convincing performance using an American voice. This demonstrated the versatility of their verbal repertoire. As with *From the Mississippi Delta*, the performers in *Flyin' West* received voice coaching. The sessions were delivered by Claudette Williams.

---

[73] John Thaxter, 'Flyin' West', *Stage*, 3 July 1997, 14.
[74] S.K., 'Flyin' West', *Big Issue*, 2–8 June 1997, 32.
[75] Brewster Interview, 31 October 2014.
[76] Ibid.

Ben Thomas's performance is noteworthy. Thomas as Frank, in addition to demonstrating a credible American voice, showed versatility and theatrical depth. His performance was a brave endeavour as he was cast in the role of the outsider and playing to an audience who may also have regarded both Thomas's character and Thomas the actor as such. The strength of Thomas's performance created a discernible hatred from the audience throughout each of his appearances. Thomas managed to display a detestable arrogance and dislike of black people with every movement he made and phrase he uttered. The critics do not appear to have appreciated Thomas's impact on the audience, as little or no mention is made of his work in the reviews.

It is in the work of Angie Le Mar, as Fannie, that the behind-the-scenes work that Brewster does in nurturing black talent is seen. Le Mars performance was judged by Aslka for her American accent: 'Although the play is set in the American West, Angie Le Mar's accent brings you down South with a jolt, South London, that is.'[77] Prior to accepting the role Brewster had commented to me, 'I am trying to get Angie Le Mar for this, but she can't decide if she wants to do it or not.'[78] Brewster wanted Le Mar as she saw her as a brave woman with real guts. Her aim was to give her the confidence to act outside of comedy and stand-up.[79] Brewster believes in giving chances and realizes that black performers need them if they are to develop their craft in British theatre.

Talawa's audience reaction to the performance was displayed at any high point by mutterings, comments, sighs and laughter. This behaviour was epitomized by a lady on my left who appeared to want to share her theatrical experience at various points throughout the performance. This was particularly the case for scenes that either showed, or made reference to, the domestic violence being suffered by Blake's Minnie and ultimately when Thomas's Frank enjoyed eating the poisoned pie. The lady exclaimed, 'Good, good, good, that's all I can say, they did the best thing with him. He didn't deserve any better than that.'[80]

Smiling, the lady then apologized to me. The fact that this audience member had become overtly involved in the show was neither a new

---

[77] Aslka, 'Flyin' West to Freedom'.
[78] Brewster Interview, 1 March 1997.
[79] Brewster Interviews, 31 October 2014 and 26 November 2018.
[80] Voice of audience member at Talawa's performance of *Flyin' West*, 28 June 1997.

experience at a Talawa performance specifically, or in black theatre generally. The black British 'dilemma' was in the fact that the lady was apologizing in case she had disturbed both my and others' viewing. Her tentative apology demonstrated that she was not quite sure whether she had acted inappropriately to a black play in the white space. Her reaction was not unique during the performance, as other audience members also contributed throughout. This behaviour was understood by the wider audience as reasonable involvement. Such reactions indicated that the audience had been drawn in and was enjoying the performance. Were all of the other audiences less audible? Why did this positive audience reaction go unmentioned by the mainstream critics? Had they seen such behaviour as a disturbance?

Talawa's production of the American plays was a multiple achievement. In addition to highlighting some of the versatility of the black talent available to contemporary British theatre at the time and providing training in this genre, there were three further successes that the company's work demonstrated. Firstly the artistic commitment to introducing this genre, secondly the ability to recognize the widespread needs of Talawa's diverse black audience and its developing mainstream followers, and finally the undertaking to produce quality black writing.

The work that Talawa produced in the American genre during the Brewster years points to an artistic and managerial flexibility that perhaps partly accounts for the company's longevity at the time. Additionally, the work highlights Brewster's awareness of the perpetual need to move Talawa's performance work forward, mirroring the black British reality that black people are generally required to develop huge flexibility in order to be successful in contemporary British society.

CHAPTER 6
STAY IN YOUR BOX

'And then to summon riffraff to mock my mother tongue.'[1]

When Brewster decided to prove that the British classics also rightfully belong to black British theatre, she was battling centuries of ingrained belief in Britain that such work was never generally meant to include black people. This notion was historically promulgated on the tenets that black people could not speak as well as whites and that, on a physical level, all things black were bad.

This knowledge fuelled Brewster's resolve and resulted in her directing five plays in this genre between 1989 and 1997. These included *Antony and Cleopatra* (1991), *King Lear* (1994) and *Tis Pity She's a Whore* (1995). The analysis of these three productions introduces several of Talawa's firsts, challenges and reviews, as well as opportunities Brewster offered others and some of the general trials and tribulations the company experienced through working in this genre; this is followed by a detailed discussion of the company's productions of *The Importance of Being Earnest* (1989) and *Othello* (1997).

The British classical genre: No voice for blacks

Dabydeen and Wilson-Tagoe demonstrate how, since biblical times, less popular language use justified the ill-treatment of its speaker. In the case they cite, those who are perceived to use incorrect language forms are also considered less worthy of living.[2] Whilst not using the specific oral language

---

[1] Ola Rotimi, *The Gods Are Not to Blame*, Talawa's rehearsal script of the company's 1989 production, 46, voice of Odewale.
[2] David Dabydeen and Nana Wilson-Tagoe, *A Reader's Guide to West Indian and Black British Literature* (London: Hansib/Rutherford, 1988), 165. Dabydeen and Wilson-Tagoe quote the Bible: Judges 12.4.

of British theatre has probably not resulted in death, performers who would not, or could not, produce the required sound could expect to have a less active performance life than those who did.

Both whilst Britain was a leading colonial power and for decades after colonial rule had ended, the oral language for British stage performance was principally the voice of the wealthy British upper middle classes, an elite group that was and remains powerful in British theatre, literature and education.³ The upper middle classes used the reference points of their own existence to provide dramatic entertainment for each other. Speech forms that did not meet this standard were generally not used centre stage. Principle amongst the excluded groups were all forms of black voice.

Documented negative opinions of black speech have existed since the 1600s, when writers sought to reduce black people to a subhuman level by suggesting they were less human than whites. This was in part achieved by likening black speech to that of apes.⁴ The black voice then has customarily been treated with disrespect and in opposition to the British stage 'standard' since Western classical performance began.

Where early black performers could produce the 'standard' speech of their white counterparts, writers of the day explained this away by stressing the physical features this particular black speaker had in common with whites. Aphra Behn's Oroonoko is described in 1678:

> His face was not of that brown, rusty Black which most of that Nation are, but a perfect Ebony, or polish'd Jett. His Eyes were the most awful, (impressive) that cou'd be seen, and very piercing; the White of 'em being like Snow, as were his Teeth. His Nose was rising and Roman, instead of African, and flat. His Mouth, the finest shap'd that could be seen; far from those great turn'd Lips which are so natural to the rest of the Negroes.⁵

For 'rusty blacks' with 'flat African' noses and 'great turn'd lips' who could produce the sound, the matter did not end there. Their colour and features, far less easy to disguise than their voice, remained a visual barrier in a

---

³Gilbert and Tompkins, *Post-Colonial Drama*, 15.
⁴Ibid. 'In 1634, Sir Thomas Herbert suggested that Africans and apes mated with each other, the evidence of this being that African speech sounded "more like that of apes than men . . . their language is rather apishly than articulately founded".'
⁵Aphra Behn, *Oroonoko: Or, the Royal Slave. A True History* (London: Will Canning, 1688), 20-1.

world where the word 'black' negated anything it preceded.[6] A world where being black justified the lowest possible status, along with the general presumptions of otherness, suspicion and being undesirable in every regard.

Chambers illustrates this idea, whilst highlighting the presence of black performers in Britain from the 1300s to the 1800s.[7] Throughout most of this period black entertainers in Britain were invariably cast as the vengeful male, whilst colour gradation was used to prove distrust of the other. This is shown in *A Midsummer Night's Dream* where Hermia is referred to as 'an Ethiop' and 'tawny Tartar'.[8]

Prior to his creation of Hermia, Shakespeare had introduced distrust of the black other in *Othello*. *Othello* also testifies to the fact that there has been a black presence in British theatre since its appearance in 1603. Whilst Othello is perhaps the clearest example of an historical black character on the British stage, the work of the black actor Ira Aldridge some two hundred years later can be seen as the real-life historical equivalent. Despite this historical black presence and the eloquence of both Othello and Aldridge, when black performers were introduced to the British and colonial stages between the 1600s and the 1850s, it was generally because their language and culture were to be used to heighten their baseness and perceived lack of intelligence. This would then justify their lowly position in society.[9]

Blacks then were customarily denigrated, abused and dehumanized at the point when Britain unusually allowed the highly articulate and talented Aldridge to have a career on the British stage, and later become widely credited as Britain's first black actor.[10] Born in New York in 1807, Aldridge made his debut performance at the Royal Theatre, London in 1825, aged 17. In addition to success in Britain, Aldridge achieved notoriety for his performances whilst touring in Europe in 1852, where he was both celebrated and honoured. He later became a British citizen in 1863.

It is thought that Aldridge came to Britain believing there was more opportunity for him here, having been attacked by a circus performer in 1822, when he was 14.[11] Since the turn of the twenty-first century, however,

---

[6]Fryer, *Staying Power*, 135.
[7]Chambers, *Black and Asian Theatre in Britain*, 10–37.
[8]Ibid., 15.
[9]This is seen in Cumberland's *The West Indian* and Bickerstaffe's *The Padlock*.
[10]Chambers, *Black and Asian Theatre in Britain*, 38–56.
[11]Ibid., 39.

it has become increasingly common for black British artists to go to America in the belief they have greater opportunity there.[12] Like Aldridge, contemporary black performers continue to be attacked both in America and in Europe.[13] It appears that the circus performers are still at large.

Surrounding the isolated success of Aldridge was the British cultural background to his performance life. This, since the Restoration, had firmly placed whites at the top of British society, with those increasingly less white to black at the bottom. Additionally, following its dominance as a slavocracy in the eighteenth century, Britain became a global power in the nineteenth century, where blackface was used in shaping a racist interpretation of black people.[14] In broad terms, they represented uninhibited sex, physicality, sensuality and ugliness; the men were excessively endowed and the woman had large breasts and posteriors.[15]

Along with the ritual denigration with which whites treated blacks came the more sinister white creation of a stereotypical personification of black people through blackface minstrelsy. With the appearance of Harriet Beecher Stowe's *Uncle Tom's Cabin* in 1852, this characterization was legitimized. This ensured blacks remained where the post-abolitionist slavocracy wanted them: the subject of ridicule. Chambers clarifies the

---

[12] After being nominated for both a Golden Globe and an Academy Award for best supporting actress in Mike Leigh's 1996 *Secrets and Lies*, Marianne Jean Baptiste moved to America and has worked consistently to date. Other black British artists currently work in and out of America as a normal part of their performance life. These include actor Idris Elba, playing Stringer Bell in the American television series *The Wire* from 2002 to 2004; Chitewel Ejiofor, nominated for the Golden Globe and the Academy Award for best actor in *12 Years a Slave* in 2014; director Steve McQueen, who won the Golden Globe for best motion picture, the Bafta for best film and the Academy Award for best picture for *12 Years a Slave* in 2014; John Boyega, who starred as Finn in *Star Wars: The Force Awakens* in 2015 and *Star Wars: The Last Jedi* in 2017 and Daniel Kaluuya, who was nominated for the Golden Globe, Bafta and Academy Award for best actor in *Get Out* in 2018, whilst American Jordan Peele won the Academy Award for best original screenplay for *Get Out* in 2018. The last example also illustrates how successful black British and black American collaborative work can be.
[13] Black American Broadway actor and singer Elijah Ahmad Lewis was physically and verbally assaulted by a white woman calling him a 'nigger' as she tried to knock his mobile phone out of his hands when he walked in the streets in Reno, USA, in January 2017: https://www.necn.com/entertainment/entertainment-news/Motown-Musical-actor-complains-of-racial-assault-in-Reno-411823505.html, accessed 22 March 2019. Similarly on 4 March 2018, black Spanish actor Marius Makon was viciously physically attacked by a white woman. She struck him in the face with a bottle telling him, 'I'm white, I can kill you, nothing will happen'. https://elpais.com/elpais/2018/03/06/inenglish/1520329317_212718.html, accessed 22 March 2019.
[14] Chambers, *Black and Asian Theatre in Britain*, 11.
[15] Ibid., 15.

Stay in Your Box

extent to which this was a strategy of external and internal, white on black, domination:

> The white body has the power to mimic the black body, to wear the black mask and, by possessing and controlling, to confirm black disempowerment. If white can become black without losing its whiteness, white can conquer anything. In such a world, where white is the universal standard, colour can even be considered ephemeral like makeup when white chooses. As such, colour can be disregarded as a marker for collective violence while that violence continues unchecked.[16]

It was at least until the late 1960s that black performance in Britain was synonymous with servile roles and little in terms of speech.[17] This treatment of black artists and black people generally was an act of oppression that served to revive, maintain and force notions of limit on contemporary black British society, both on and off stage. If black people were only seen in subservient roles, the myth that they were incapable of occupying any other roles in society could successfully be perpetuated. They were then not shown as speaking because wider society did not want to hear their voice. After all, if society listened to their message, it might have to respond.

To avoid the prospect of ever hearing a genuine black voice, and in line with the blackface minstrelsy of one hundred years earlier, the BBC with the new medium of television aimed to ensure anti-black stereotypes flourished with its *Black and White Minstrel* Show. This aired on BBC primetime television for two decades from 1958 to 1978. Audiences were continually fed the notion that black merited humiliation because black people were inferior, childlike, funny, hideous and cuddly, in that submissive gollywog kind of way.

Silencing the black voice strategically continued in wider society, which had a foolproof system in place, one which was guaranteed to get all black people when they were young enough to, on the whole, be irreversibly damaged. This was achieved through the British education system which treated African-Caribbean immigrants as 'trainee whites and equated their non-standard

---

[16]Ibid., 56.
[17]Cameron, *Blackgrounds* Interview, May 1997.

speech with antisocial and deviant behaviour'.[18] This would keep the 'trainees' down until their white apprenticeship, which most failed by leaving school with little or no qualifications, was complete. This was unsurprising as it is very hard to really get to grips with being white when you are black.

Having arrived in Britain at 17, Brewster was unaffected by the imposed limitations of this very British secondary education. Her Caribbean British education had not sought to divide and conquer in precisely the same way. In her mind then, the British classics were as natural a choice for her to direct as any other genre. When she did this at Talawa, her decision highlighted that black theatre need not be limited to the performance of black plays.

By doing this work when she did, Brewster afforded black actors both a training ground and the opportunity to professionally access the great leading roles within a genre they would generally be excluded from. White actors also benefited as they explored the work within a black setting. At the time, this practical study of any aspect of black theatre was unavailable in British drama schools. It was a shrewd move on Brewster's part to add work from the British classical genre to Talawa's repertoire, as it automatically expanded the language of black theatre to incorporate the 'highest' quality 'standard English' speech.

This 'standard English' speech is now the native speech of all contemporary black Britons born here. Additionally, the importance of 'standard English' speech forms will often have been drilled into them by their black British 'norm enforcer' parents.[19] It is common for second and third generation black British parents to want their children to sound British. This is a throwback to the negative treatment the first and second generation parents received in the British education system: the very same system that, with each passing generation, has become less able to exploit black Britons, as it increasingly fails to defeat them.

The version of the Caribbean language that third and fourth generation black Britons speak is a further diluted variety of that of their parents and grandparents. It is questionable whether these later generations would cling onto their ancestors' language if they were simply accepted as British, without the qualifying 'x generation' and 'black' labels. How many generations will have to pass on before white British society perceives

---

[18]Yasmin Alibhai-Brown, *Who Do We Think We Are: Imagining the New Britain* (London: Penguin, 2001), 160-2.
[19]Inchley, *Voice and New Writing 1997 - 2007*, 88.

the 'black' to have washed off? Whilst this third-generation-onwards black British speech is also used by their white counterparts, there are no qualifying adjectives specifically designed to exclude these white Britons from society. Although these generations of black Britons have 'standard' speech as their first language, some may choose to identify themselves more closely with Caribbean speech styles at times of their choosing. The bicultural nature of their existence affords them this option. This is a powerful use of language which states, 'I always understand you, but I decide when you understand me.'

This ability to take linguistic control was mirrored in Brewster's work in this genre, by her subversion of notions of limitation regarding blackness. As the plays were not originally intended for black actors, their bodies in these roles automatically gave the parts new meaning. This was most marked where the actors' colour affected the meaning of the text. These inevitable changes played into Brewster's determination to broaden the scope of this genre to more readily include black artists. They also supported her belief that great plays can be taken from any perspective, including that of black directors.[20]

By daring to tackle the British classics, Brewster's work made the audible statement to black actors that they were allowed to do it all. She explains:

> With the Shakespearean thing, it was important for black actors to realize they could do this with affirmation and without having to pretend they were white. [This] was happening a lot with Shakespeare, they come and strut around and they think that if you look at them long enough you'd believe they're white. Why? White people don't strut around in the hope that you'll believe they're black, do they?[21]

Additionally, Brewster knew this genre of work was an intrinsic part of her heritage and by extension all black Britons. She ensured that her company members knew this. Bartholemew points to one of her techniques for getting this message across: 'Actors who worked with her on Shakespeare plays blithely recall how she would haul out from nowhere a classical painting depicting images of black figures – in order to hammer home the fact of black people's participation in European civilisation and art.'[22]

---

[20]Brewster Interview, 31 October 2014.
[21]Ibid.
[22]Bartholemew, 'Homeless, but Not Rootless', 10.

Talawa Theatre Company

By making the British classics a staple of Talawa's developing repertoire, the company was not attempting to create a contemporary version of the RSC. This was, rather, part of the by-product of the commitment to produce wide-ranging performance work. Brewster did however have a clear intention to ensure Talawa could not only be defined by the African and Caribbean work it had done. She believed that productions of the classics would help to cement Talawa as a black British theatre company.[23] Accordingly, she did not give these productions a black slant. They simply had black actors. She explains the transparent mainstream opposition to her work in this genre: 'People only act funny about black actors playing Shakespeare because it's England's greatest export. It's like having a black woman playing the queen and I don't see anything wrong with that.'[24]

What Brewster is highlighting is a mainstream commitment to exclude black people from what makes white Britain white. The reality of course is that even, and perhaps more so, in British subcultures, the habits of the mainstream are quietly mastered. Brewster was certain that cultural exclusion zones would not apply to her or Talawa, and that it was time the mainstream heard classical English from black British mouths.

Antony and Cleopatra

Antony and Cleopatra ran from 16 May to 15 June 1991 at the Bloomsbury Theatre, London and Everyman Theatre, Liverpool. It is the first all-black production in the available documented history of British theatre and it allowed Brewster to present her audience with the reality of a black queen, in Dona Croll. She also provided a black Antony in Jeffrey Kissoon and a mixed race Octavius Caesar in Ben Thomas. Mark Borkowski comments, 'Stagings of Shakespeare's work with black casts in the past have been rare: in the 1930s, Orson Welles directed the famous "Voodoo" "Macbeth"; in the 1970s, there was "Umabatha", the Zulu version of the play; and in the early 80s, the National Theatre staged a mixed cast "Measure for Measure".'[25]

This was Brewster's first Shakespeare production with Talawa and 'blackness' would not be presented as an overt theme. These were black

---

[23]Brewster, 'Talawa Theatre Company 1985 - 2002', 87–105.
[24]Harry, 'The Voice Interview: Yvonne Brewster, Enter, Stage Left!', 19.
[25]Mark Borkowski, press release prepared for *Antony and Cleopatra*. See Talawa's production archives, *Antony and Cleopatra*, publicity file.

Stay in Your Box

actors telling a story about characters that are ordinarily represented by white artists. Historically, casting Cleopatra as white was preferable to showing a black Queen of Egypt. Her origins would, however, have made it impossible for her to have been white, despite audiences having been offered her in Elizabeth Taylor and white others. Antar Mason comments, 'you really can't believe that Elizabeth Taylor looked like Cleopatra.'[26] This does not mean that she should not have played her, but in a world where white can be black, presumably black can be black too?

Brewster had a clear aim: 'I really wanted to see a Cleopatra that looked like she was Egyptian.'[27] In casting Croll, Brewster met with outside challenges based on the leap she offered Croll from playing maids in Shakespeare to now playing a queen.[28] Brewster knew, however, that unless she took a chance on her actors, they would be even less likely to be cast in similar roles under a white director in the future.

Brewster also ran the additional risk of limiting her audience. White audiences could see white actors doing Shakespeare every day of the week. Would Talawa's performance bring the acceptable amount of 'blackness' to the show to be both inoffensive and exotic to white audiences? Would black audiences feel connected enough to the work to support it? Jeffrey Wainwright's comments on the show illustrate the unfair burden placed on black theatre practitioners by the mainstream:

> It may be that we have rapidly learnt to expect too much of our black theatre companies. We have come to look for newly exciting, uninhibited acting styles – an anticipation which in itself may rest upon stereotypes – and less naturalistic staging which we think in some vague way might draw upon ritual. More reasonably we hope that their approach to the European classics will produce radically new perspectives and references to surprise us.[29]

With this in mind, along with Brewster's actors using RSC pronunciation and no attempt at an African-Caribbean voice to stamp the company's 'blackness' onto the play, Talawa was not doing what the mainstream

---

[26] Antar Mason, 'From Hip-Hop to Hittite: Part X', 385.
[27] Brewster, *Blackstages* Interview, July 2002.
[28] Chambers, *Black and Asian Theatre in Britain*, 191.
[29] Jeffrey Wainwright, 'An African Queen', *Independent*, 30 April 1991, 14.

expected of black theatre. Brewster's focus was to illustrate her belief that the play is all about messages.[30] Her general approach catered to what is expected of a Shakespeare play. This was necessary if Talawa was to be able to continue to work within this genre without stereotypical expectations, or producing the kind of impossible work Wainwright refers to.

Brewster was giving Talawa the possibility of later performing within the genre without having to live up to a set style. This would also afford the company the scope to experiment with its approaches to Shakespeare and other classics in later productions. Due to the mainstream perception of Talawa and Brewster's daring to produce Shakespeare, it was perhaps inevitable that the press would be keen to provide a plethora of comments.

Richard Philips described the set design as 'a simple one. Almost too simple: There's a line of steps, a wall, a backdrop. And that's about it'.[31] Philip Key, agreeing that the set is simplistic, explains why he finds this problematic: 'Unfortunately it is not a great help with narrative drive. Rome and Egypt are played out in the same space as the battles that occur and even the costumes – fun as they may be make it difficult to judge who exactly is whom.'[32] On top of that, Key felt the delivery of the language was the main issue: 'No-one on stage seems quite aware of what they are doing, the words often delivered in a tum te tum style.'[33] He also describes Brewster's direction as 'simplistic' in her choice of staging techniques,[34] and Wainwright comments, 'as a conceptual re-interpretation Yvonne Brewster's production is disappointing.'[35]

The reviewers' comments on some of the lead performances were no more favourable. Phillips writes, 'Not all of the speechifying is clear. Renu Setna's Enobarbus is often garbled.'[36] After a general comment that 'the acting is uneven,'[37] Wainwright states, 'Renu Setna, trying a more fastidious than gruff Enobarbus, is not convincing.'[38] Equally he is underwhelmed

---

[30] Brewster Interview, 26 November 2018.
[31] Richard Philips, 'Antony and Cleopatra', *Liverpool Echo*, 25 April 1991, 38.
[32] Philip Key, 'Unsolved Mysteries – The Tale Included', *Daily Post*, 25 April 1991, 9.
[33] Ibid.
[34] Ibid.
[35] Wainwright, 'An African Queen', 14.
[36] Philips, 'Antony and Cleopatra', 38.
[37] Wainwright, 'An African Queen', 14.
[38] Ibid.

with Kissoon's Antony, stating, 'Mr Kissoon does not entirely solve the paradox of a man overwhelmed by Cleopatra.' As for Croll's press night performance, Wainwright describes it as 'just snatching at the role'.[39] Finally, Key sums up Croll's performance as getting 'the loud treatment from Dona Croll. Not so much seductive as aggressive.'[40]

Reckord, in partial agreement with the critics, offers an explanation for Croll's work:

> There is such a long tradition of white actors doing Shakespeare that there are thousands of them to choose from and you get a handful of people who are really good. With black actors ... there are a dozen to choose from. I saw Dona Croll do Cleopatra and she is a wonderful actress and ... she wasn't wonderful. I wondered whether there wasn't a combination of [an] inferiority complex just because of the ... situation that they're [black actors] in, and that they don't have the exposure ... She couldn't shine. She's as good an actress as anybody, she should shine in that sort of part, but it's a question of context, of experience, of confidence.[41]

This did not apply to all Brewster's performers, as is illustrated by the reviewers' comments on Ben Thomas playing Caesar. Key writes, 'Only Ben Thomas's Caesar makes an impression, his anguish over his friend's desertion only too clear.'[42] Philips agrees: 'He (the character Caesar) is played by Ben Thomas, another forceful character and the most understandable.'[43]

Additional success was in the fact that Brewster had intentionally provided the exposure and the chance for her performers to develop the performance toolkit Reckord refers to. By doing this work, Brewster was also creating a body of professional black actors who could later be called upon, both in mainstream and black theatre, to take on these kinds of roles. Had she not done this, would Thomas, although already significantly accomplished, have been able to appear in Talawa's next classical production, this time however quite accidentally, as King Lear?

---

[39] Ibid.
[40] Key, 'Unsolved Mysteries – The Tale Included', 9.
[41] Reckord, *Blackgrounds* Interview, April 1997.
[42] Key, 'Unsolved Mysteries – The Tale Included', 9.
[43] Philips, 'Antony and Cleopatra', 38.

Talawa Theatre Company

King Lear

Between 16 March and 16 April 1994 Talawa performed *King Lear*, the company's fifteenth production and second British classic, in Talawa's home at the Cochrane.[44] For Ukaegbu, the show 'challenged conventional views about *other* races as outsiders and questioned the actions of especially those in authority who instead of using their positions to create racial harmony use different kinds of excuses to justify racism'.[45]

The depth of what Brewster was trying to achieve, along with the West End setting, gave black theatre practitioners confidence that black theatre was now being taken seriously by the mainstream. Where black performers were not customarily seen in the majority of West End shows, as remains the case, with the exception of musical performance work, Brewster put them centre stage, in the centre of London, in their own home.

It was planned that Norman Beaton, of *Desmond's* fame, would play King Lear. When he became too ill Ben Thomas took over the role at a week's notice, armed with Brewster's absolute confidence in him that he was a brilliant actor, and that he was not going to let her down.[46] Brewster also had to replace other cast members who dropped out once they realized Beaton was not going to be able to perform. By happenstance, this then led to the mixed cast that Brewster took through the production. Brewster explains, 'The diverse cast was a result of panic.'[47]

In addition to casting Thomas, Brewster also cast David Harewood as Edmund. Nervous about delivering Shakespeare, Brewster had to develop his confidence in this area. Despite his efforts, it was another aspect of his performance, quite out of his control, that was focused on by a radio host interviewing Brewster. The host questioned, 'But isn't it such a bad example for all those boys in Brixton to have this black actor play Edmund, because he's such an unsympathetic character?'[48] Brewster left the interview.

Harewood's performance had the opposite effect, however, on Vanessa Redgrave, who cast him as Antony in her version of *Antony and Cleopatra*

---

[44]The production also played at the Nia Centre, Manchester, the Queens Theatre, Barnstable and The Playhouse, Oxford.
[45]Ukaegbu, 'Talawa Theatre Company: The "Likkle" Matter of Black Creativity and Representation on the British Stage', 139.
[46]Brewster Interview, 31 October 2014.
[47]Ibid.
[48]Brewster, *Blackstages* Interview, July 2002.

(1997). Nicola Stockley was equally impressed and cast him as Othello. With this latter production, Harewood became the first black man to play Othello at the National Theatre (1997). Having since forged a successful career in Hollywood, Harewood explains that he has not worked in Britain since 2008. He believes he was not getting work in Britain because directors did not know what to do with a black man with received pronunciation. Additionally, he reveals producers were told that 'Critics would slam a production with a black leading actor'.[49]

Although Thomas was now playing the lead, Beaton's image was still used in the publicity as it was too late to change it. In the poster, Beaton wore a crown made of pound notes. This was seen as a visual tribute to him. Similarly Ukaegbu attributes Thomas playing Lear as 'the first black actor in Britain to achieve this status since Ira Aldridge's highly acclaimed one night performance in Hull in June 1859'.[50] There were of course firsts decades before Thomas, and since Aldridge, in this classical genre.[51] The firsts of the 1950s, however, are little publicized because the mainstream generally regards the classics as out of bounds to blacks.

This generally tacit notion was revealed to Brewster in 1980. Whilst appearing as Tituba in the National Theatre production of *The Crucible*, she overheard a conversation between the then artistic director Peter Hall and a friend. The thrust was that black actors could not be expected to do Shakespeare as they are just not suited to it.[52] Twenty years later, and six years after Talawa's *King Lear*, David Oyelowo became the first black man to play an English king at the RSC when he played Henry IV (2000). He explains how he spent weeks defending the casting because, in relation to his playing the role, an Oxford don had said, 'We open ourselves up to ridicule if we allow black people to play those kinds of parts.'[53]

Talawa was eight years old and enjoying positive theatrical recognition when the company performed *King Lear*. The black theatre-going community's appreciation of the range of work that Talawa had given them was shown when, just before the production, the company received

---

[49] *Black Hollywood*, BBC1, 27 October 2018.
[50] Ukaegbu, 'Talawa Theatre Company: The "Likkle" Matter of Black Creativity and Representation on the British Stage', 129.
[51] Edric Connor played Gower in *Pericles* for the RSC at Stratford in 1958 and Paul Robeson played Othello at Stratford in 1959.
[52] Brewster, 'A Short Autobiographical Essay Focusing on My Work in the Theatre', 395.
[53] *Black Hollywood*, BBC1, 27 October 2018.

the accolade of 'Performing Arts Company of the Decade' from *The Voice* newspaper.[54] Brewster was inspired to continue to deliver and made a conscious attempt to put her own mark on *King Lear*, as well as expand the performance range of her actors, by setting the production in 2001, with a mostly black population. She decided a new language form should be found to reflect the time and ethnicity of the community.[55]

The language developed from extending a range of present-day British accents. The performers were required to work on developing their perceived and imaginary evolution of vowel sounds from the present-day cockney accent, until they touched upon a sound that worked for their specific character. Each actor found a sound that both brought the character to life in an original way, and that harmonized with the other voices.[56] Brewster employed Cicely Berry for three days of voice coaching for the production. Whilst her language strategy outlined above can be seen to complement her ambition to produce original work, the use of a classical voice coach suggests that the performers were also partly steered into producing the traditional RSC style. This mixing of both forms was successful in terms of the audience response.

Brewster recounts how, when Harewood's Edmund stated 'To both these women have I pledged my love, now which one shall it be, shall I take one, both, or neither?' he met the roar of a black woman in the audience: 'Typical black man!'[57] Whilst she may have been responding to the message alone, it is also possible Harewood's language use triggered her response, as it was reminiscent of an aspect of her own. Had Edmund been white would the woman in the audience have made a similar comment?[58]

Brewster dedicated this historic performance to the inspiration of Norman Beaton. She cast him to play Lear after Beaton had told her, 'before

---

[54]Talawa's production archives for *King Lear*; see publicity flyer and programme for the production.
[55]Brewster Interview, 21 February 1998.
[56]Ibid.
[57]Ibid.
[58]This paragraph is an edited version of the original written in my doctoral thesis in 1999. My thesis was published in the University of Warwick online library in 2001. Rodreguez King-Dorset has accepted that sections of my Ph.D, including my discussion of this production of Talawa's *King Lear*, were plagiarised by him in 'his' text *Black British Theatre Pioneers: Yvonne Brewster and the First Generation of Actors, Playwrights and Other Practitioners* (McFarland & Co., 2014). Rodreguez King-Dorset has admitted his plagiarism and the book has subsequently been made unavailable.

I die I have to do King Lear and I've seen your shows and I think it's you.'[59] Once cast, Beaton turned up at Brewster's house at 11.00 am on a Saturday morning. He was chauffeur-driven in a white Rolls Royce, dressed in white linen and drunk. His vision was that King Lear should be the head of a Credit Union. His three daughters would be working for him and stealing the money that the black people brought in.[60]

When Beaton became ill, and then too ill to do the production, Brewster describes this as 'one of the most emotional times of my entire life'.[61] Beaton saw the show, the first half from the back of the auditorium with Brewster beside him. She had slipped him in and held his hand as he cried and told her, 'I'm supposed to be on that stage.' He continued, 'I would have done anything to have played King Lear.' When Brewster helped him out in the interval he said, 'So you mean to say, Yvonne, that I never got the chance to play King Lear?'[62] She never saw him again.

This production of *King Lear* was not the one Brewster had planned. It did, however, bring its own production and then post-production success when it was selected, along with the RSC and the National Theatre, as part of a series of trial videos for the national video archive of stage performances. The videos were housed at London's Theatre Museum, which also wanted Talawa, with this production, to take part in an exhibition being prepared on interpreting Shakespeare.[63]

Brewster's changing genres and dipping into the British classics gave Talawa an edge that was being appreciated as the company went from strength to strength. With this upward trajectory, Talawa was being described variously as 'the internationally renowned Talawa Theatre',[64] 'Britain's leading black theatre group',[65] and, with its next classical production, *Tis Pity She's a Whore*, 'Britain's leading black theatre company'.[66]

---

[59]Brewster Interview, 26 November 2018.
[60]Brewster Interview, 31 October 2014.
[61]Ibid.
[62]Ibid.
[63]Archival video performances of Talawa's *King Lear* and *Othello* were housed as permanent features at the Theatre Museum. They are now held at the Victoria and Albert Museum, in the Theatre and Performance Archives, along with all of Talawa's work.
[64]Harry, 'The Voice Interview: Yvonne Brewster, Enter, Stage Left!', 19.
[65]Bartholemew, 'Homeless, but Not Rootless', 10.
[66]Anon, 'Tis Pity She's a Whore', *What's On in London*, 8 November 1995, 57.

Talawa Theatre Company

Tis Pity She's a Whore

For three weeks from 1 to 18 November 1995, Talawa presented its nineteenth production and third British classical drama with John Ford's 1633 Jacobean play *Tis Pity She's a Whore*, at the Lyric Theatre Hammersmith, London.

With this show, Talawa wanted to remind audiences that it was not a one-trick pony. The critics suggest the production exhibited a lack of clarity in terms of what Talawa was trying to achieve: 'History will applaud Talawa for its many groundbreaking coups de theatre, but this is certainly not one of them';[67] 'Whatever Talawa director Yvonne Brewster was aiming for – despite programme notes – remains obscured and the result is desperately wide of the mark.'[68]

It is difficult for such mainstream comments not to give rise to some questioning: How much of this response reflects stereotypical African-Caribbean references not being met? Are the comments based on frustration with Talawa's conventional performance? As this type of work has been done without African-Caribbean references for centuries, must black performers be obliged to add them now? Should white critics define the work of a black theatre company by indirectly expressing the notion that, 'If you have to do our classics, do a black version to show how different we are. This will keep our stereotypes alive and kicking'? Whilst the critics are unlikely to state this, is the next best thing to write about how uninspired they are by the work? Along with shaping future efforts, this type of commentary could potentially contribute to stopping classical British performance featuring blacks at all.

The reviews continue: 'the acting does not have the passion to match the picturesqueness. Almost everyone in Parma is guilty of underacting or overacting.'[69] Does this mean, 'Almost everyone in Parma is guilty of being black and not singing and dancing?' Or are we simply left trying to justify reviews that have an intention beyond offering a critical evaluation?

The under- or over-acting may refer to actors playing two characters and consequently using two ways of speaking. This is seen with Andrew Dennis playing Grimaldi and Poggio, Simon Clayton playing Bergetto and the Cardinal, and Hassani Shapi playing both Friar Bonaventura and Donado. The acting oral 'extremes' are those of developing performers differentiating between their multiple characters by using significantly contrasting speech styles.[70]

---

[67] Phil Gilbey, 'Tis Pity She's a Whore', *Stage*, 9 November 1995, 12.
[68] John O'Mahony, '"Tis Pity She's a Whore", *Time Out*, 8–15 November 1995, 133.
[69] Anon, 'Pity It's a Bore', *The Times*, 4 November 1995, 19.
[70] This is a common technique for actors performing multiple roles in the same production.

Brewster had intentionally used the production as a forum to give new actors experience in this genre. Aware of their general lack of experience with this work, Brewster comments on the lack of preparedness of some actors at audition, including the woman who was dressed as a whore and had not read the play.[71] It was precisely because of this kind of occurrence that Brewster knew she had to use her position to allow capable, talented performers the opportunity to learn this aspect of their craft.

Both Phil Gilbey and John O'Mahoney continue and express the view that the actors struggle with the text, do not understand the subtleties of the play, and that consequently it is impossible for them to express the nuances. Gilbey writes, 'And when the action takes place the reading of the lines is often undistinguished. Giovanni and Annabella seem content to deliver their words without injecting passion and they are not alone in failing to fire the script.'[72] O'Mahoney comments, 'others have barely grasped their lines and display nothing more than a grim determination to reach the end.'[73]

Whilst the critics' comments generally reflect their disappointment in the lack of experience on the part of some of the performers, there is, however, some good news. One cast member is positively singled out by the press:

> Don Warrington's excellent Vasques shows us how pitifully underused he was in 'Rising Damp', and what a crying shame it is there haven't been good television roles since he played that good-natured token black man smiling amiably at the prejudices of those around him. But then how many television roles have there been since then for good actors who happen to be black?[74]

Michaels's remarks accurately point to a gulf between excellent actors 'who happen to be black' and the limited work they get because of their skin colour. Her comments may also refer to her acceptance of Warrington in this serious role. We had already been told to take him seriously in *Rising Damp* and so we do not expect to see him breaking out into calypso and whining his waist. Although the comments are about television at the time, the same was true for British theatre back then.

---

[71] Brewster Interview, 26 November 2018.
[72] Gilbey, 'Tis Pity She's a Whore', 12.
[73] O'Mahoney, 'Tis Pity She's a Whore', 133.
[74] Melissa Michaels, 'Tis Pity She's a Whore', *What's On in London*, 8 November 1995, 54.

This situation has changed unimaginably since 1995 with every current sitcom and soap opera portraying various forms of 'minority' life in Britain. Precisely because of this, Melissa Michaels's question still stands: 'How many television roles have there been since then for good actors who happen to be black?' In addition to the quality of his performance, Brewster's decision to cast Warrington also gave the younger black performers access to a mentor-type performer. His body of work indicated to them that they could also be successful. Brewster herself paid a price for this because Warrington's attitude knocked her confidence:

> I'm not sure how supportive he was; behind his amenability there was a slight disdain and he would always come up to me and give me slightly wonderful advice about various things. One day one of the actors said to him, 'Why don't you give yourself the advice?' With Don, he would a bit English, I mean [his] grandiosity, he would try to tell you that you're a load of shit really, without actually saying so. [He would say] 'But my dear, I'm ever indebted to your creativity'. It's just his attitude because he was brought up with all of these white actors who go in for that kind of 'oh my dear chap' kind of thing.[75]

Despite how she felt, Brewster was able to keep her eye on the bigger picture and focus on the many complimentary strands of what she was trying to achieve through this performance, both on and off stage. Some of this was picked up by Lyn Gardener: 'Perhaps it's not an inspired production but it is an intelligent and eminently watchable one, and it's a pleasure to see Talawa consolidating its reputation for tackling the classics and developing a coherent performance style.'[76] Gardner's acknowledgement that Talawa's work at the time was maturing in the right direction was welcome. The fact that she gave the impression it had a place performing the classics on the British stage was a breath of fresh air in an otherwise generally discouraging environment.

Brewster's bravery in this genre is particularly shown in her decision to take on Oscar Wilde's *The Importance of Being Earnest* (1989) and Shakespeare's *Othello* (1997). For each production Brewster knew the reception from the mainstream press would serve as a marker of how ready theatre land was, at that time, to share its white plays with blacks not even

---

[75]Brewster Interview, 26 November 2018.
[76]Lyn Gardner, 'Tis Pity She's a Whore', *Guardian*, 7 November 1995, s2.10.

pretending to be white. Typically, Brewster had clear aims for taking these risks. These included to illustrate that her black actors could play Victorians, as well as Shakespeare's most demanding roles. Her directorial decision not to adapt any of the language in Wilde's play, along with her decision to cast black actors other than Othello in Shakespeare's play, revealed the extent to which Brewster wished to challenge her audience and the mainstream.

The Importance of Being Earnest

Talawa presented its version of the Oscar Wilde classic at the Tyne Theatre, Newcastle and London's Bloomsbury Theatre between 19 April and 13 May 1989. The production also toured Britain and was Talawa's first foray into classical theatre and the company's fifth production in total.

It was because of Antony Everett's report to the Arts Council on *O Babylon* (1988) and his comment that he could see 'every penny [of the funding] on stage' that the Arts Council decided to make Talawa one of its regulars. Brewster was called to an Arts Council meeting and offered an annual subsidy for middle-scale touring theatre for three years. She had previously received project funding only. Whilst happy, Brewster's immediate concern was that she would not be able to do anything else. Concern shifted to the Arts Council when Brewster stated, having accepted the funding, that her next production would be *The Importance of Being Earnest*. She clarified, 'Wilde was Irish and despised the English, so I would like to have a look at Lady Bracknell as a vulgarian.'[77] The suggestion she should aim to closer meet the needs of the black community met with: 'I'll do *The Importance of Being Earnest* with a black cast.'[78] Her 'In fact, we'll have no white people in it at all' clarified her intentions for this quintessentially English play.[79]

Brewster felt that Wilde's attack on English snobbery performed by black actors was just what the black community needed. They and black actors had been seen as voiceless minstrel-types for long enough. The contemporary laugh would rest with Talawa, as the English would be ridiculed by both the Irish and blacks, the very people the Victorians regarded as least fitting of Victorian status: 'It's social comedy and it really is taking the piss out of

---

[77]Brewster Interview, 26 November 2018.
[78]Ibid.
[79]Ibid.

the Brits which I love, because I love the Brits, but I love to take the piss of them as well.'[80]

Talawa learnt to have a specific aim, beyond the purely creative, for doing work in the classical genre. This was because the mainstream eyes on the company encouraged a feeling that Talawa would have to justify itself in this or any other genre that was not 'obviously black'. Talawa's production of *The Importance of Being Earnest*, in addition to presenting black Victorians, aimed centrally 'to try and impress the British theatrical community with their own text'.[81]

The Importance of Being Earnest was preceded by three Caribbean and one African production and was ground-breaking in that it moved Talawa away from the kinds of so-called 'black' work that the company had become associated with. It would potentially attract new audiences, as well as help Talawa to become established in the mainstream as the only black British theatre company performing British classics at the time.

Additionally, the production would provide new opportunities for black actors. Whilst there is little contemporary documented evidence that black performers are not deemed suitable for classical roles, the fact they hardly appeared in them at the time, and still do not regularly feature in them on the British stage, suggests they are still seen to be less appropriate for them than their white counterparts. Oscar James comments, 'We are not even given a chance to fail, which is why this company is so important in allowing black actors a chance at the classical.'[82]

With black actors in 'white roles' Talawa provided evidence of the genuine possibility of colour crossover in theatre. This straightforward movement of physically black actors into roles historically played by whites on the British stage deeply impacted the black performers: 'You had to remind yourself especially with this all black production that you are not the people it was intended for, you are yourself, so you must use your own life as the emotional bedrock for the characters.'[83]

Thomas's notion that this type of work was not intended for black performers put an additional burden on the company to produce a

---

[80]Brewster, *Blackstages* Interview, July 2002.
[81]Ben Thomas, Personal Interview by David Johnson, London, 3 September 2000.
[82]Quoted in Keith Duston, 'Importance of Being Oscar', *Sunday Sun*, 9 April 1989, 27.
[83]Thomas Interview, 3 September 2000; Thomas Interview, 5 July 2019.

particularly impressive performance, despite the company's lack of experience in this genre. This highlights the perpetual pioneering burden that Talawa has to live with. With so few black theatre companies, the work always has to be exemplary, or it will quickly be disregarded by the mainstream.

With the introduction of the British plays to its repertoire, Talawa showed both the right and ability to perform all work that made up its multicultural theatrical heritage. Thomas explains, 'you can as a black theatre company do what supposedly is English work and it still works.'[84] This particular idea is aided in *The Importance of Being Earnest* by the fact that some central aspects of Victorian thought are mirrored by Talawa as an institution, thus making the work even more relevant to the company. The most obvious is the Victorian notion that man has the power to effect and positively change his environment.[85]

Once Talawa had established itself as a company that primarily focused on black work, it maintained control of its own future by launching itself into the classical genre whilst continuing to work within the genres of African, Caribbean and American plays. Talawa's work in the classics, having introduced many performers and audiences to the idea of black actors performing a range of roles, demonstrates Brewster encouraging black theatre practitioners to work in all areas of British theatre, and British audiences to accept and expect them.

During the Victorian era, blacks were regarded, along with the Irish and other 'lower classes' in Victorian science and literature, as childlike, unreasonable, irrational, excitable, superstitious, godless, criminal, filthy, excessively sexual and coming from unknown dark territories.[86] Due to how successfully such notions have been embedded into the British psyche, real movement away from such engrained ideas remains questionable. These ideals would not however be reflected in Talawa's performance, although the company followed rather than adapted the script. In spite of the negatives above, Brewster is clear why the work should be done:

---

[84]Thomas Interview, 3 September 2000.
[85]See the Victorian and Victorianism site: http://landow.stg.brown.edu/victorian/vn/victor4.html (accessed 2 September 2000). George P. Landow states, 'In science and technology, the Victorians invented the modern idea of invention – the notion that one can create solutions to problems, that man can create new means of bettering himself and his environment.'
[86]Douglas Lorimer, *Colour, Class and the Victorians: English Attitudes to the Negro in the Mid-Nineteenth Century* (Leicester: Leicester University Press, 1978).

> Black theatre has as many facets as any other sort of theatre, and the ambitions held by black theatre practitioners are probably not much different from anyone else in this challenging business; but because opportunities for realizing these ambitions are much fewer and certainly farther apart, so much depends on the success or failure of every endeavour. This is even more true if the black theatre practitioner is attempting to interpret what has been seen for centuries as the rightful property of others. It is important, indeed vital, that black companies continue to celebrate and to investigate the wealth of non-European material which exists, as this is the ultimate source of their inspiration. However, [when presenting non-'black' plays] they must always expect to defend their work from the ever present question, HOW RELEVANT IS THIS TO YOU?, meaning if the obvious connection of colour is not immediately apparent, the matter of common humanity is irrelevant. This is debilitating and suggests that the questioner would prefer us to exist culturally in a cocoon. The good and great work from all cultures belongs to everyone. A Wole Soyinka play should be as important a source of inspiration to the Norwegians as Strindberg is to the English.[87]

The programme information, mentioning both Ira Aldridge and Samuel Morgan Smith, as well as confirming how long black people have been performing in this genre, suggests that both must have been outstanding performers, given the degree of racism between 1782 and 1866 when they respectively started performing in Britain.[88] Talawa's programme information continues, 'The success of these 2 black men seems to suggest that England provided a safe and creative haven for the talent of black performers in the 19th Century. We wish to test this theory in 1989.'[89] Contemporary British audiences then were invited to accept Talawa's black performers depicting life in the shires, English manners and Victorian

---

[87] Production programme, *The Importance of Being Earnest*, 6.
[88] Production programme, *The Importance of Being Earnest*, 6. By the end of his career, which spanned four decades, Ira Aldridge had played Richard III, Shylock, Hamlet, Macbeth, King Lear, Othello and most of the major Shakespearean roles in Britain and in Europe. Samuel Morgan Smith was born in Philadelphia in 1833 and died in Sheffield in 1882. He arrived in England from America to set up his own theatre company in Gravesend in 1866. He successfully produced and acted in a wide range of plays from Shakespeare to contemporary work.
[89] See Talawa's production archives for *The Importance of Being Earnest*, production programme, 6.

values, and question the extent to which historical, inherent and sometimes tacit racism still existed.

A critical reception

The audience response to the production was as varied as the range of work that Talawa had produced to date. Thomas explains:

> It was a wonderful response. I think that there might have been some particularly ethnic orientated comments about how could black people do this obviously white play, but then they saw the confidence that we did it in. One of the reviews, which for me was one of my best I've ever had, and I didn't even understand what it meant, said, 'Ben Thomas is more blue book than any actor I have seen before.'[90]

The blue book referred to is a handbook of middle class Victorian behaviour. Thomas's ability to epitomize it shows how the appropriate manners can be learnt by others. This challenges the worthiness white Victorians gave this behaviour, whilst illustrating the arbitrariness of the Victorian codes of good breeding.

The media response echoed some of Thomas's perceptions. Alex Renton comments, 'I cannot remember another where the actors seemed to perform and live each scene with such ease.'[91] Similarly, David Isaacs states, 'The standard of the performance is high.'[92] Other critics focused on various aspects of what they saw as a colour issue. As Talawa had not highlighted colour, such commentary materialized because this 'white play' had an all-black cast.

Nicholas De Jongh believes that 'Short of finding herself in bed with a manservant or two, Lady Bracknell could scarcely have envisaged anything worse than to find herself, and her associates being impersonated by blacks'.[93] De Jongh's notion of 'impersonation' may suggest the black actors are playing at being something that is entirely anathema to black existence, that it should remain so and that this type of 'impersonation' is

---

[90] Thomas Interview, 3 September 2000; Thomas Interview, 5 July 2019.
[91] Alex Renton, 'Something Wilde', *Independent*, 18 May 1989, 18.
[92] David Isaacs, 'Skills Sweep Doubt Away', *Journal*, 21 April 1989. No page number available.
[93] Nicholas De Jongh, 'The Importance of Being Earnest', *Guardian*, 18 May 1989, 28.

hugely offensive to the real Lady Bracknells of this world. A subtext to this, unintended or otherwise, is that to avoid offence, Talawa should not attempt such classics in this way. What the critic describes as Lady Bracknell's worst imaginings neatly points to the failure of the mainstream press, at the time, to understand either the relevance of such work to Talawa, or Talawa's relevance in all its forms to the British stage and wider British society.

Similarly, though clearly well-intentioned, Armistead's comments reveal her feelings towards black Britons doing 'non-black' work. She writes, 'There is something oddly disarming about seeing the black theatre establishment investing time, talent and energy in a play that is so much a part of white theatre tradition, without any perceivable intention to subvert or reinterptret it.'[94] Her comments, and in particular the words 'oddly disarming', are really rather condescending to both the performers and her black readers and give rise to a series of questions: Is the entirety of the black performer's work reduced to skin colour when no overt attempt is made to 'blacken' the performance? Can black performers not be appreciated for their acting skill alone? Is the mainstream incapable of recognizing that this work is part of black theatre tradition both in Britain and internationally?

The facts of the slave trade and British colonial rule widely succeeded in forcing African and then Caribbean blacks to be stripped of everything they were. This was replaced with everything they were not, and included British theatre traditions. Black people then have had white British theatre thrust upon them for a long as they have been in contact with whites. How can it not be claimed as part of their theatre too? De Jongh's revelations are reminiscent of the reaction Brewster et al. received in Jamaica after studying abroad, and which led her to set up The Barn theatre. It did not matter how many of the correct hoops they had jumped through, they were just not allowed in by the island's white theatre-makers.

When mainstream critics present notions that black British theatre practitioners ought to be so divorced from traditional British theatre that they should not want to perform it in its original form, their message is a reminder that the theatrical mainstream can only accept them if their work is overtly stereotypical to white eyes. This type of outdated performance would ensure that these practitioners never become British without the 'black'. Additionally, they will be denying themselves part of what is equally theirs.

---

[94]Claire Armistead, 'The Importance of Being Earnest', *Financial Times*, 18 May 1989, 7.

Those who insist on being bemused by this kind of performance ignore the impact of the British Empire on both those black people who were colonized and then came home to Britain, and on those that were born and raised here. It seems that their blackness is not seen as part of their ever-changing bicultural existence, but necessarily viewed as the sum total of who they are. Dennis Barker quotes Brewster citing a white audience member regarding *The Importance of Being Earnest*: 'Oh mah deahh! I reahhly don't know what they are going to do with this, because it is so utterly, utterly English.'[95] Presumably the speaker sees Talawa as 'utterly, utterly black' and ignores the cultural and linguistic fluidity that all blacks in Britain negotiate from the day they arrive or are born there.

From a subordinate position in British society, black people are forced to examine and fully understand white people, until this becomes instinct, in the same way that a child learns to normalize and deal with the unpredictability of a schizophrenic parent. This is, in a word, survival. It should then not be so surprising to see black actors playing white characters as credibly as black ones. This would not work the other way round because white people were not enslaved for centuries and then forced to live subordinate lives to black people for hundreds of years thereafter. The daily survival of whites has therefore not depended on really knowing and understanding blacks. Kasi Lemmons explains, 'We know white people a lot better than most white people know black people.'[96] In her writing on Teer, Thomas provides an explanation for Lemmons's comment. She states:

> The culture shock many whites experience at an NBT production is due to the self-enforced isolation from black culture, in worship as well as in daily chores. Living as a minority in a hegemonic society necessitates disguise in order to succeed or even to exist, so blacks learn white ways in their efforts to adapt; but whites almost never have occasion to observe black life, let alone understand it.[97]

Applied to a British context and Talawa, how would black actors not be able play archetypal white characters?

---

[95] Dennis Barker, 'A Black Look at Oscar Wilde', *Guardian*, 13 May 1989, 2.
[96] *Black Hollywood, They've Got to Have Us: Black Film Is Not a Genre* (2018), [TV programme] BBC1, 20 October.
[97] Thomas, 'Barbara Ann Teer: From Holistic Training to Liberating Rituals', 349.

Talawa Theatre Company

Contemporary black Victorians

In a press release before the production, Brewster stated, 'My aim is not to attempt a West Indian version of the play but to stage this Oscar Wilde classic with black actors.'[98] The black actors would ensure their credibility as English upper middle class Victorians by adopting the appropriate speech. De Jongh confirms the sense in this strategy: 'The revelation of this production is that the sight of black actors inhabiting the skins and minds of upper middle class white Victorians does not seem strange or perverse. As long as they sound right you accept them. Elocution transcends colour.'[99]

The 'standard English' of the text reflects the voice of the white English upper middle class. This voice is abandoned by Gary McDonald playing Jack Worthing and Juanita Waterman playing Gwendolen. The former moves from black British to a slightly cockney sound, the latter from the required upper middle class sound to a distinct cockney voice. Lane, the Manservant, played by Christopher Tajah, adopts a general northern voice.

Whilst both black British and West Indian performers produced accurate voice work, De Jongh singles out Thomas for praise: 'Ben Thomas's elegant Algernon Moncrief, a smooth aesthete done out in a crisp moustache and cream suit, manages the authentic Wildean noise and cultivates the right langour and artifice.'[100] Thomas explains his ease at delivering the voice:

> I am a particularly Anglicized black man. I am quite an English Englishman despite coming from Yorkshire, which allowed me not to be worried about the text in any shape or form as it was familiar to me. I was able to relax the other actors into not being afraid of what that text was about. Similarly, I learnt a wider freedom of expression from them.[101]

Along with Thomas, Jamaican Leonie Forbes produced an accurate voice in her role as Miss Prism, despite not being British or living in England. She was however born and raised in Jamaica during colonization and learnt how to deliver colonial speech and manners. Both Forbes and

---

[98] See Talawa's production archives, *The Importance of Being Earnest*, publicity file.
[99] De Jongh, 'The Importance of Being Earnest', 28.
[100] Ibid.
[101] Ben Thomas, Personal Interview by David Johnson, London, 30 August 2000; Thomas Interview, 5 July 2019.

Thomas then demonstrated they were able to accommodate their language to suit the upper middle class Victorian characters of the script and simultaneously illustrate their verbal repertoire. Their skin colour paled into insignificance.

White words black mouths

Talawa's decision to concentrate on its right and 'nativeness' to perform the play without changing the original language of the text meant that some sentences in the play took on a new meaning as the actors were black, and performing in a contemporary setting.

When Williams's Cecily tells Thomas's Algernon, 'What wonderfully blue eyes you have', followed by 'I hope your hair curls naturally', the audience laughs. Thomas does not have blue eyes and indeed, like all black men, has hair that curls naturally. In this unintended context it is as if she is asking him if he is a real black man, as perhaps this is what she is really after. She regards hair texture as one way of gauging the black authenticity she requires. There is further irony in Williams's Cecily's latter comment as Thomas, at the time of Talawa's performance, had artificially curled hair. Thomas explains, 'This is another dimension of the Afro-Caribbean story of hair curl being straight and so on, so when black people were in the audience that meant much more to them.'[102]

When Williams's Cecily later states, 'When I see a spade I call it a spade', to which Waterman's Gwendolen replies, 'I am glad to say that I have never seen a spade', the racial connotations for the British audience are many: 'half of the audience screams with delight, the black half, the other half questions if the performers realize what they just said. Cecily is saying, "When I see a nigger I call it a nigger".'[103] Following Thomas's suggestion, Waterman's Gwendolen's later comment of 'I'm glad to say I've never seen a spade', for Talawa's audience, means 'I'm glad to say I've never seen a nigger.'

This highlights the wealth of additional layers of meaning that automatically evolve with black actors in these roles. The connotations go significantly beyond skin colour. Whilst this in itself is not problematic,

---

[102] Thomas Interview, 30 August 2000; Thomas Interview, 5 July 2019.
[103] Ibid.

by not changing the language, Talawa is rising above the superficial as the meaning of the text is clear. The inherently racist nature of the language of the text, as understood by a contemporary audience and expressed by black performers, cannot be transferred to a black cast without momentarily affecting the original meaning. Brewster is proud when she explains that she did not change a single word in the script.[104] This layered interpretation could lead black theatre companies to avoid the issue of questions that arise naturally when performing British classics. They may instead prefer to adapt the language and performance of traditionally 'white' plays.

The above quotes may promote an idea that, in the eyes of the mainstream, this is not appropriate work for black performers. This is suggested by Isaacs's summing up of the media response and the expressions of doubt that he came across about the production. He writes, 'I feel bound to say, however, that some of them have also been tinged with malice and expressed in tones overtly racist.'[105] The racist attitude towards Talawa's production of the *The Importance of Being Earnest* was being expressed by the mainstream loud enough for critics who did not share the same opinion to both know about it, and feel it important enough to comment on it in their own reviews.

In spite of the 'conflict' between the black skin of the performers and the language of the text, Brewster's resolve to do the production was beneficial in that it proved that if black actors were given the chance, they were as capable in this genre as their white counterparts. Thomas outlines additional advantages: 'It meant that there might be a credible competition now. The other thing was that the other black theatre companies that existed in those days, and don't now, got extra confidence that they could be experimental too in whatever they wanted to do.'[106]

Brewster knew that doing this production would be a risk and she was prepared to take it. This was her way of ensuring that excellent black performers, who would be overlooked by the mainstream, got the opportunity to play these classic roles: 'It's part of our job, to give black actors a chance to play parts that no-one else would cast them in.'[107] Just as

---

[104]Brewster, *Blackstages* Interview, July 2002.
[105]Isaacs, 'Skills Sweep Doubt Away'. No page number available.
[106]Thomas Interview, 3 September 2000.
[107]Brewster, *Blackstages* Interview, July 2002.

Brewster later discovered that Beaton wanted to play Lear, she knew that Mona Hammond wanted to play Lady Bracknell and she seized her chance to make this happen with this production.[108]

Hammond herself acknowledges that it was because Brewster took the chance on her as Lady Bracknell that she was then cast as Aase in *Peer Gynt*, that she was at the National Theatre for two years where she did *The Crucible* and *Wind in the Willows*, and then a New York production of *Macbeth*. From this she secured an American agent:

> Talawa filled the gap of not only doing black productions with black actors but giving them the opportunity to do classical work. For me, classical work is the challenge. She [Brewster] provided another outlet for actors to work in and create. Places like the RSC and the National weren't doing it often enough. I really honestly believe that Talawa had something to do with what's happening today, and I am very proud of it. I'm very proud when I see David Harewood, play Othello and Adrian Lester, do *As You Like It*, and all the Shakespeare that he's doing now, *Hamlet*. I've seen progression in the right direction.[109]

The success of Brewster's production included the compliments of Wilde's grandson Merlin Holland. Having attended the show with his mother, he gave Brewster a copy of Wilde's collected plays, in which he wrote, 'You have given back 25 years to my grandfather's play. Brilliant.'[110] It is with the benefit of many more years' experience and hindsight that Brewster questions and answers, 'I wonder if I would have chosen to direct this play, of all the plays, with an all-black cast if I had second sight of the outrage it would cause? Perhaps not.'[111] British theatre generally owes a debt of gratitude to Brewster that she did. Black theatre practitioners are more specifically indebted to her for broadening their legitimate repertoire by her indomitable staging of British classics. By the time Brewster decided to do a production of *Othello* in 1997, Talawa's audience and the mainstream had come to expect the unexpected from the company.

---

[108] Brewster Interview, 26 November 2018.
[109] Hammond, *Blackstages* Interview, August 2002.
[110] Brewster Interview, 26 November 2018.
[111] Brewster, 'A Short Autobiographical Essay Focusing on My Work in the Theatre', 394.

Talawa Theatre Company

O to hell go Othello

Talawa's production of Shakespeare's *Othello* ran from 9 October to 1 November 1997 at the Drill Hall, London. This was Talawa's twenty-third production in total and its fifth work within the British classical genre. By the time Talawa performed *Othello* the company had been in existence for twelve years. During this period many black theatre companies had come and gone while Talawa had remained. Part of the reason for Talawa's longevity was due to the fact that the company was innovative in the nature of its creative work, marked not least by its occasional forays into classical performance.

Whilst performing Shakespeare was no longer a novelty for Talawa, a production of *Othello* could be regarded slightly differently because of the fact that of all Shakespeare's plays *Othello* was the most obvious one for the company to do. A new black company choosing to do it would have been predictable. Talawa waited until the company was established before taking it on. It would then be longer awaited than expected.

Through her production, Brewster questions whether blacks who reach Othello's level of success are blind to the fact that white society's acceptance of them depends on its race and other rules being adhered to.[112] She was thus pointing to social integration being a charade and identifying racism as the reason for a black man's demise in white society. Ukaegbu explains, 'the production placed culpability for racism on both public and private spheres ... by indicating that his [Othello's] contributions to Venetian society were by far superior to those of his white accusers put together ... and how ugly racism manages to dilute and destroy a pure emotion like love.'[113]

It is Brewster's colour casting that gives the clearest picture of her aim to make the work inimitably her own. Evident in this production are the five white cast members.[114] Brewster's decision to use these performers complemented the traditionally white roles she had given to black performers. With a mixed race cast, she could challenge and highlight the stereotypes that persist around black people in an original way.

---

[112]Ukaegbu, 'Talawa Theatre Company: The "Likkle" Matter of Black Creativity and Representation on the British Stage', 138.
[113]Ibid.
[114]The following roles are played by white performers: Brabantio (Peter Mair), Desdemona (Paula Stockbridge), Iago (Dominic Letts), Lodovico (Peter Mair) and Rodrigo (Ian Driver).

Casting Paula Stockbridge as Desdemona created unforeseen problems for Talawa. The Drill Hall's artistic director, Julie Parker, was concerned that Talawa's choice may lead to negative publicity for the production which would in turn impact on the Drill Hall. As the production opened shortly after the death of Princess Diana, the creative management of the Drill Hall was concerned about perceived references being made to her through Stockbridge's Desdemona. This was conceivable in that Stockbridge's Desdemona wears army fatigues whilst at sea. This image is loosely reminiscent of Princess Diana crossing minefields in Angola. Princess Diana and Stockbridge's Desdemona shared a further link: Desdemona certainly, and Princess Diana allegedly, are each in love with a black man. This causes Desdemona's death and is rumoured as part of the reason for Princess Diana's. Brewster put Parker's mind at rest:

> Your letter seeks a written assurance that no 'quasi' characterisation of the Princess of Wales will be presented or 'indeed any direct or indirect references' to her will be made. None will. It has never been the view of the Creative Team or intimated by any member of our staff, that the characterisation of Desdemona be that of 'a quasi Princess Diana'.[115]

Whilst any likeness to Princess Diana was purely accidental, Brewster based aspects of her portrayal of Othello on the American football star OJ Simpson. Talawa's production programme consists almost entirely of the specifically designed research package that compares Othello and the OJ Simpson trial.[116] The comparisons illustrate how both men were required to shed their blackness for whiteness in order to succeed.[117]

---

[115]Letter from Yvonne Brewster to Julie Parker (artistic director of the Drill Hall), 2 October 1997. See Talawa's production archives, *Othello*, correspondence file.
[116]Talawa's research package for the production of Othello made up 90 per cent of all additional non-advertising and biographical information of the production programme. The package consists of an unpublished essay by Austin Clarke, 'Orenthal and Othello: Phobogenic statements made in the opening statement and in the prologue of the play, Othello', 1997.
[117]Clarke, 'Orenthal and Othello', 23. All of the comparisons attempt to show how both men replace cultural 'blackness' with 'whiteness'. For example, like Othello, Simpson is seen as having 'erased his oppositeness with his speech'. Clarke continues, 'This "white" voice, or this "whitening" of speech, which is more than an articulation of language, is the deliberate attempt to be clothed in the colonialist's rhetoric and culture.'

In white-directed productions of the play, it is usual for the actor playing Othello to be very dark, whether by the use of make-up or his natural hue. Brewster presents a mixed race Othello in Ben Thomas. Thomas's Othello's mixed race identity has the effect of watering down the effect of Shakespeare's racist language. Othello's negative traits, attributed to his physical blackness, do not describe the light-skinned Othello we see before us. What is understood from this is that the white characters' negative language in reference to Thomas's Othello's blackness are aimed at making him an outsider despite his skin colour not being far removed from their own. Also, by Americanizing Thomas's Othello, Brewster achieves the effect of making him sound like the outsider the white characters need him to be.

In addition to casting Othello as a mixed race man, Cassio is played by Michael Buffong, Emilia by Sam Adams, and Bianca by Amantha Edmead. The blackness of the performers changes the dynamics of the central relationships. The fact that Buffong's Cassio is also black means that two of the most prominent and likeable men in the play are black. Brewster gives her audience two positive black male role models. This extinguishes all possibility of Buffong's Cassio being drawn as good and white, in opposition to Thomas's Othello's badness being understood as an inherent component of his blackness. Any redeeming features or negative traits such as Othello's jealousy and Cassio's tendency to drink, and all other comparisons on and off the battlefield, cannot be colour-based in a straightforward black versus white sense.

Similarly, debates along the lines of 'the blacker the man the worse he is' would be counter-productive in this particular comparison as Buffong's Cassio is darker than Thomas's Othello. Brewster's idea to cast Cassio as a black man stemmed from her grandfather, Ba. He thought it would be easier on Othello if it were another black man that was accused of sleeping with his wife: 'if it was pokey old Rodrigo, he would just kick him up his arse, so make him black.'[118]

Buffong's Cassio, the physically blackest man, is the most deservedly victorious by the end of the production. The blackest man, then, has the best soul. Directly below him is the light-skinned Thomas's Othello who, although he has murdered his wife, can be forgiven as he was misled. Below him is the

---

[118]Brewster Interview, 26 November 2018.

white Letts's Iago who has no redeeming features. With this interpretation of the colour hierarchy, the further racial dynamic relevant to the contemporary audience of black-on-black conflict is presented to the contemporary British audience. This is instigated and encouraged by the white Letts's Iago between the two black men, Thomas's Othello and Buffong's Cassio.

Buffong's Cassio's physical blackness also creates new dynamics with regard to his relationship with Edmead's Bianca. Both are cast in negative and stereotypical roles. As a black prostitute on the British stage, where black female performers are rarely featured, Edmead's Bianca is reminiscent of the historical black female sexy dancer types. The relationship also illustrates that Buffong's Cassio is immoral and oversexed, and needs the services of a prostitute. Whilst the same may be said if both characters are played by white performers, they have the reassurance that white performers are seen in a range of roles and usually within the same play. More positively, in his minimal relationship with Adams's Emilia, Buffong's Cassio is seen to be another good black man, along with Thomas's Othello, in the eyes of the less powerful black maid.

Further statements on racial dynamics are offered by the fact that the weakest male characters in Brewster's production are kept white. Letts's Iago is generally jealous of black men. This would not be apparent in traditional productions where all characters, other than Othello, are usually white. His jealousy is a psychological weakness. Brewster adds to this by choosing a white performer who is considerably physically smaller than all the black men in the production. Although he causes death and destruction in their lives, Letts's Iago also unintentionally succeeds in replacing one black general for another. He thus empowers another black man. The second is darker than the first.

Letts's Iago's jealousy is of black men's status, success and lifestyle. This is coupled with his frustration that he is no match for their physical and sexual prowess. Brewster has made the stereotype of the black man's physical and sexual power an overt and additional object of the white man's jealousy. This is further demonstrated by the fact that Brewster gives Letts's Iago a black wife.

Within the context of this racially mixed production, Letts's Iago's general lack of respect for Adams's Emilia, despite his marriage to her, appears to be racially engendered. He has little regard for her as a human being because he does not see her as his equal. In more traditional performances this is seen as his attitude towards women generally. Here the suggestion is that her colour causes him to treat her negatively. The tacit notion that he treats her badly because he sees himself as inferior to the male members of her race seeps through Letts's performance. He is violent whilst she remains passive during their lovemaking. During these scenes he is nervous of her and aware that she can overpower him if she chooses to do so. She allows him to live the fantasy of appearing dominant, although they both know she is in control.

Whilst Letts's Iago's racism towards blacks is multilayered in Talawa's production, his general behaviour towards the white characters is no more favourable. This is seen with his manipulation of Driver's Rodrigo. Seen perhaps as the other significant white man in Talawa's production, Driver's Rodrigo's all-around weakness is what helps him to fade into the background. Brewster's production then divides the men into strong and black, in Thomas's Othello and Buffong's Cassio, and weak and white, in Letts's Iago and Driver's Rodrigo. This is uncommon in contemporary British theatre and would impact the black male audience unused to seeing themselves portrayed in positions of power. The general reaction to Talawa's *Othello* is documented in the company's archival video of the performance, as well as in the audience response, and the production reviews of the show.

Audience response

From outside the theatre, the audience was invited into the show by Thomas's Othello's answer phone message, which played on a loop. It explained that he was away in the desert for four months.[119] Whilst this caused amusement, the audience's general enjoyment of the show is illustrated by the many occurrences of unpredictable laughter during the performance.

This occurs when Letts's Iago manipulates Thomas's Othello with the idea his wife is having an affair. His 'Lie with her, on her, what you will' elicits laughter from the audience. The same happens when Stockbridge's Desdemona realizes she is about to be killed and says 'I am not yet to die' and Thomas's Othello responds with 'Yes presently'. The collective laughter is a response to casual language use in highly emotionally charged situations. It also highlights that black audiences often go to the theatre to interact with the performers.

---

[119]Brewster Interview, 26 November 2018.

The collective laughter recurs whenever physical scuffles result in one character looking physically weaker than another. When Thomas's Othello demands proof of Stockbridge's Desdemona's betrayal, he lifts Letts's Iago from the floor with one hand. The audience finds his show of brute strength hilarious and ignores his emotional pain. There is a similar response when Driver's Rodrigo attempts and fails to kill Buffong's Cassio. In the same way, when Edmead's Bianca physically moves Letts's Iago out of the way so that she can try to stab Buffong's Cassio, the resulting audience laughter may be partially because the black woman shows herself to be physically stronger than the white man. It may also be due to Brewster's production once again generally presenting the white man in an unusually weak position.

The fact that the audience laughs aloud at many 'serious' points during the performance, along with delivering rapturous applause at the end, points to the degree to which the audience has been entertained. There is also active oral audience participation during the show. Thomas comments, 'I remember that on one occasion when I was about to kill Desdemona someone shouted out something like, "If you don't get out he's going to kill you, and you foolish girl, you should never give men like that a chance."'[120]

This kind of response was not uncommon throughout the run, which according to Thomas pointed to the extent to which some of the audience members remained engaged. Thomas highlights this reaction as typical of Talawa's audiences: 'When some of my white friends came to see the show, they didn't know what to think about people shouting out. They said to me, "Wasn't it terrible, spoiling it for the whole audience!" I said they were loving it, they pay their money, they do what they want and that's that at Talawa.'[121]

Thomas's explanation neatly expresses the call-and-response nature of black theatre. Participation is not rude, it is expected. Whilst this is a tacit aspect of Brewster's work, Teer set out to intentionally adapt the call and response of religious sermons and filter it into theatre. Her work was 'governed by an unwritten code of taste that, while welcoming spontaneous outbursts by all parties and the use of intimate phrases expressing solidarity, prevented demonstrations from becoming unruly'.[122] Similarly, Brewster welcomes her audience's reactions. As black British lives revolve around

---

[120] Thomas Interview, 3 September 2000; Thomas Interview, 5 July 2019.
[121] Ibid.
[122] Thomas, 'Barbara Ann Teer: From Holistic Training to Liberating Rituals', 349.

the key group rituals found in family and the church, like Teer's audiences, Brewster's black audience has a developed understanding of the tacit rules of audience behaviour, and instinctively knows how far to go.

White audience members also participated. Brewster recalls being challenged by an older white man who could not understand why Desdemona was being played by an actress in her thirties. He saw her as a flower of English youth destroyed by a black man. Brewster explained that she saw it differently; Brabantio had tried unsuccessfully to marry Desdemona off before. Desdemona was disinterested in suitors until she met Othello, as he excited her.[123] The man wanted to continue the discussion during the performance. He was engaged, but did not know the tacit rules of call and response within the black British theatre context.

Production reviews

Talawa promoted the show in three ways. Firstly the press would be invited to do pre-show 'exclusive' interviews with Brewster as *Othello* was billed as her last Talawa show.[124] None of the papers approached took up the offer. Secondly the show was being performed by Britain's leading black theatre company.[125] The final strategy was to advertise Talawa's new *Blackgrounds* oral history project as part of the *Othello* publicity.[126]

The production press pack sums up the result of the three approaches aimed at encouraging media and public interest. Cameron Duncan explains, 'The response, particularly from the national media, was disappointing, especially on the review front. However, I have found that the national critics are often unwilling to commit to a Talawa theatre production and this was no exception, sadly.'[127] This shone a light on the ever-continuing uphill struggle that Brewster faced. No explanation was given for the press silence. Was this a synchronized collective act of racism? Was this directed at Talawa and black theatre generally, or a body blow aimed at Brewster herself?

---

[123]Brewster Interview, 26 November 2018.
[124]Cameron Duncan PR, production press pack for Talawa's *Othello*, 1. The following papers were contacted: *Stage, Telegraph, Independent, Guardian, Radio 4 Kaleidoscope, Sunday Times, The Times*. See Talawa's production archives, *Othello*, publicity file.
[125]Ibid., 2.
[126]Ibid., 3.
[127]Ibid., 4.

Stay in Your Box

The final comment in the press pack points to the majority of the write-ups simply stating that the production is happening, with only two commenting further. In the first review the show received, which is in part blamed for the later lack of response from other papers,[128] Dominic Cavendish comments, 'Sad to report then, that what should be a crowning glory is nothing to write home about.'[129] In a later review Sam Marlowe comments:

> There is a ham-fisted feel to the whole production. The crass stereotyping of Desdemona (played by Paula Stockbridge) as a Sloane Ranger in Barbour jacket and loafers robs her of individuality and renders her death a matter of indifference to us. Michael Buffong as Cassio seems profoundly ill-at-ease, while Ben Thomas is a plodding Othello. There is a severe lack of pace generally, and little sense of growing misunderstandings, mental torment and imminent disaster.[130]

The reviews are drawn in stark contrast to the fact that *Othello* was, at the point of performance, one of Talawa's biggest box office successes.[131] This suggests that the negative response from the white media did not best reflect the experience of Talawa's audience. It also calls into question, once again, how it was possible that the audience and the press responded so differently to the same work. Perhaps expectations were widely opposed or, as indicated by the press pack, the press did not want to see Brewster exit with a successful production. Did they really think their silence would stop her legacy?

The language of the text versus the colour of the performers: Even Cassio is black

The impact of the language of the performance, versus the colour of the actors delivering it, was central to the work. This was ignored by the press. Hugh Quarshie illustrates how for the contemporary black performer the language of *Othello* presents challenges:

---

[128]Ibid., 1. Duncan PR, 'If we had had a good review in *Time Out* then I think I could have encouraged one or two critics to come along.'
[129]Dominic Cavendish, 'Othello', *Time Out*, 15–22 October 1997, 144.
[130]Sam Marlowe, 'Othello', *What's On in London*, 22–29 October 1997, 53.
[131]Thomas Interview, 3 September 2000.

Othello is given lines to speak which might have been quite unremarkable for a white Elizabethan actor in black make-up, but which, particularly for a modern black actor, are problematic. He must make no comment when his wife effectively says, 'I know he's as ugly as sin, but he has a beautiful mind' ('I saw Othello's visage in his mind').[132]

The contemporary black Othello, working with an all-white cast, would be expected to get on with delivering, and coping with, the impact of such language. With Talawa's mixed cast, however, racially offensive language is automatically reinterpreted. The burden of problematic language is handled by the whole cast and multiple interpretations are offered. This is seen when Letts's Iago tells Mair's Brabantio that 'the old black ram is tupping your white ewe'; the disgust that Letts's Iago is meant to impart with his statement is taken with a pinch of salt. This is because he is married to Adams's Emilia who is black. How disgusted can he really be by cross-cultural sexual activity? Similarly, when he claims Thomas's Othello and Stockbridge's Desdemona are 'making the beast with two backs', this is what he does with his wife. As Thomas's Othello is the product of mixed parentage, there can then be no mystery as to the type of human being that results from a black and white union. Brabantio need not be so afraid after all.

When Letts's Iago expounds on the nature of women for the benefit of three black people – Adams's Emilia, Thomas's Othello and Buffong's Cassio – his statement, 'If she be black and there to have a wit, she'll find a white that shall her blackness fit', refers to his own life. In productions where Emilia is white, Iago's comment is not founded in fact and is loutish bravado. Similarly, his comment to Driver's Rodrigo, 'we work by wit and not by witchcraft', appears founded because of his black connections, or ridiculous precisely because of them. His toast to Buffong's Cassio, 'to the health of black Othello', is turned on its head. Buffong's considerably darker Cassio must wonder what colour he is described as.

In traditional English productions of *Othello*, some comments define or cast aspersions on a character's social status. Brewster's mixed casting gives these same comments an extra edge when spoken by a black performer.

---

[132]Hugh Quarshie, 'Second Thoughts About Othello', based on Quarshie's 'Hesitations on Othello', given by the author as the Birthday Lecture at the Shakespeare Centre, Stratford upon Avon, 24 April 1998, 13.

Such remarks also allow Brewster's audience to reflect on the lack of development between historical and contemporary negative views on black people. Where Adams's Emilia questions Stockbridge's Desdemona, 'Who would not make their husband a cuckold to make him a monarch?' her 'free' attitude to infidelity may be seen as a part of her blackness. Whilst the black wife thinks little of an infidelity that brings reward, the white wife remains faithful. When she asks Thomas's Othello, 'What should such a fool do with so good a wife?' there is a suggestion that the black man, from a black woman's perspective, and by extension all other people, is not good enough for the white woman. Her comment and traditional performances of the play invite the suggestion that the black man, despite his ability to excel, both on and off stage, is inadequate in white society. Any white man with none of Othello's skill is deemed superior to him, by dint of his skin colour.

Playing Othello: The actors' perspective

There were two physical dimensions that would make it difficult for Thomas to be a credible Othello without traditional stereotypes being broken. The first was Thomas's light skin colour as discussed above. Secondly was Thomas's youthful appearance. Whilst Thomas was in his early forties at the time of the performance, traditional productions often have Othello played by older performers. The young looking light-skinned Othello was not the most obvious physical choice.

Similarly, for Thomas the role of Othello was not his first choice of Shakespearean roles: 'I resisted it, I was resentful personally, because it's the cage I expected people to want me to sit in occasionally, to play the black Shakespeare role. The part of yourself you use to make it authentic, your blackness, doesn't fit. It's a white man with paint on his face.'[133] Another part of Thomas's resistance was based on the burden he feels the role carries with it. He could not ignore the fact that unlike his white counterparts, he was not at liberty to play the role without the possibility of the negative aspects of Othello's character, and the play generally, appearing representative of all black men. Thomas states:

> Othello is bound up in so much bigotry. It seems to pander even to today's audience about their prejudices; put an alien in a position of

---

[133] Thomas Interview, 3 September 2000; Thomas Interview, 5 July 2019.

authority and they'll screw it up. On the sexual side of things, anything that is exciting and exotic might steal away our most beautiful prizes. It's not a story that I think is necessarily as interesting as some of the others, particularly if you and your race are cast in the role of the thief.[134]

Thomas chose to approach the role with the idea of making a difference and attempted to show that Othello 'was not a fool but had just been foolish'.[135] With this in mind, Thomas developed his character's history so that his Othello would make sense within the context of the range of behaviour he displays in the play. Negative behaviour could not be attributed to his blackness, but rather related to concrete personal facts. So in order to justify his killing of Stockbridge's Desdemona, Thomas's Othello was made a Muslim.

As a Muslim the death of evil was a good thing. In spite of his intentions, efforts and insights, Thomas was, however, unable to give the audience the Othello he wanted to: 'I played a character that I couldn't be proud of because he was less of a man than I wanted him to be, and I couldn't make him an icon with a flaw. His flaws were too great, we would have had to totally change the play.'[136] Is it reasonable then that Thomas should feel he has to change the characters he plays so that they are perfect rather than human, in order to ensure that black men are more fairly represented?

Quarshie echoes Thomas's thoughts: 'if a genuinely black actor plays Othello does he not risk making racial stereotypes seem legitimate or even true?'[137] He goes further: 'Of all the parts in the canon, perhaps Othello is the one which should most definitely not be played by a black actor.'[138] This comment is reasonable with the knowledge that Othello was perhaps never meant to be a real black man, but was rather to remain a white impersonation of one. This is supported by the fact that Shakespeare suggests Othello behaves negatively because he is black. This would make the role unattractive to black actors and illustrates that they were never really expected to play it.[139]

---

[134]Ibid.
[135]Ibid.
[136]Ibid.
[137]Quarshie, 'Second Thoughts About Othello', 4.
[138]Ibid.
[139]Ibid., 8.

Stay in Your Box

As it seems Othello was originally intended for a white actor and white audience, it can be argued that when played by a black actor, he is perhaps required to shed himself of all vestiges of his natural 'blackness' in favour of impersonating a black man to a remit and description prepared for, and aimed at, feeding the prejudices of whites. I made that comment in 2000. Brewster told me in 2018:

> I saw Olivier do his Othello, with the lip out. I didn't last. I kind of couldn't stand it. Then I saw Paul Scofield doing it. That was awful as well, not as bad as Olivier though, that wouldn't happen now. But when you see Adrian [Lester] doing Othello, you wonder why his body language is so white, and you wonder whether he was made to do that. That's something that worries me. It's a taking away of what is essentially yours and that's terrible. That's racism at its most violent. To be successful, to get on the National Theatre stage, as a non-white actor, you have to become more white.[140]

Acutely aware of the dilemma of playing Othello, Brewster helped with his characterization in her production through her direction of Iago. Iago could not be played as a cockney joker as Othello would not believe him: 'Iago was a seriously vicious, intelligent public school person who thought it [Othello's career and marriage] was not right.' It was more than simple jealousy.[141] This was hatred, the kind of hatred that Shakespeare may have felt towards Othello. It was Brewster's grandfather, Ba, who taught her to say 'O to hell go for Othello'. This is what he felt Shakespeare was saying to this black man: 'O to hell go, you old black fool. That's why he [Shakespeare] made him into a dithering thing that froths at the mouth. He doesn't like him.'[142] Shakespeare ensured that by giving Othello epilepsy, he would have an insurmountable physical flaw. This would mean that for all his strength and success, he could be weak, vulnerable and unpredictable at any given point. He could only be allowed to go so far. This characterization continues to be a clear illustration of the black man's plight in contemporary white society.

---

[140]Brewster Interview, 26 November 2018.
[141]Ibid.
[142]Ibid.

Similarly, Baptiste details the black actor's predicament in playing the part, and that he could not accept the notion that Othello would fall for Iago's trick. He had to create his own reasons to explain Othello's stupidity. Baptiste imagined Iago in love with Othello, and becoming nastier when Othello marries Desdemona. He thinks the handkerchief storyline should be swapped for a condom. This would signify something was very wrong. He comments, 'Othello is very difficult for a black actor to play. More so than a white actor.'[143] A white actor would not have to justify the character's flaws and stupidity. He could rest assured that Othello would not be seen as a reflection of him, or other white men.

Quarshie suggests a possible solution to the black 'dilemma' of playing Othello: 'perhaps black actors could simply decline to play the role on the grounds that it should only be played by a white actor, with or without black make-up. This would of course have the merit of allowing black actors to play Iago.'[144] Whilst black actors should be able to play the role of Iago, this should not be instead of playing Othello or anything else. It is certainly more beneficial for black performers and black theatre companies to continue doing this play, rather than avoiding it. Such productions would create the opportunity for the outdated elements of the work to be challenged creatively and would eventually allow black actors to feel less burdened whenever they perform the play.

Talawa's performance of *Othello* impacted mainstream theatre and helped to fuel the debate as to whether the role of Othello is the preserve of one particular race. Brewster's production, running at the same time as the National Theatre production starring David Harewood as Othello, highlighted that black actors have the skills to take on this part. This was not welcomed by factions of the mainstream press. John Gross writes,

> I don't know whether anyone has actually decreed that the part of Othello should only be played by black actors, but such is the convention which has come into force in contemporary theatre. It is a serious restriction on artistic freedom, and its chief practical effect is that Othello now gets produced less often than any of the other major Shakespeare tragedies.[145]

---

[143] Baptiste, *Blackstages* Interview, September 2002.
[144] Quarshie, 'Second Thoughts About Othello', 22.
[145] John Gross, 'Moor with Added Value', *Sunday Telegraph*, 21 September 1997, 11.

Gross fails to acknowledge that where a character has been created specifically to make a comment on his blackness that character may also be played by a black actor on the contemporary British stage. His notion of a convention that only black performers can play the part appears to stem from two 1997 London productions of the show. An identical lack of support from the white mainstream is seen in David Lister's comments in reference to the National Theatre's production of *Othello*:

> no white actor with a similar background would be playing the lead in a Shakespeare tragedy at the NT. Harewood, 32, has never yet acted in a national company or West End play, but has starred in British regional theatre and in *Antony and Cleopatra* off Broadway. Meanwhile the role is barred at the highest level to every white actor in the country.[146]

Lister's comment demonstrates part of the attitude that Talawa and all black theatre practitioners are up against from the mainstream. Whilst this attitude may encourage marginalization, Talawa and black Britons in general increasingly refuse to be sidelined. Lister continues, 'it's a great shame to deprive white actors of one of the most demanding roles in the repertoire.'[147] His use of the emotive verb 'deprive', in relation to white actors on the British stage, illustrates an attempt to make the playing of Othello a political issue from a white perspective. The reality of course is that it is black lives that have been deprived and politicized in all areas of British life since the beginning of white domination of blacks with the transatlantic slave trade.

Harewood looks back twenty-one years to when he made history as the first black man to play Othello at the National Theatre. It is not the achievement that sticks in his mind, but the battle to be accepted and Lister's article.[148] Harewood's solution to combat this racism was to move to America and make a success of his acting career. If similar opportunities were available to him in Britain as in America, he may well have stayed. He was in effect driven out by racism as epitomized in Lister's article.

---

[146]David Lister, 'Can It Be Wrong to "Black Up" for Othello?', *Independent*, 7 August 1997, 13.
[147]Ibid.
[148]*Black Hollywood*, BBC1, 27 October 2018. Harewood discusses Lister's article.

Talawa Theatre Company

The range of attitudes towards the performance of the character Othello suggests that the interest and thought the role provokes, for black and white theatre practitioners alike, makes the part too important for it not to be staged by any particular racial group. More generally, Talawa's performances of the British classics enriched British theatre by showing how black culture and experience can give multiple meanings to the traditional text, thereby making it more relevant to a contemporary setting. Brewster's work encouraged the growth of Talawa's audience by making the classics accessible to both the black community and the mainstream, and simultaneously helped the company to reflect the important role of black British theatre in the national and international arena. This went some way to reaching the day when performances of the British classics with black actors are no longer seen as a novelty, but as an everyday event in British theatre and globally.

CHAPTER 7
DON'T TELL MASSA

'As a black creative person in today's society, I believe it's even harder than it was. They're telling you how to be recognized now. They're making decisions for you.'[1]

The contribution to black British theatre and identity

Talawa's theatrical roots are shown to have originated in Africa, developed through slavery in the Caribbean generally and Jamaica specifically, and progressed in Britain through the pioneering work of post-war black British performers. It is against this backdrop, and following her permanent return to Britain in 1971, that Brewster co-founded Talawa for its 1986 production of *The Black Jacobins*. Under Brewster, the company made a considerable and innovative contribution to the contemporary British stage through the voice it gave to black British theatre.

The body of performance work achieved between 1986 and 2001 illustrates the breadth of genres Brewster legitimately claimed under the black theatre umbrella. This was marked by the magnitude of shows produced in the four distinct genres of African, American, British classical and Caribbean theatre. Brewster's choices vastly expanded what had previously been seen as black theatre. The themes explored in each genre also gave Talawa's audience an introduction to parts of its history rarely seen on the British stage.

By performing in voices from Africa, America, Britain and the Caribbean, Talawa shone a spotlight on the range and complexity of language within the black British community. Brewster's insistence on the production of accurate speech in performance is testament to her awareness of the close

---
[1] Brewster Interview, 26 November 2018.

link between language and specific cultural identity. In portraying a range of black lives, she distinguished varying communities and characters within them by speech style.

Both the extent and specificity of Talawa's productions directly benefited individual black British performers. The work allowed them to develop in culture-specific, as well as mainstream, styles of work. They were provided with a training ground and acting opportunities that still widely remain unavailable to them. Additionally, white performers gained an understanding of black British theatre by working with Talawa.

Brewster remembers a young Femi Oguns being brought into Talawa's youth theatre. He went on to found Identity Agency Group and Identity School of Acting (2006), where he represents and develops black actors, amongst others.[2] One such actor was John Boyega, originally from South London, now famed for his roles in the *Star Wars* franchise. Boyega comments on his appearance as Finn in *Star Wars: The Force Awakens* (2015): 'The fans have spent so many years away from their beloved *Star Wars*, and the first person to pop up, he's got hair that you can't necessarily run a comb through.'[3] It is partly due to Brewster that Oguns and Boyega take the baton forward. They now normalize blackness in Hollywood and everywhere else they go.

In addition to setting performers on a successful path, perhaps Talawa's greatest contribution to black British theatre in the Brewster era was establishing a home for black theatre in London's West End. The three-year residency at the Cochrane provides a tangible example to black artists that reaching the West End is not beyond a black British theatre company. Brewster set the precedent. The trials and tribulations can be learnt from to secure and maintain a second central London home. It is time.

An inevitable and strategically managed by-product of Talawa's contribution to British theatre was the wider questions the carefully selected work raised on the broader issues of black British identity. Black audiences were offered up aspects of their lives in performance. Their culture was visible, their language was audible, they witnessed themselves from the inside out. The mainstream also experienced them, and from a black perspective. Brewster's work was instrumental then in helping to define black British history, culture and language to itself and the wider mainstream through performance. Gus Edwards explains the need for these

---

[2] Brewster Interview, 31 October 2014.
[3] *Black Hollywood,* BBC1, 13 October 2018.

theatrical contributions: 'We must assert our unique cultural perspectives. And the most dynamic forum we have for these assertions lies in our performative expression. So it is very important that we not allow it to be codified or tamed by obeisance to the dictates of the social majority.'[4]

An appreciation of this assertion of black cultural identity on the British stage was seen in the black media's response to the shows. Talawa was at the centre of all its artistic discussion, from reviews and features on Brewster and other Talawa performers to awarding accolades to the company. More widely, the recognition of Talawa's significant contribution in performing black British identity is illustrated by the increased backing it gained in receiving first small- then middle-scale funding. As the longest surviving black British theatre company both during Brewster's era and to date, Talawa has secured a place for itself in contemporary British theatre history. This success and longevity came, at least initially, from Brewster's knowing herself and the conviction she expresses in her statement, 'Don't believe a word they tell you, believe what you know to be true in yourself.'[5]

The end

Brewster decided to take a year out from her commitments to Talawa in 2000. This became two years as she acted in BBC1's television series *Doctors* between 2000 and 2002. Discovering that she had a heart condition in 2002, life had decided that a return to Talawa was not an option. Whilst ill, Brewster put in an application to the Arts Council for a new home for black theatre at the St James Theatre in Victoria, London. She explains:

> I was fed up with Nick Kent telling me this is what you people ought to do, and Philip Headley, although he wasn't so patronizing. They can't help it because they like to help. If you have some place that is yours you know you will lose it if you choose the wrong things. There's a dynamic there that makes you very careful, but also makes you understand what it is to have something that you're responsible for.[6]

---

[4]Edwards, 'Part IV Performance Introduction', 314.
[5]Brewster Interview, 31 October 2014.
[6]Brewster Interview, 20 November 2018.

Brewster was not alone in this exercise and remains indebted to Floella Benjamin, Mo Mowlam and many others for their efforts. Despite her best intentions, Brewster found she was the subject of hostility from black people who complained, in writing, to the Arts Council about the possibility that she may pull the project off.[7] Brewster contextualizes this behaviour:

> It must be part of some of the left over colonial thing that exists in some of us. We believe that we have to kowtow to massa and then massa will give us something, so we run and tell tales on our fellow slaves. It happened all the time in slavery, people running off and trying to make good with massa by making it bad for their own people, thinking they would never be found out. Those were the ones that were often found hanging from trees.[8]

Whilst discussions for the St James Theatre were in progress, Thomas as acting artistic director at Talawa received a warning phone call out of the blue, from a white theatre director. He was told, 'Nothing against you Ben, but I'm going to use every breath in my body to stop that building.'[9] How could this not be against Thomas who had acted frequently for Talawa, helped secure the Cochrane and was now holding the fort? Or had the caller deemed it reasonable to disrespect him in this way because he was a black man running a black company, and should have no aspirations of securing a theatrical home, let alone one next to Buckingham Palace?

Brewster gained £7 million in assets for the project and could see Talawa's new home getting closer by dint of her endless grafting, delivering after-dinner speeches, being bolshie and having a great administrator in Angela McSherry. Despite this, the Arts Council ditched the project on the grounds that the paperwork was incorrect. Brewster's theory is that they got cold feet because they mistakenly thought the black community was behind the project.[10] She clarifies the lack of understanding for what she was trying to achieve and the inescapable institutional racism around it:

---

[7]Ibid.
[8]Ibid.
[9]Brewster Interview, 31 October 2014.
[10]Ibid.

Who's calling the shots? It's not one of our BLAME, LAME, BARMEY BAME people. It's white people. I think they [the board at the time] thought we were a community centre. In England, just because you are black, you get prescribed and ethnically minoritied as black or some other word. You must have an adjective. How come we don't say the White National Theatre, which it undoubtedly is? The sort of black theatre I wanted at St James is not supposed to happen in England. No, that would be too much power. The theatre people want to tell you what is good for you. It's not only in theatre, it's also in which schools you should send your children to, what churches you should attend, the jobs you should have, how many of you should be on television. England has a greater hurdle to jump than a lot of other countries in this respect because England was more colonial than everybody else.[11]

The predictable failure of the St James Theatre project signalled to Brewster that after seventeen years at the helm, Talawa needed a new artistic director to take the company forward.[12] In the early 2000s, however, there was a lack of black theatre directors with the experience to take on the artistic directorship of the company.[13] Those of African-Caribbean descent who had the appropriate experience did not initially express an interest.[14] This was then followed by a succession of artistic directors in post.[15]

Brewster's era at Talawa proved to be only the beginning of what the company would have to offer contemporary British theatre generally. It also set the stage for the company's continued development under the ensuing artistic directors and ensured that black British theatre companies, due to Brewster's legacy, could no longer be seen as a novelty, or out of place on the British stage. Brewster is acutely aware of having passed on what

---

[11]Ibid.
[12]Brewster Interview, 20 November 2018.
[13]Catherine Ugwu, 'Talawa Theatre Company: Towards 2001 – A Paper for Board Discussion and Decision' (unpublished, prepared for Talawa's Board, March 1999), 2.
[14]Ibid., 3.
[15]2001: director Topher Campell. Left immediately. 2001: playwright Bonnie Greer. Remained in post for three months. 2002 to 2005: director and playwright Paulette Randall. 2005 to 2006: actor Ben Thomas was the interim artistic director. 2006 to 2011: director Pat Crumper. 2011 to present: director Michael Buffong.

she dedicated so much of her life to creating, and that the contemporary black British theatre revolution she played an instrumental role in forging is now in the capable hands of British-born blacks to professionally explore, develop and stamp their own complex identity on. As for advice to the current and future artistic directors of Talawa, Brewster simply has this: 'To thine own self be true.'[16] To the rest of us there's this: 'You're not over until you're over, and when you're over you're still there because what you did lives after you, I think.'[17]

---

[16]Brewster Interview, 26 November 2018.
[17]Brewster Interview, 31 October 2014.

IMAGES

Talawa Theatre Company
Presents

An Echo in the Bone

by
Dennis Scott

Directed by
Yvonne Brewster

Designed by
Sue Mayes
Lighting by
Richard Moffatt

With
Allister Bain   Joanne Campbell   Lenny Edwardes
Malcolm Frederick   Mona Hammond   Kwabena Manso
Gary McDonald   Ellen Thomas   Faith Tingle   Leo Wringer

THE DRILL HALL ARTS CENTRE
16 Chenies Street London WC1
Box Office Tel: 01-637 8270 ◆ Goodge Street
Access for people with disabilities. Bar & Restaurant
Free childminding for under 5s Friday & Saturday Evenings

24 JUNE - 19 JULY 1986 TUE - SAT at 8pm

Theatre Royal Stratford East and Talawa Theatre company present
The Dragon Can't Dance
a calypso carnival musical play by Earl Lovelace
Theatre Royal Stratford East
Box Office 081·534 0310
29 June–4 Aug

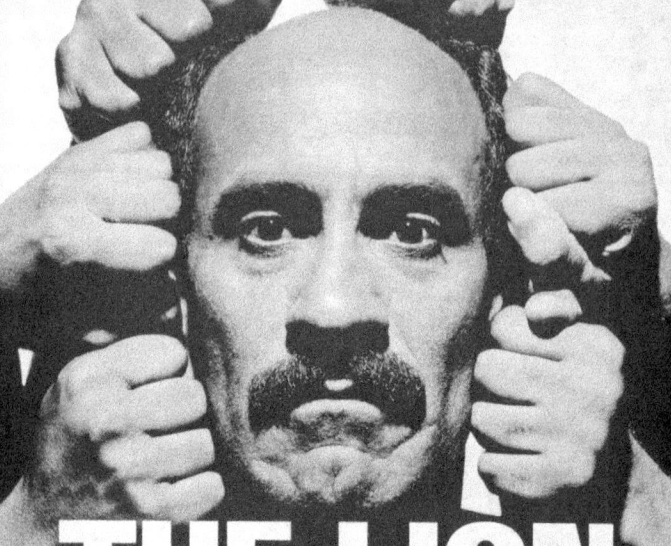

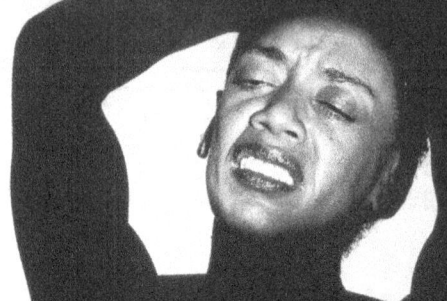

TALAWA
at THE COCHRANE

and
CONTACT THEATRE COMPANY
present

FROM THE MISSISSIPPI DELTA
by Dr. Endesha Ida Mae Holland
directed by Annie Castledine

BOX OFFICE 071-242-7040
Thursday 1st April - Saturday 1st May at 7.30pm
Tuesday 6th April at 7.00pm
Ticket prices: £7.00 / £10.00 / £12.00 / Preview and Concessions £5.00

THE COCHRANE THEATRE
SOUTHAMPTON ROW LONDON WC1B 4AP
Just 1 Minute from Holborn Tube

Co-Directed by Sue MacLennan. Designed by Iona McLeod. Music: Helen Glavin. Lighting by Nick Beadle
Dialect Coach: Charmian Hoare. Performed by Pauline Black, Josette Bushell-Mingo, Joy Richardson

The Merseyside Everyman Theatre and
Talawa Theatre Company Present

ANTONY & CLEOPATRA

by William Shakespeare

**THURS 16th MAY -
SAT 15th JUNE - 7.30 p.m.**

Preview - Wed 15th May - 7.30 p.m.
Matinees - Thur & Sat - 2.00 p.m.
Press Night - Thur 16th May - 7.00 p.m.

Tickets - £7.50, £9.50, £11.50
BOX OFFICE: 071- 387 9629

Bloomsbury Theatre
15 Gordon Street, London, WC1

PHOTOGRAPHER: GAVIN EVANS

The Merseyside Everyman Theatre and
Talawa Theatre Company Present

ANTONY & CLEOPATRA

by William Shakespeare
**THURS 16th MAY -
SAT 15th JUNE - 7.30 p.m.**
Preview - Wed 15th May - 7.30 p.m.
Matinees - Thur & Sat - 2.00 p.m.
Press Night - Thur 16th May - 7.00 p.m.

**Tickets - £7.50, £9.50, £11.50
BOX OFFICE: 071- 387 9629**

Bloomsbury Theatre
15 Gordon Street, London, WC1

PHOTOGRAPHER GAVIN EVANS

BIBLIOGRAPHY

Abrahams, Roger D. *The Man-of-Words in the West Indies, Performance and the Emergence of Creole Culture*. Baltimore and London: John Hopkins University Press, 1983.

Adams, L. Emilie. *Understanding Jamaican Patois: An Introduction to Afro-Jamaican Grammar*. Kingston: Kingston Publishers Limited, 1991.

Adi, Hakim. *Black British History: New Perspectives*. London: Zed Books, 2019.

Aikens, Nick and Elizabeth Robles. *The Place Is Here: The Work of Black Artists in 1980s Britain*. London: Sternberg Press, 2019.

Alibhai-Brown, Yasmin. *Who Do We Think We Are?: Imagining the New Britain*. London: Penguin, 2001.

Allen, Robert. *The Reluctant Informers*. New York: Anchor, 1975.

Alleyne, M. *Roots of Jamaican Culture*. London: Pluto Press, 1988.

Allsopp, Richard. *Dictionary of Caribbean English Usage*. Oxford: Oxford University Press, 1996.

Anderson, Carol. *White Rage: The Unspoken Truth of Our Racial Divide*. New York: Bloomsbury, 2017.

Anderson, I. and F. Cundall, eds. *Jamaica Proverbs*. Kingston: Institute of Jamaica, 1910, reprinted, Shannon: Irish University Press, 1972.

Arends, Jacques, Pieter Muysken and Norval Smith, eds. *Pidgins and Creoles: An Introduction*. Amsterdam: J. Benjamins, 1995.

Ashcroft, Bill, Gareth Griffiths and Helen Tiffin. *The Empire Writes Back: Theory and Practice in Post Colonial Literatures*. New York: Routledge, 1989.

Baker, C. *Foundations of Bilingual Education and Bilingualism*. Clevedon Philadelphia: Multilingual Matters, 1993.

Bame, Kwabena N. *Come to Laugh: African Traditional Theatre in Ghana*. New York: Lillian Barber Press, 1985.

Banham, Martin, Errol Hill and George Woodyard, eds. *The Cambridge Guide to African and Caribbean Theatre*. Cambridge: Cambridge University Press, 1994.

Baugh, J. *Black Street Speech, Its History, Structure and Survival*. Austin: University of Texas Press, 1983.

Baxter, Ivy. *The Arts of an Island: The Development of the Culture of the Folk and Creative Arts in Jamaica, 1494–1962*. Metuchen: Scarecrow Press, 1970.

Beckford, George and Michael Witter. *Small Garden . . . Bitter Weed: Struggle and Change in Jamaica*. Kingston: Institute of Social and Economic Research, 1991.

Beckwith, Martha. *Jamaica Proverbs*. New York: Negro University Press, 1970, original 1925.

Behn, Aphra. *Oroonoko: Or the Royal Slave. A True Story*. London: Will Canning, 1688.

Bibliography

Benjamin, Ione. *The Black Press in Britain*. London: Trentham Books Limited, 1995.
Bennett, Louise. *Jamaican Dialect Poems*. Kingston: Gleaner Co. Ltd., 1948.
Bennett, Louise. *Lulu Says, Dialect Verses with Glossary*. Kingston: Gleaner Co. Ltd., 1952.
Bennett, Louise. *Laugh with Louise*. Kingston: City Printery, 1961.
Bennett, Louise. *Jamaica Labrish*. Kingston: Sangster's Book Store Ltd., 1966.
Bennett, Louise. *Anancy and Miss Lou*. Kingston: Sangster's Book Store Ltd., 1979.
Bennett, Louise. *Selected Poems*. Kingston: Sangster's Book Store Ltd., 1982.
Bennett, Louise. *Aunty Roachy Seh*. Kingston: Sangster's Book Store Ltd., 1993.
Bhopal, Kalwant. *White Privilege: The Myth of a Post-Racial Society*. Bristol: Policy Press, 2018.
Bickerstaffe, Isaac. *The Padlock*. Cork: Anon, 1770.
Boakye, Jeffrey. *Black, Listed: Black British Culture Explored*. London, Dialogue Book, 2019.
Boas, Franz. *Race, Language and Culture*. London: Collier Macmillan Publishers, 1940.
Bowen, George R., ed. *Jamaica Dialect Verses*. Kingston: The Herald Ltd., 1942.
Braithwaite, Edward Kamau. *Contradictory Omens: Cultural Diversity and integration in the Caribbean*. Kingston: Savacou Publications, 1974.
Brathwaite, Edward Kamau. *Jamaica Poetry: A Check List, Books Pamphlets and Broadsheets 1686–1978*. Kingston: The Herald Limited, 1979.
Brathwaite, Edward Kamau. *History of the Voice: The Development of Nation Language in Anglophone Caribbean Poetry*. London and Port of Spain: New Beacon Books, 1984.
Brinkhurst-Cuff, Charlie, ed. *Mother Country: Real Stories of the Windrush Children*. London: Headline Publishing Group, 2018.
Bull, John. *British Theatre Companies 1965 - 1979*. London: Bloomsbury, Methuen Drama, 2016.
Burgess, T. and H. Rosen. *The Language and Dialects of London School Children*. London: Wardlock Educational, 1980.
Burns, Elizabeth. *Theatricality: A Study of Convention in the Theatre and in Social Life*. London: Longman, 1972.
Carlson, Marvin. *Performance: A Critical Introduction*. London: Routledge, 1996.
Cassidy, Frederic G. *Jamaica Talk: Three Hundred Years of the English Language in Jamaica*. London: Macmillan, 1961.
Cassidy, F. G. and R. B. Le Page. *Dictionary of Jamaican English*. Cambridge, London and New York: Cambridge University Press, 1985.
Chamberlin, J. Edward. *Come Back to Me My Language: Poetry and the West Indies*. Urbana and Chicago: University of Illinois Press, 1993.
Chambers, Colin. *Black and Asian Theatre in Britain: A History*. Oxon: Routledge, 2011.
Cooper, Carolyn. *Noises in the Blood: Orality, Gender and the 'Vulgar' Body of Jamaican Popular Culture*. London: Macmillan, 1993.

Bibliography

Cooper, Wayne F. *Claude McKay: Rebel Sojourner in the Harlem Renaissance. A Biography*. New York: Schocken Books, 1987.

Cornell Paul, Martin Day and Keith Topping. *Classic British TV 2*. London: Trentham Books Limited, 1995.

Coupland, Nikolas and Adam Jaworski. *Sociolinguistics: A Reader and Coursebook*. London: Macmillan, 1997.

Cumberland, Richard. *The Fashionable Lover, The West Indian and The Brothers*. Perth: Morison and Son, 1771.

Dabydeen, David, and Nana Tagoe-Wilson. *A Reader's Guide to West Indian and Black British Literature*. London: Hansib/Rutherford, 1988.

Dalphinis, Morgan. *Caribbean and African Languages: Social History, Language, Literature and Education*. London: Karia Press, 1985.

Dance, Daryl Cumber. *Folklore from Contemporary Jamaicans*. Knoxville: University of Tennessee Press, 1985.

Dance, Daryl Cumber. *Conversations with Contemporary West Indian Writers*. Leeds: Peepal Tree Books, 1992.

Daniels, Therese, and Jane Gerson, eds. *The Colour Black: Black Images in British Television*. London: British Film Institute, 1989.

Davies, E., T. Jupp and C. Roberts. *Language and Discrimination*. London: Longman, 1992.

Deakin, Nicholas and others. *Colour, Citizenship and British Society*. London: Panther Books, 1970.

Devonish, Hubert. *Language and Liberation: Creole Language Politics in the Caribbean*. London: Karia Press, 1986.

Diangelo, Robin. *White Fragility: Why It's so Hard for White People to Talk About Racism*. Boston: Beacon Press, 2018.

Dodgson, Elyse. *Motherland: West Indian Women in Britain in the 1950s*. London: Heinemann, 1984.

Duggan, Patrick and Victor Ukaegbu, eds. *Reverberations Across Small-Scale British Theatre: Politics, Aesthetics and Forms*. Bristol: Intellect, 2013.

Durham, P. and L. E. Jones. *The Negro Cowboys*. New York: Dodd, Mead, 1965.

Eddo-Lodge, Reni. *Why I'm No Longer Talking to White People About Race*. London: Bloomsbury, 2017.

Edwards, V. *West Indian Language, Attitudes and the School*. Derby: National Association for Multi-racial Education, 1977.

Edwards, V. *Language in a Black Community*. Clevedon: Multilingual Matters, 1986.

Ellis, R. *The Study of Second Language Acquisition*. Oxford: Oxford University Press, 1994.

Elsom, John. *Post-War Theatre Criticism*. London: Routledge, 1981.

Fairclough, Norman. *Language and Power*. Harlow: Longman, 1989.

Fanon, Franz. *Black Skin, White Masks*. London: Pluto Press, 1986.

Fasold, Ralph. *Introduction to Sociolinguistics, Vol. 2: The Sociolinguistics of Language*. Oxford: Basil Blackwell, 1989.

Figueroa, John J. ed. *An Anthology of African and Caribbean Writing in English*. Oxford: Heinemann, 1982.
Fryer, P. *Staying Power: The History of Black People in Britain*. London: Pluto Press, 1984.
Fuller, Michael. *'Kill the Black One First': A Memoir*. London: 535, 2019.
Gainor, J. Ellen, ed. *Imperialism and Theatre: Essays on World Theatre Drama and Performance*. London and New York: Routledge, 1995.
Gates, Henry Louis, Jr. *The Signifying Monkey: A Theory of Latin American Literary Criticism*. New York: Oxford University Press, 1988.
Giddens, A. *Modernity and Self-Identity, Self and Society in the Late Modern Man*. Cambridge: Polity, 1991.
Gilbert, Helen and Joanne Hopkins. *Post-Colonial Drama: Theory, Practice, Politics*. London and New York: Routledge, 1996.
Gilkes, Michael. *Creative Schizophrenia: The Caribbean Cultural Challenge, The Third Walter Rodney Memorial Lecture*, December 1986. Warwick: Centre for Caribbean Studies, University of Warwick, 1986.
Gilroy, Paul. *Small Acts: Thoughts on the Politics of Black Cultures*. London and New York: Serpent's Tail, 1993.
Gilroy, Paul. *The Black Atlantic: Modernity and Double Consciousness*. London and New York: Verso, 1993.
Godiwala, Dimple, ed. *Alternatives Within the Mainstream: British Black and Asian Theatres*. Newcastle: Cambridge Scholars Press, 2006.
Goulbourne, H. Teachers. *Education and Politics in Jamaica 1892–1972*. London: Macmillan Caribbean, 1988.
Grant, Cy. *Blackness & the Dreaming Soul: Race, Identity and the Materialistic Paradigm*. Edinburgh: Shoving Leopard, 2007.
Gumperz, J., ed. *Language and Social Identity*. Cambridge: Cambridge University Press, 1982.
Harris, R. and F. Savitzky. *My Personal Language History*. London: New Beacon, 1988.
Harrison, Paul Carter, Victor Leo Walker and Gus Edwards, eds. *Black Theatre: Ritual Performance in the African Diaspora*. Philadelphia: Temple University Press, 2002.
Harte, Joe, ed. *Black People and the Media: Equality in Employment and Training: Policies and Practice*. Warwick: Warwick Printing Company Ltd., 1988.
Hazzard-Gordon, Katrina. *Jookin': The Rise of Social Dance Formations in African American Culture*. Philadelphia: Temple University Press, 1990.
Hewitt, R. *White Talk Black Talk, Inter-Racial Friendship and Communication Amongst Adolescents*. Cambridge: Cambridge University Press, 1986.
Hill, Errol. *Shakespeare in Sable: A History of Black Shakespearean Actors*. Amherst: University of Massachusetts Press, 1984.
Hill, Errol. *The Jamaican Stage 1655 – 1900: Profile of a Colonial Theatre*. Amherst: University of Massachusetts Press, 1992.
Hirsch, Afua. *Brit(ish): On Race, Identity and Belonging*. London: Vintage, Penguin Random House, 2018.

Bibliography

Holmes, Janet. *Introduction to Sociolinguistics.* London: Longman, 1992.

hooks, bell. *Yearning, Race, Gender and Cultural Politics.* Boston, MA: South End Press, 1990.

Inchley, Maggie. *Voice and New Writing, 1997 - 2007: Articulating the Demos.* Basingstoke: Palgrave Macmillan, 2015.

James, C. L. R. *Black Jacobins, Toussaint L'ouverture and the San Domingo Revolution.* London: Alison & Busby, 1980.

Jelly-Schapiro, Joshua. *Island People: The Caribbean and the Word.* Edinburgh: Canongate, 2018.

Johnson, D.V. *The History, Theatrical Performance Work and Achievements of Talawa Theatre Company* 1986–2001, University of Warwick, Ph.D thesis, 2001.

Joseph-Salisbury, Remi. *Black Mixed-Race Men: Transatlanticity, Hybridity and 'Post- Racial' Resilience.* Bingley: Emerald Publishing, 2018.

Katz, Loren W. *Black People Who Made the Old West.* New York: Cromwell, 1977.

Katz, Loren W. *The Black West.* New York: Open Hand Publishing, 1987.

Kerr, David. *African Popular Theatre: From Pre-Colonial Times to the Present Day.* London: James Currey. 1995.

King, Bruce. *Derek Walcott and West Indian Drama.* New York: Clarendon Press, 1995.

Knight, Franklin W. and Colin A. Palmer, eds. *Identity, Race, and Black Power in Independent Jamaica: The Modern Caribbean.* Chapel Hill: University of North Carolina Press, 1989.

Laguerre, Michel S. *Voodoo and Politics in Haiti.* London: Macmillan, 1989.

Le Page, R. B., ed. *Creole Language Studies II.* London and New York: Macmillan, 1961.

Lewis, Rupert. *Marcus Garvey: Anti-Colonial Champion.* London: Karia Press, 1987.

Lorimer, Douglas. *Colour, Class and the Victorians: English Attitudes to the Negro in the Mid-Nineteenth Century.* Leicester: Leicester University Press, 1978.

Lott, Eric. *Love and Theft: Blackface Minstrelsy and the American Working Class.* New York: Oxford University Press, 1993.

Lovelace, Earl. *The Dragon Can't Dance.* Harlow: Longman, 1981.

Luckett, Sharell D. and Tia M. Shaffer. *Black Acting Methods: Critical Approaches.* Abingdon: Routledge, 2017.

Mais, Roger. *Brother Man.* Oxford: Heinemann Caribbean Writers Series, 1974.

Marshall, Herbert and Mildred Stock. *Ira Aldridge the Negro Tragedian.* London: The Camelot Press Ltd., 1958.

Matthews, David. *Voices of the Windrush Generation: The Real Story Told by the People Themselves.* London: Blink Publishing, 2018.

Matura, Mustafa. *Six Plays: As Time Goes By, Play Mas, Independence, Welcome Home Jacko, Nice Meetings.* London: Methuen, 1992.

McKay, Claude. *An Autobiography: A Long Way from Home.* London: Pluto Press, 1985.

Bibliography

McMillan, Michael. *Theatre Writing Associate, Black Writing: A Guide for Black Writers*. London: London Arts Board, 1998.

Milling, Jane. *Modern British Playwriting, the 1980s, Voices, Documents, New Interpretations*. London: Methuen, 2012.

Morrison, Lionel, ed. *Black People Human Rights and the Media*. London: Black Rights UK with the assistance of the Commission for Racial Equality, 1989.

Mühlhäusler, Peter. *Pidgin and Creole Linguistics*. Oxford: Basil Blackwell Ltd., 1986.

Murray, Douglas. *The Strange Death of Europe: Immigration, Identity, Islam*. London: Bloomsbury, 2017.

Nettleford, Rex. *Caribbean Cultural Identity: The Case of Jamaica. An Essay in Cultural Dynamics*. Kingston: Institute of Jamaica, 1978.

Nettleford, Rex, ed. *Jamaica in Independence: Essays on the Early Years*. London and Kingston: Heinemann Caribbean, 1989.

Ngugi, wa Thiong'o. *Decolonising the Mind: The Politics of Language in African Literature*. London: James Currey, 1986.

Olaniyan, Tejumola. *Scars of Conquest Masks of Resistance: The Invention of Cultural Identities in African and African - American and Caribbean Drama*. New York and Oxford: Oxford University Press, 1995.

Olusoga, David. *Black and British: A Forgotten History*. London: Macmillan, 2016.

Omotoso, Kole. *The Theatrical into Theatre: A Study of Drama and Theatre in the English-Speaking Caribbean*. London and Port of Spain: New Beacon Books, 1982.

Ong, Walter J. *Orality and Literacy: The Technologizing of the Word*. London: Routledge, 1982.

Owusu, Derek. *Safe: On Black British Men Reclaiming Space*. London: Trapeze, 2019.

Owusu, Kwesi. *The Struggle for Black Arts in Britain: What We Consider Better Than Freedom*. London: Comedia Publishing Group, 1986.

Paget, Henry and Paul Buhle, eds. *CLR James's Caribbean*. Durham, NC: Duke University Press, 1992.

Paiewonsky, Isidor. *Eyewitness Accounts of Slavery in the Danish West Indies also Graphic Tales of Other Slave Happenings on Ships and Plantations*. New York: Ford University Press, 1989.

Pavis, Patrice, ed. *The Intercultural Performance Reader*. London and New York: Routledge, 1996.

Pennycook, Alistair. *The Cultural Politics of English as an International Language*. London: Longman, 1995.

Pickering, Michael. *Blackface Minstrelsy in Britain*. London and New York: Routledge, 2016.

Pinker, Steven. *The Language Instinct*. London and New York: Penguin, 1994.

Pits, Johny. *Afroeuropean: Notes from Black Europe*. London: Penguin, 2019.

Rampton, Ben. *Crossing: Language and Ethnicity Among Adolescents*. London: Longman, 1995.

Bibliography

Rees, Roland. *Fringe First: Pioneers of Fringe Theatre on Record*. London: Oberon, 1992.

Rheeders, Kate. *Some Traditional African Beliefs: A Beginner's Guide*. London: Hodder and Stoughton Educational, 1988.

Roberts, Peter Arthur. *West Indians and Their Language*. Cambridge: Cambridge University Press, 1988.

Rohlehr, Gordon. *Calypso and Society in Pre-independence Trinidad*. Port of Spain: G. Rohlehr, 1990.

Romaine, Suzanne. *Pidgins and Creole Languages*. London: Longman, 1988.

Rose, Tricia. *Black Noise: Rap Music and Black Culture in Contemporary America*. Hanover and London: Wesleyan University Press, 1994.

Rosenthal, Judy. *Possession, Ecstasy and Law in Ewe Voodoo*. Charlottesville and London: University Press of Virginia, 1998.

Rust, Brian. *London Musical Shows on Record 1897-1976*. Middlesex: General Gramophone Publications Ltd., 1977.

Saakana, Amon Saba and Adetokunbo Pearse, eds. *Towards the Decolonisation of the British Education System*. London: Frontline Journal/Karnak House, 1986.

Saunders, Graham. *British Theatre Companies 1980 - 1994*. London: Bloomsbury, Methuen Drama, 2015.

Saunders, Malcolm. *Multicultural Teaching: A Guide for the Classroom*. London: McGraw-Hill Book Company UK Ltd., 1982.

Schechner, Richard. *The Future of Ritual Writings on Culture and Performance*. London and New York: Routledge, 1993.

Sebba, Mark. *London Jamaican*. London and New York: Longman, 1993.

Sekyi, Kobina. *The Blinkards*. London: Heinemann, 1974.

Selvon, Sam. *The Lonely Londoners*. Essex: Longman, 1995.

Smith, David J. *Racial Disadvantage in Britain: The PEP Report*. Harmondsworth: Penguin Books, 1977.

Smitherman, Geneva. *Talkin and Testifyin*. Boston: Houghton Mifflin, 1977.

Stone, Carl. *Class Race and Political Behaviour in Urban Jamaica*. Kingston: Institute of Social and Economic Research, 1973.

Stone, Judy S. J. *Theatre Studies in West Indian Literature*. London and Basingstoke: Macmillan, 1994.

Thomas, Lundeana Marie. *Barbara Ann Teer and the National Black Theatre: Transformational Forces in Harlem*. New York: Routledge, 2016.

Thomas, J. J. *The Theory and Practice of Creole Grammar*. London and Port of Spain: New Beacon Books Ltd., 1969.

Tomlin, Liz and Graham Saunders. *British Theatre Companies: 1995 – 2014*. London: Bloomsbury, Methuen Drama, 2015.

Tompsett, A. Ruth, ed. *Black Theatre in Britain*. Amsterdam, The Netherlands: Harwood Academic Publishers, 1996.

Trudgill, Peter. *Sociolingusitics: An Introduction to Language and Society*. London: Penguin, 1974.

Trudgill, Peter. *Dialects*. London: Routledge, 1994.

Tynan, Kenneth. *A View of the English Stage 1944-1965*. London: Methuen, 1984.

Bibliography

Wallace, Michelle. *Black Popular Culture*. Seattle: Bay Press, 1992.

Walmsley, Anne. *The Caribbean Artists Movement 1966–1972: A Literary and Cultural History*. London and Port of Spain: New Beacon Books, 1992.

Watson, G. Llewellyn. *Jamaican Sayings: With Notes on Folklore, Aesthetics, and Social Control*. Tallahassee: Florida A&M University Press, 1991.

Wells, C. J. *Jamaican Pronunciation in London*. Oxford: Basil Blackwell, 1973.

Whytelaw III, Boulé. *Think Like a White Man: Conquering the World . . . While Black*. Edinburgh: Canongate, 2019.

Widdicombe, Sue and Robin Wooffit. *The Language of Youth Subcultures, Social Identities in Action*. London and New York: Harvester Wheatsheaf, 1995.

Wiley, Ralph. *Why Black People Tend to Shout: Cold Facts and Wry Views from a Black Man's World*. New York: Penguin, 1992.

Williams, Mance. *Black Theatre in the 1960s and 1970s: A Historical-Critical Analysis of the Movement*. Westport: Greenwood Press, 1985.

INDEX

Abbensetts, Michael 122–3
accuracy
  linguistic 9, 134, 137–41, 148–9
  of voice 99
Adams, Sam 137
Aderin, Susan 113
Afari, Yasus 23
African-Caribbean
  artists in Britain 2, 49
  cultural history 91–4
  language 97
  movement 103
  music 103
  non-spoken performance vocabulary of
    'All A We Is One' (song) 112–21
    colonialism 103–9
    Voodoo 103–9
  people (*see* black)
  speech forms 123
  voices 7, 123, 185–6
African drama ritual 13–21
  birth 14–15
  killing of newborns 14
  suicide 14
  welcome 14–15
Albee, Edward 144
Aldridge, Amanda Ira 36
Aldridge, Ira 36, 179–80, 189, 198
Ali, Jamal 64, 70
All A We Is One 112–21
All God's Children 35
All My Sons (Miller) 144
Alternatives Within the Mainstream: British Black and Asian Theatres (Godiwala) 1
American 82, 84
  accents 9, 137–8, 143, 148–9, 157–8, 175
  black 12, 20, 75
  genre, refusing exclusion from 143–6
  works 146–76
American Buffalo (Mamet) 144

Anansi and Brer Englishman (Young) 70
Angelou, Maya 55
Annie 145
Annobil-Dodoo, Freddie 134–9
antilanguage speech 6–8, 30, 33, 100–1, 148
Antony and Cleopatra 49, 85, 177, 184–7
Archibald, Douglas 31
Armatrading, Joan 50
Armistead, Claire 86, 200
arson 65, 88
Asian theatre 2, 76
As Time Goes By (Matura) 64
Athill, Diana 47
Atkins, Robert 35
Audience Design Framework 8
Aunty Roachy Seh 30

Bacchae, The 51
Back Street Mammy (Cook) 67
Baker, Josephine 26
Baker, Tom 60
Baku, Trinidadian Shango 137
Bamboula 16
Ban, George 39
Baptiste, Marianne Jean 180 n.12
Baptiste, Thomas 54
Baraka, Amiri 69
Barker, Clive 64
The Barn theatre company 60–3
Bear Up (Bennett) 28
Beaton, Norman 53, 71, 75, 80, 96–7, 188
Beautiful 145
Beauty and The Beast 145
Beckford, Laura 113
Beckonsale, Richard 126
Bee, Sandra 135, 137, 139–40
Beef, No Chicken 133–4, 137, 140–1
  directing language 134–41
Behn, Aphra 178
Bela, Nana 21–2
Belafonte, Harry 88
Bell, Allan 8

Index

Bell, Madeline 39
Bellas Gate Boy (Rhone) 62
Belle Fanto (Roach) 31
Ben Dung (Bennett) 29
Benjamin, Floella 50
Bennett, Louise 23, 27–33
BiBi Crew (1980s–present) 67
Billington, Michael 153
birth rituals 14–15
black
   Africa 4
   American culture 75
   Britons 4–5, 32, 66–8, 93, 97–8,
      117–18, 121, 128–33, 182–3
   diaspora 3, 88
   identity 3–5, 128–33, 221–3
   language forms 5, 11, 96, 102–3, 126,
      133, 138, 140, 155
   performers in Britain 177–84
   racism 36, 38–40, 59, 64, 67, 69–70,
      73, 85, 88, 95, 108, 188, 198–9,
      206, 210, 212, 217, 219, 224
   Victorians 202–3
   voice 9–10, 156, 177–84
Black, Pauline 156–7
*Black and Asian Theatre in Britain: A
   History* (Chambers) 2
Black and White Minstrel Show 181
black British theatre 1–3, 13, 33–55,
   64–9, 221–3
Black Experience Arts Programme 79
Black Feet in the Snow (Ali) 64
Black Girl in Search of God 54
Blackgrounds 33–4
Black Jacobins, The (James) 77, 79, 81,
   94–5, 102–3, 106–11
Black Mime Theatre (1984-97) 66
Black Pieces (Matura) 64
Blacks, The 70
Blackstages 33–4
Black Theatre Cooperative (BTC) 66,
   74–5
Black Theatre Forum (BTF) 66, 76–9
Blackwood, Derek 77
Blake, Syan 171
Blood, Sweat and Fears 78
Blood Wedding (Lorca) 67
blue book 199
Bogarde, Dirk 36
Boulaye, Patti 49

Bovell, Brian 100
Boyega, John 180
Branson, Richard 119
Brathwaite, Edward Kamau 48, 51
Bread 40
Breeze, Jean Binta 63, 77, 147–52
Brer Nancy 70
Brewster, Yvonne 1–12, 32–4, 42, 47, 55,
   221–6; *see also* Talawa Theatre
   Company
   and Barn theatre company 60–3
   beginnings 57–60
   birth 3
   black British voice 96–7
   black identity, work on 3
   with BTC 74–5
   with BTF 76–9
   and Carib Theatre 72–4
   with Dark and Light company
      70–1
   directing language 134–41
   drama school training 59–60
   Open House show 63
   racism and 59
   role in making of black British
      theatre 64–9
   study/training 57–60
Britain, black people in 4–5, 32, 93, 95,
   97–8, 117–18, 121, 182–3
   black theatre in 103–9
   black theatre practitioners in 95
British Theatre Companies 1980-1994
   (Saunders) 1
Britons 32, 66–8, 93, 97–8, 117–18, 121,
   128–33, 182–3
Brown, Colette 124–6
Brown, Georgina 93
Brown, Lennox 20
Bugsy Malone 145
Bullwinkle, Jean 73
burden of representation 9–11
Burrows, Derek 23
Burton, Richard 39
Bushell-Mingo, Josette 158–9
Buy a Tram (Bennett) 28
Bythewood, Gina Prince 153

Cairns, Ellen 174
calypso 12, 39, 76, 105, 112–21
Cameron, Earl 33–7

Index

Cameron, Margaret Cheer 25
Cameron, Norman 27
Carew, Jan 48
Caribbean Artist's Movement, The
 (Walmsley) 51
Caribbean Artist's Movement (CAM) 51
Caribbean language 6, 99
Carib Theatre 31, 47, 48, 66, 72–4
Carlson, Marvin 66
Carnival 12–13, 16, 76, 109–10, 112–21
 as black-controlled event 116
 manhood 118–19
 music 112–16
 physical violence in 117–19
 self-reflective criticism, tradition
  of 120
 songs 112–15
 sponsorship 118–19
 superficial aspects of 120–1
 Trinidad 112–21
Carstens, Johan Lorentz 16
Carter, Corinne Skinner 76
Carter, Steve 40
Castledine, Annie 154–5, 158–9
Cat on a Hot Tin Roof (Williams) 144
Cattouse, Nadia 39, 49, 54
Cavendish, Dominic 213
Césaire, Aimé 27, 40
Charles, Stafford 160
choreopoem; *see Love Space Demands, The*
 (Shange)
Christopher, James 171–2
Chubb, Ken 73
Chungh, Teerth 87
Cindy-Ella 39
Cirpriani, Andrew 48
Clarke, Yvonne 31
Clayton, Simon 192
Clayton, Sonji 167
Cleage, Pearl 143, 162–6, 169, 172
Cliff, Jimmy 63
Clorindy, the Origin of the Cakewalk 145
Cochrane Theatre 82–90
Collie, Ian 105
Collins, Joan 39
colonialism 12, 103–9
Colour Bar (Bennett) 29
coloured 37, 94, 165
'Come Out In The Road Warrior' (song)
  113–14
Connery, Sean 49

Connor, Edric 48
Connor, Pearl 33, 47–55
Constab Balldads (McKay) 28
Constance, Zeno 20
Contemporary Black British Playwrights:
 Margins to Mainstream
 (Goddard) 2
continuum 124, 126–7, 131
Cook, Trish 67
Cooper, Carolyn 30
Coronation of an African King, The
 (Garvey) 27
Coup, The (Matura) 64
Courtship and Marriage 29
Craft, Eddie 38
Creole 4, 24–5, 28, 95, 110, 115, 127–8
Croll, Dona 187
Cron, Richard 69–70
Crossman, Harry 35
Crucible, The (Miller) 144, 189, 205
Cumberland, Richard 24
Curry, Michael 18
Cus Cus (Bennett) 29

Dabydeen, David 177–8
Dahl, Mary Karen 109, 128
'Dance Dragon' (song) 113
Dark and Light Theatre Company
  69–71
Dark Days and Light Nights (Ali) 70
Dark Disciples, The 51
Dear Princess 29
Death of a Salesman (Miller) 144
De Camp, David 124, 127
de Cordova, Rafael J. 28–9
Deeper the Roots 36
de Jongh, Nicholas 76, 199–202
de Juan, Jorge 15
Delicate Balance, A (Albee) 144
De Lisser, Herbert George 27
Della (Reckord) 31, 43
Dennis, Andrew 192
Departure in the Dark (Hillary) 31
Desmond 41, 45
Dessalines (Laird) 100–2, 104–7
De Victory Parade (Bennett) 29
Dexter, Felix 67
Domingo, Anni 165
Don't Gas the Blacks (Reckord) 44
Douglas, Paul Keens 23
Downpression Get a Blow 32

Index

Dragon Can't Dance, The (Lovelace)   76, 109–11, 137
   calypso   112–21
   carnival   112–21
   chosen ethnicity   109–10
   music   112–21
   performance, oral language of   110–12
Dream Girls   145
Dreardon, Basil   36
Duchess and the Two Dukes, The   36
Duck Variations (Mamet)   144

Echo in the Bone, An (Scott)   20, 91–4
Edmund (Mamet)   144
educational opportunities   4, 131
Edwards, Bryan   17
Edwards, Gus   16
Ejiofor, Chitewel   180 n.12
Elmina's Kitchen (Kwei-Armah)   92–3
England Is De Place For Me (Gideon)   67
Entertainments National Service Association (ENSA)   36
equality   17
Espejel, Inigo   80
Ethelred Marlow (Ogilvie)   27
Ethnic, Felicity   67
ethnicity   109–10
Ethnic Minority Arts Policy   66
Evans, Edith   55
Evans, Victor Romero   75
Evaristo, Bernadine   71
Everett, Antony   195
Evolution of the Blues (Hendricks)   69

Falconer, John   73
Fame   145
feminism   143
Fight Against Slavery, The   65
Findlay, Jim   137
Fishing (Randall)   76
Fishman, Joshua A.   6
Fitzgerald, Ella   57
Five Guys Named Mo   86
Fix Up (Kwei-Armah)   98
Flesh to a Tiger (Reckord)   43, 47
flexing   97
Flyin' West (Cleage)   143, 162
   critics' response   171–4
   eye-witness account   174–6
   heritage facts   163–74
Forbes, Leonie   61

For Black Boys Who Have Considered Homicide When The Streets Were Too Much (Mason)   148
For Colored Girls Who Considered Suicide When The Rainbow Is Enuf (Shange)   148
Ford, John   191
For the Reckord   47
Fox Hole Parlour   36
Francis, Geff   112–14, 117–20, 137–8, 141
Frederick, Malcolm   75
Freedom Road   39
From the Mississippi Delta (Holland)   143, 154–62
   Black, Pauline   156–7
   Bushell-Mingo, Josette   158–9
   critical reception   159–62
   delta voices   154–6
   Richardson, Joy   157–8
frontier   162–4, 169

Gardner, Lyn   194
Garvey, Marcus   26–7
Gideon, Killian   67
Gideon, Llewella   67
Giles, Howard   8
Give the Gaffa Time to Love You (Reckord)   44
Glass Menagerie, The (Williams)   144
Glengarry Glen Ross (Mamet)   144
Goat, Or Who Is Sylvia, The? (Albee)   144
Gods Are Not To Blame, The   65
Gone with The Wind   3
Goodman, Lizbeth   143
Grant, Cy   33, 37–42
Grease   145
Greater London Arts Association (GLAA)   77
Greater London Council (GLC)   65
Green Book   155
Guyanese accent   97, 99

Haagensen, Richard   15
Hair   50
Hall, Peter   189
Hallam Theatre Company   24
Hammond, Mona   49, 54–5, 64–5, 80, 97–9, 205
Hands, Terry   70
Hanson, Charlie   74

253

Index

Harder They Come, The 65
Harewood, David 188–9
Harlem Renaissance 26–7
Harris, Naomi 155
Harrison, Rex 49
Hart, Cedric 137
Hart, Jean 104–5
Haynes, David 104
Hazemore, Keith 104
Hendricks, Jon 69
Henry, Lenny 99
heritage 27, 32, 103, 105–7, 121, 125, 129–30, 135, 137–8, 163–71
Hero's Welcome, A (Pinnock) 67
Hibbert, Sydney 61
Hilaire, Patricia 71
Hill, Errol 28–9, 31, 46
Hillary, Samuel 31
Hines, Winsome 171
Holder, Ram John 45, 49, 51, 137
Holland, Endesha Ida Mae 143, 154–6, 159–61
Holland, Merlin 205
Home of the Brave 39
'Hooligans in Port of Spain' (song) 114
Hopkinson, Slade 31
Hughes, Langston 26
Hurston, Zora Neal 26
Hutchinson, Joan Andrea 23
Hyatt, Charlie 64

Ice Cold in Alex (John) 55
If Beale Street Could Talk 155
Igweonu, Kene 81, 86, 143
Importance of Being Earnest, The 177, 194–9
  audience response 199–201
  black Victorians 202–3
  white words black mouths 203–5
Inception 37
Inchley, Maggie 6, 9, 89, 93, 98, 102
In Dahomey 145
Institute of Contemporary Arts (ICA) 64
Interpreter, The 36
Ipi Tombi 145
Issacs, Samuel Abraham 57
It's Not My Fault Baby: A Play in Dialect 62

Jacob, Judith 75
Jamaican patois-speaking theatre 32
Jamaican speech 99, 126
Jamaican theatre 23–7
  artistic movements 26
  artists 26
  developments in 25–7
James, C. L. R. 48, 77, 79, 94–5
James, Horace 49
James, Oscar 113, 118
Jane's Career (De Lisser) 27
Jericho (Ali) 70
Jesus Christ Superstar 50
Jeyifo, Biodun 23
John, Errol 39, 48, 54–5
Johnson, Iris 57
Johnson, Linton Kwesi 32
Jonkunnu 92
Jules, Jenny 105
Jumbie Street March (Wilson) 70
Junction Village (Archibald) 31

Kalipha, Stefan 122
Kaluuya, Daniel 180 n.12
Kataki (Wincalbert) 69
Kay, Janet 75
Kean-Dawes, Jennifer 30
Keane, Shake 23
Kent, Nick 89
Key, Philip 186
Khalifa, Stefan 64
Kidman, Nicole 36
killing of newborns 14
King Lear 177, 188–91
Kwan, Nancy 49
Kwa Zulu 145
Kwei-Armah, Kwame 92–3, 98

Labat, Pere 16
Laine, Cleo 39
Laird, Trevor 100–7
La Mar, Angie 67
'La Marseillaise' 103–4, 106
Lamb, Robert 70
language
  African-Caribbean 97
  Caribbean 6, 99
  forms 5, 11, 96, 102–3, 126, 133, 138, 140, 155

Index

oral language of performance
    'it ain't reach yet'   110–12
    'speaky spokey'   122–8
    'we speak black'   95–103
overt   6, 21, 27–30, 33, 101, 110, 120, 125
sociology of   6–8
style as audience design and related
    theories   8–9
of text *vs.* colour of performers   213–15
Lawrance, Tamara   101
Lawson, Mark   89
Lecture on Heads, The (Stevens)   28
Leigh, Mike   180 n.12
Le Mar, Angie   165, 175
Le Page, R. B.   9, 100
Lemmons, Kasi   160
Levy, Andrea   99
Lewis, Elijah   180 n.13
Liberated Woman (Reckord)   44
linguistic
    accommodation   8, 100–3
    behaviour   8–9, 100–3
    of black British people   10–12, 31–3,
        96–100
    Brewster's approach   134–41
    Caribbean   112, 125
    forms   122–8
    identity   96–7
    of native Trinidadian speech   111
    sophistication   127, 149–50
Lion, The (Abbensetts)   122, 128
    black identity, notions of   128–33
    performance, oral language of   122–8
Lion King, The   145
Lippo the New Noah   64
Little Shop of Horrors, The   145
Lonely Londoners (Selvon)   123
Long Song, The (Levy)   99, 101–2
Look Back in Anger (Osborne)   47
L'Ouverture, Toussaint   96–7
Lovelace, Earl   76, 109–10
Lover, The (Pinter)   65
Love Space Demands, The (Shange)   143, 146
    dancing dialogue   150–4
    oral language of performance   148–50
    psyche   150–4
    structure of   146–7
Love Thy Neighbour   52
Lowden, Jack   101
'lunatic balls'   16

McBurnie, Beryl   47
McDaniel, Hattie   3, 10
Mack, Tara   33
McKay, Claude   26, 28
Mackintosh, Cameron   86
MacLennan, Elizabeth   44
McPherson, Douglas   171
McQueen, Steve   180 n.12
Mahone, Sydné   3
Makon, Marius   180 n.13
Mamet, David   144–5
'Man Alone' (song)   113–14
Man From the Sun, The   39
Manley, Carmen   54
Manley, Michael   63
marginalized black communities   2–3, 7,
    157; *see also* black
Marie-Jeanne   97–9, 105
Marijuana Affair, The   65
Markle, Meghan   18
Married (Bennett)   29
Marsh, Elspeth   39
masculinity   118, 128, 130–1
Maskarade (Jonkonnu)   20, 91–4
Mason, Ketih Antar   148, 184
Mass Wedding (Bennett)   29
Matura, Mustapha   40, 64, 74–5
Maud, Mongo   18
Maxwell, Marina Omowale   20
Medea in the Mirror   134
Meeks, Amina Blackwood   23
Mendez, Greta   135–7, 151
Methuen, Paul   62
Midsummer Night's Dream, A   179
militants   19
Miller, Arthur   144
Milling, Jane   79
Mini, Nana   22
Mirren, Helen   37
Miss Julie (Strindberg)   61–2
Miss Lou's Views   29
mixed race   101, 103, 162, 166,
    168–9
monolingual patois speech   127–8,
    138–40, 149–50
Monroe, Carmen   80
Moon Dance Night (White)   77
Moonlight   155
Moon on a Rainbow Shawl
    (John)   55

Index

Morgan, Prince 151
Morris, Mervyn 23
Motown 145
mulatto 101, 105
Murray, Andrew C. 29–30
Murray, Douglas 46
Murray, Henry Garland 29–30
Murray, William Coleman 29–30
Mutabaruka 23
'muthafucka' 149
My Father Sun Sun Johnson 65

Naipaul, Vidia 48
Nansi, Bru 22
National Black Theatre (NBT) 10, 106
nationalists 19
Negroes 17, 19
Nettleford, Rex 128
New Hardware Store, The (Lovelace) 76
Nielsen, Hans 18
'niggah' 149
Night of the Iguana (Williams) 144
Nine Nights tradition 91
non-spoken performance vocabulary 112–21
   'All A We Is One' (song) 112–21
   colonialism 103–9
   Voodoo 103–9
North West Frontier 49
Nri, Cyril 113
Nsue, Nansi 15

O Babylon 195
Obeah 16–17, 105–6
Observer, The 37
Odedina, Abiodun 82, 86
Ogilvie, G. 27
Olaniyan, Tejumola 116
Oldendorp, Christian Georg Andreas 14–15, 17
Ole-Time Tram (Bennett) 28
Olivier, Laurence 38–40, 49, 51, 217
On a Tramcar (Bennett) 28
One Soja Man (Ogilvie) 27
Open House show 63
oral language of performance
   'it ain't reach yet' 110–12
   'speaky spokey' 122–8
   'we speak black' 95–103
Oshodi, Maria 78

Othello 177, 179, 194, 206–20
   actors' perspective 215–20
   audience response 210–12
   language of text *vs.* colour of performers 213–15
   production reviews 212–13
Our First Baby 29
Ové, Horace 122
overt language behaviour 6, 21, 27–30, 33, 101, 110, 120, 125
Oyelowo, David 189

Padlock, The (Bickerstaffe) 24
Paiewonsky, Isidor 21–2
Palumbo, Lord 83, 87
Party, The 51
Pass Fe White (Bennett) 29
patois 29–33, 57–8, 92, 98, 122, 127–8, 138–9, 149–50
Peele, Jordan 180 n.12
Peer Gynt 205
Penn, Sean 36
Pericles 49
Petrified Forest, The 35–6
Phango, Peggy 76
Philips, Anton 72, 76
Philips, Bob 104
Philips, Judy 72
Phillips, Caryl 67
pidgins 24, 95–6, 100
Ping Pong, The (Hill) 31
Pinnock, Winsome 67
Pinter, Harold 65
Pixley, Dick 134
Poke, Gregory 43
Pool of London, The 36
Porgy and Bess 145
Porkpie 45, 45 n.106
Posse, The (1992-4) 67
post-traumatic slavery disorder 13–55
   Bennett, Louise and 27–33
   black British theatre 33–55
   Jamaican theatre (1700s–1980s) 23–7
   post-war pioneers 33–55
   rituals 13–21
   storytelling 21–3
poverty 125
Powell, Enoch 5, 40, 128
Powell, Wesley 63

Index

Powesland, Peter 8
Prescott, Paul 39
Priestly, Patricia 61
pronunciation 154, 162, 185–6, 189
Pyramid Process 166–7

Quashie, Hugh 127
Queen, The 37

Raas (Lamb) 70
racism 36, 38–40, 59, 64, 67, 69–70, 73, 85, 88, 95, 108, 188, 198–9, 206, 210, 212, 217, 219, 224
Raisin in the Sun 75
Rand, Jimi 70
Randall, Pauline 71, 76
recitals 28
Reckord, Barry 31, 33, 42–7
Reckord, Lloyd 44, 46
Redemption Song (White) 67
Redgrave, Vanessa 188–9
Rees, Roland 64
Registration (Bennett) 29
representation, burden of 9–11
Return To My Native Land (Césaire) 27, 40
Reverberations Across Small-Scale British Theatre (Duggan and Ukaegbu) 1
Rhone, Trevor 31, 61
Richardson, Joy 157–8
Richardson, Tony 43, 44, 49
Richmond, Doyle 75
Ring Ding (1969–80) 30
rituals 13–21
    birth 14–15
    killing of newborns 14
    suicide 14
    of Voodoo 106–7
    welcome 14–15
Rivers, Sharon 155
Roach, Eric 31
Road, The (Soyinka) 85
Roaming Jamaicans (Garvey) 27
Robeson, Paul 79
Rock in the Water (Pinnock) 67
Romeo and Juliet 65
Rose, Jason 70, 77
Rose, John La 51

Rose Bruford raining College of Speech and Drama 47, 58–61, 63, 71–2
Rose Slip, The (Archibald) 31
Rough Riding Tram (Bennett) 28
Royal Air Force (RAF) 37
Running Dream (Cook) 67

St Joan (Shaw) 60
Saint Luke Passion 50
Salkey, Andrew 48, 51
Samarth, Alaknanda 33
Sapani, Danny Kwasi 124–6
Saturday Night Fever 145
Savory, Elaine 116
Schechner, Richard 105, 110
Scot, Dennis 91
Seawife 39
Secret Life of Bees, The 153
Secrets and Lies (Leigh) 180 n.12
Seduced (Rand) 70
self-reflective criticism 120
Semper, Nina Baden 49
Sexual Perversity in Chicago (Mamet) 144
sexual voice 149–50
Shange, Ntozake 143, 146–9, 152–3
Shapi, Hassani 192
Shirley, Don 155
Show Boat 145
Signifying Monkey, The (Gates) 93
Simpson, OJ 205
Sinclair, Madge 122
Skinner, Coreen 49
Skyvers (Reckord) 44
Slave, The Baraka, Amiri 69
Slavery from Hut to Mansion (Garvey) 27
slavocracy 14–18, 21, 33, 180–1
Smile Orange (Rhone) 62, 64, 65
Smith, Alan 89
Smith, Samedi 104
Smith, Samuel Morgan 198
sociology of language 6–8
Solja Work (Bennett) 29
Songs of Jamaica (McKay) 28
Soyinka, Wole 40, 85
Spawning of Eels, A (Hopkinson) 31
Spencer, Charles 93
standard English speech 7, 28, 30, 58–60, 66–7, 95–9, 102, 110, 122–5, 128, 134–5, 138–9, 157, 182, 202
Statement of Regret (Kwei-Armah) 98

257

Index

Stevens, George Alexander 28
Stewart, Marie 89
Stockley, Nicola 189
storytelling 21–3
   ideas 23
   women in 21–3
Stowe, Harriet Beecher 180
Strange Death of Europe, The (Murray) 46
Strange Fruit (Phillips) 67
Street Car Named Desire, A (Williams) 144
Streetwise 72
suicide 14
Susan Proudleigh (De Lisser) 27
Suzy Wong 49
'Sylvia Ain't Have No Man' (song) 113

Talawa Theatre Company 1, 66, 79–82;
   see also Brewster, Yvonne;
   individual plays
   audiences 85
   Beef, No Chicken 133–4
   black identity in 6
   body of work 81
   Dragon Can't Dance, The 109–10
   Echo in the Bone, An 91–4
   funding 81–3, 82 n.108
   language of production 95–103
   Maskarade 91–4
   residency at Cochrane 82–90
   work 81–2
Tan-Up Seat (Bennett) 28
Tara Arts 2
Taste of Honey, A (Delaney) 44
Taylor, Elizabeth 184
Teer, Barbara Ann 10, 19, 88, 106
Temba (1972–93) 66
Tenant, The (Cron) 69–70
Tennant, H. I. 36
Thaxter, John 141
Theatre of Black Women 66, 71–2
Theatre Royal Stratford East 86
13 Death Street Harlem 36, 38
Thomas, Ben 83, 175, 187–8
Thomas, Ellen 76
Thomas, Trevor 64
Thriller 145
Tiata Fahodzi 3
Tina 145
Tis Pity She's a Whore 177, 191–5
Titanic 145

Tjon, Henk 20
Tonight show 39
Trip to Coontown, A 145
'Tro Me Out A She Yard' (song) 113
Trotman, Bill 23
Twisted Knots (Ali) 70
Two Little Indians 49

Ukaegbu, Victor 1, 81, 86, 91, 188–9, 206
'Umabatha' 184
Umoja (1984–6) 66
Uncle Tom's Cabin (Stowe) 180
Universal Negro Improvement Association
   (UNIA) 26
Upon Westminster Bridge (Bennett) 32

verbal repertoire 6–7, 97–100, 111–12,
   125–6, 149, 157–8, 174, 182, 203
Victorian behaviour 199
Victory (Bennett) 29
View From The Bridge, A (Miller) 144
voices 6
   African-Caribbean 7, 123, 185–6
   black 96–7, 177–84
   sexual 149–50
Voodoo rituals 12, 103–9

Walcott, Derek 48, 133
Walker, Rudolph 50, 52
Warner, Earl 32
Warrington, Don 126
Webber, David 126–7, 163, 165–6
'We Believe In Miracles' (song) 114
Welch, Elizabeth 39
welcome rituals 14–15
Welles, Orson 184
West Indian, The (Cumberland) 24
West Indian Lady's Arrival in London, A
   (Cameron) 25
West Indians 24, 38, 46, 52, 96, 128
West Indian slavery 17
West Indian Standard speech (WIS) 124
Where There Is Darkness (Phillips) 67
White, Edgar 67, 77
White Pickney (Bennett) 29
White Witch of Rose Hall, The (De Lisser)
   27
Whiting, Andrea 151
Who's Afraid of Virginia Woolf? (Albee)
   144

Index

Whylie, Dwight   134
Wiley, Ralph   117
Williams, Claudette   136–7
Williams, Joan   71
Williams, Tennessee   144
Wilmott, Diane   87
Wilson, T. Bone   70
Wilson-Tagoe, Nana   177–8
Wincalbert, Shiman   69
Wind in the Willows   205
Windrush scandal   118
Wire, The   180
Wiz, The   145
women storytellers   21–3

Woods, The (Mamet)   144
Woung, Billy   61
Wynter, Sylvia   20, 91

X (Reckord)   44

Yerma (Lorca)   15
Yoruba culture   85
You in Your Small Corner (Reckord)   44
Young, Manley   70

Zacca, Munair   61
Zoo Story, The (Albee)   61–2
Zuwanie, Edmond   36